Additional Praises for

No Boundaries: How to Use Time and Labor Management Technology to Win the Race for Profits and Productivity

"In our current economic climate, every employer should seriously evaluate what workforce management tools are necessary to ensure that the business is managed effectively and efficiently. This book was not written to sell the next latest and greatest tech tools to manage time and attendance. Instead, Disselkamp very effectively provides guidance regarding what workforce management tools should be in place and how you as an employer can ensure that the use of these tools positively impacts your organization's bottom line."

—Andy Brantley, President and Chief Executive Officer, College and University Professional Association for Human Resources (CUPA-HR)

"The concepts and ideas presented in this book are very timely as today's organizations face serious difficulties effectively managing and using large volumes of data readily available in an increasingly complex corporate, government, and non-profit world. Workforce Management Technology offers a "holistic approach" for organizational management, thereby increasing productivity and higher return on technology investments and transparency."

—Jorge Haddock, Dean, School of Management, George Mason University

"As an experienced government and industry executive, I have learned that labor costs drive business results. Lisa Disselkamp reveals the potential for using Time and Labor Management Technology to meet profit goals for a business or cost targets for a government entity. Lisa provides insights and subject matter advice that is smart, useful, and strategic."

—Fred Schobert, Award-winning government manager of large and complex programs and Fortune 500 industry executive responsible for meeting business-line revenue and profit goals

"Lisa Disselkamp offers sound advice for the successful implementation of Time and Labor Management Technology. Her focus on deploying everywhere, changing the workflow, capturing the benefits, auditing, and gathering the right data from the beginning, match my own experience in healthcare IT implementations."

—John D. Halamka MD, CIO, Beth Israel Deaconess and Harvard Medical School

No Boundaries

No Boundaries

How to Use Time and Labor Management Technology to Win the Race for Profits and Productivity

LISA DISSELKAMP

WILEY

John Wiley & Sons, Inc.

Published by John Wiley & Sons, Inc., Hoboken, New Jersey.
Published simultaneously in Canada.

The first edition of this book, *Working the Clock: How to Win the Race for Productivity and Profits with Workforce Management Technology*, was published in 2007.

For general information on our other products and services or for technical support, please contact our Customer Care Department within the United States at (800) 762-2974, outside the United States at (317) 572-3993 or fax (317) 572-4002.

Wiley also publishes its books in a variety of electronic formats. Some content that appears in print may not be available in electronic books. For more information about Wiley products, visit our web site at www.wiley.com.

Library of Congress Cataloging-in-Publication Data:

Disselkamp, Lisa, 1962–
    No boundaries : how to use time and labor management technology to win the race for profits and productivity / Lisa Disselkamp.
        p. cm.
    Includes index.
    ISBN 978-0-470-49706-7 (cloth)
    1. Personnel management—Technological innovations.   2. Success in business.
I. Title.
    HF5549.5.T33D57 2009
    658.3–dc22

                                                            2009005658

Printed in the United States of America.

10 9 8 7 6 5 4 3 2 1

To my husband, Ed

Contents

Foreword

In today's ever-changing economy, the area of spend (commonly referred to as "labor") is both the most scrutinized and nonmeasured category in organizations both large and small worldwide. As Human Resources, finance, and operations professionals deal with shrinking budgets, a rapidly changing workforce, and, most important, a focus on doing more with less, the measures and metrics that are outputs of workforce management become the crucial elements in executives' key performance indicators and executive dashboards on a daily basis.

These factors, combined with the changing technology dynamics, the changing demographic of the workforce, and a focus on global economies, make workforce management and the transformation, automation, and optimization of the function one of the most important functions in many boardrooms.

In this new edition of her book, Lisa Disselkamp does an amazing job of giving readers a tour through this fascinating world in a clear, succinct, and action-oriented approach. She begins by helping us understand what the impact of labor data can truly be on an organization. She then drives us to challenge our collective selves to realize that any organization, small or large, has a need for automation of these processes. Another key concept that Lisa drives home in the first part of *No Boundaries* is the realization that these types of automation and technologies do not just benefit the typical human resource and payroll departments, but do and will have a continued impact on operations and lines of business on a daily basis.

One of the major misnomers around workforce management technology and automation that needs to be dispelled is that the only organizations that benefit from automation are traditional blue-collar, hourly workers. As the world continues to shift from a manufacturing economy to a knowledge economy, the need for managing, measuring, and optimizing labor is actually even more important. In a manufacturing economy, the automation of time entry, rules administration, and accurate labor laws are important and will continue to be served by these types of technologies. Going forward, the measurement and metrics around true professional services work, such as number of customers served during a shift, the number of hours worked on a project, or the demand for more IT resources based on demand, will truly separate the good from the great companies in optimizing the "people chain"—the right people in the right place at the right time with the added dimension of at the right cost.

Speaking of cost, Lisa moves into an insightful discussion on building a business case for these types of technologies. Once again, this needs to be a true "business" case, not a human resources or payroll business case. Many organizations start these processes with the simple mentality of automation of manual processes. This is a fine approach if taking your most likely broken processes and "technologizing" them is what you are trying to do. To build a true business case, understand Lisa's point about a "mission" and objectives upfront and live that like a religion. Most deployments of systems such as this go wrong when organizations stray from the "mission" and end up with nothing more than they have today. Finally, be sure to market your "mission." This book lays out a brilliant framework from building your mission and we, oftentimes, forget to tell the world about it before, during, and after our achievements. Market, market, market your mission!

We need more books like this in the marketplace. *No Boundaries* provides its readers with "action-based" templates, tools, and ideas to turn a vision into a reality. The reality and vision that is painted comes to life from understanding the beginnings of this fascinating science of measuring labor to the automation and deployment of technology to assist us in reaching our vision of how to measure our results and continue to optimize the way business is done in the world today.

The world of human resources, payroll, and adjacent functions are oftentimes seen as supporting functions to the organization. After reading this book, one realizes that the opportunity in front of us all is simply amazing and truly has *No Boundaries*. Enjoy.

Jason Averbook

Chief Executive Officer, Knowledge Infusion

Preface

A nyone working with time and labor management technology knows that the industry is populated with professionals from a broad range of backgrounds. I've never met anyone who sought out this career or dreamed of working with workforce data, time clocks, and labor requirements. We each found our way here via an unintentional course of events. My own story is no different.

This is both good and bad for the industry. It's good because we have benefited from the assimilation of so many different vocations and experiences. It's bad because the absence of a recognized profession has positioned the technology off the radar of most industry leaders, strategists, and academics. It all happened quickly and quietly.

The rapid advancement of the technology resulted in experts from a variety of special sciences being tapped on the vendor side to give input into the development of the software and devices. Consultants like me joined in to fill the void where skilled resources have been needed to select, install, manage, and optimize these products. Similarly, on the customer side, people stepped into this arena because of some overlap with their primary job, because of a particular need, or because there was no one better to take on the responsibilities of workforce management systems. The outcome has been a fast-moving evolution of the technology to satisfy business demands along a hierarchy, which, I would assert, is not far from Maslow's hierarchy of needs. At the lowest level, the market has demanded tools for survival—information, efficiency, and accuracy. Next come compliance (safety) and security, followed by collaboration and better communication (belonging) and empowerment (self-fulfillment). Finally, very mature organizations have begun to call for higher-level tools to improve performance and achieve excellence (self-actualization) and to realize their full potential for success.

Though vendors have long articulated the time- and cost-saving benefits of automated time and labor management technology, many system owners have been slow to use the tool to align themselves with the strategic goals of the organization. The end user has struggled to understand the potential of this technology to be an essential, powerful source of greater profitability.

What is missing is a comprehensive definition of what this technology is designed to accomplish and how the parts and pieces complement one another (or conversely, how the absence of each part and piece inhibits the functionality of the others and the overall mission). People on both sides are experts at supply or demand within a singular vein of business need. Business people require more of X and vendors supply it. The industry zeroes in on things that are urgent and painful. No one has successfully articulated that the technology as a package has become a distinctive specialty.

That single-line-of-sight focus has resulted in a lot of very sophisticated tools that meet discrete needs within the business. Time clocks have become highly intelligent collection devices, providing two-way communication, security features, and instant data transfer. Scheduling systems have graduated to highly intelligent, logic-driven workload generators and staffing tools. And reports have morphed into dashboards, giving business analysts the tools they need.

But what has lagged is a comprehensive understanding of how these very sophisticated tools need to change the way we do business. They are not simply tools of automation and efficiency. The systems do not elevate business processes unless the processes fundamentally change once they have been configured. The applications themselves do not change the organization. What was not managed or was poorly managed before the technology arrives will still be undermanaged if the owners do not understand how the technology should be used to achieve some clearly defined measures of success. Highly elaborate and optimized processes and decision making can occur, but someone in the organization has to know what those business opportunities and outcomes are and be able to map how they are going to be achieved with the technology.

The development of the technology has outpaced the development of a body of knowledge around this technology. Anyone working with time and labor management systems needs a comprehensive understanding of the opposing side of the equation: operational requirements (business), application features (technology), rules and regulations (environmental constraints), employee needs and behaviors (human), and organizational objectives (strategic, financial, and operational). This book is designed to fill that gap.

With any emerging technology the language around that technology must evolve as well. You may have picked up this book because some of the terms in the title are unfamiliar or you aren't sure what is implied relative to your business. Of course, you want to know what this book is about. And you need to know if the information is relevant to you and your organization.

No Boundaries explores the evolution of time and labor management technology and demonstrates how its implementation can help you and your organization win the race for profits and productivity.

Just a few years ago we simply called these new systems time and attendance. That was at first basically all they did. Then the name changed slightly to timekeeping and scheduling systems, reflecting the manual business processes they began to replace. "Human capital management" surfaced and quickly became an amalgamation of numerous human resource specialties. It appealed to those who wanted to build credibility for a new approach to labor by relating it to capital asset management—a well-respected business function. Human capital made these functions and systems seem more tangible.

Time and labor management technology is also known as workforce management technology (WMT). The technology is the evolving centerpiece of managing workers, activity, and cost. It is the best tool for treating human capital as a valuable asset. WMT systems encompass many different technologies and business solutions designed to help organizations effectively administer their labor-related processes. The cornerstones of these systems are the timekeeping and scheduling components. This is where labor activity and cost converge. WMT becomes a virtual workspace where decisions are made and activity is tracked and projected, telling the company where it is headed and whether or not it is on target—financially, operationally, and strategically.

This book goes beyond a general discussion of electronic time sheets, Web-based scheduling modules, and modern data collection devices to the specific features that become the tools to influence how labor is deployed and to balance what companies spend on labor against an improved output. It will introduce you to sophisticated analytical and process tools that add a new dimension to business intelligence and process improvement.

This book is the "workforce mechanic's" guidebook on the tools that are needed; it is also an instruction manual on how to use these software, hardware, and network tools to tune up your labor productivity and budgets. Presented from the angle of the business problem *first*, the book is designed to show how the systems help companies fix their problems and move forward. In discussing how these tools are being effectively used in various industries, I present case studies of companies that have had success with these systems. In an effort to help you build a broad understanding of the many ways these applications can solve business problems, proactively resolve key issues, and transform the organization, I also list specific business problems and then show you how various time and labor management technology applications resolve those issues. Throughout, the benefits, key ideas, and best practices are identified.

Discerning how well a product fits the business's requirements and objectives is so important that much attention is given to things to consider when purchasing and implementing a new system. In particular, I explain how "mission-based configuration" (a phrase I coined) is the key to successfully aligning the system's mission with organizational goals. The book will also take you from concept to delivery by illustrating how to build a business case to win executive support and financial backing, while planning for a project or purchase. And then on to how best to implement.

Toward the end of the book, we discuss the evolution of time and labor management as a profession and as a new business unit on the horizon. WMT systems effectively manage huge sums of money. In many organizations labor costs are the single largest expense. But without a WMT system they may be the least "managed" costs, largely because outside entities took the first steps to dictate how labor would be paid. A payroll system alone is merely an administrator for these outsiders, none of whom created their rules in the interest of the employer. A paper-based schedule is an antiquated solution to complex staffing issues that allows managers to work in isolation and under the radar but directly impacts the bottom line. WMT puts the employer in the driver's seat, using what he knows about his operations and resources to make certain the work gets done most efficiently and effectively. This is visible mission-driven workforce economics. And WMT systems are better at enforcing all the rules and regulations too, altogether resulting in more profits. Those who administer these systems and deploy them as a strategic asset will themselves become more strategic and vital to the operations side of the house.

Finally, because businesses themselves evolve, the technology is discussed relative to mergers and acquisitions and succession planning.

This book is about a smarter way to run your business. Time and labor management technology creates actionable data—information that people will use to improve the way the business operates. It is a long-overdue replacement for yesterday's unsophisticated workforce management habits. So bring everything you know about business, but be prepared to look at things from a refreshingly new perspective, and get ready to find opportunities to win the race for productivity and profits.

Acknowledgments

I would like to thank Lynne Gaines for encouraging me to write this second book and for sharing my passion for getting the message out about time and labor technology.

Since being an author is far from my day job, I would like to express my appreciation to Kelly O'Connor, my development editor, who worked skillfully to make the content of this book easily understandable. She worked under a very aggressive timeline and made certain that the project met everyone's expectations.

I would also like to thank the software and hardware vendors and their customers for sharing their stories, including their successes and their difficulties. Some have chosen to remain anonymous so that the whole story could be told. I appreciate their willingness to share their journeys with you. I am very appreciative of the many industry researchers and specialists who shared their expertise and who are also working to meet the market's growing demand for ever more powerful workforce management tools. Jen Neumann was especially helpful behind the scenes as a key liaison and "go to" person. All of us in this business get charged up talking about this new technology and what we know it can do and have seen it accomplish. I hope our enthusiasm is contagious so that you will catch it too.

Michael (Mike) R. King deserves special recognition; his contributions to the section of this book on business case development and ROI were invaluable. During the years we've known each other, over lunches, via late night e-mails, and during the times we worked side by side, he has imparted his tremendous business acumen and encyclopedic knowledge of project management.

The team of professionals at Athena Enterprises and our partners contributed as well with research, fact checking, white papers, anecdotes, and encouragement. Every day, we work together to bring great workforce management technology success stories to life.

Finally, I want to thank my family for their unending support and patience and for taking on an extra chore or two when deadlines loomed. Without you I would not have the energy to get it all done or the distraction that makes it all worthwhile.

No Boundaries

The Emergence of Workforce Management Technology and What It Can Do for Your Business

CHAPTER 1

How I Got Started in Time and Labor Management Technology

We each bring our own history into our work every day. While we may look back and realize we didn't plan to end up where we are now, we are very much a product of all of those past experiences—planned or unplanned. Variety in your background can be a strong suit, making you the "out of the box" thinker among your peers. Looking at things a little differently can provide inspiration and lead to discovering valuable correlations others may have overlooked. It can put you ahead of the curve.

Time and labor management processes were asleep for a very long time—stagnating from a lack of technology and integration. But the information age recently woke this giant up, and I was there to see it begin to happen. I took my own proverbial nap for a while from the industry and returned to find the technology well on its way to becoming a major force in business. This chapter follows that journey as well as my own awakening to the power of time and labor management technology.

An Uncharted Career Path Takes Off

I got my start in time and attendance technology when I landed a job at an airline (pun intended) in the payroll department shortly after I finished college. But it wasn't a job I'd been preparing for. With a degree in Japanese and in international management, my goal was to work in international trade. That's right—I wanted to be an import/export specialist helping companies expand their businesses in the Far East.

Remember the "Japanese Miracle"? The concept emerged back in the 1980s when I was still in school. It may seem like ancient history now, but Japan was then the place where business was manifesting tremendous quality improvement and market growth. All a person had to do was open the business pages of a daily newspaper to see headlines about an alarming

3

and rapidly growing trade imbalance between Japan and the United States. My calling in life seemed clear. I didn't want to be just an interpreter or a translator, but I did want to be fluent in a second language. So, out of patriotic fervor and a sense that few others would be able to offer this skill set, I majored in Japanese and simultaneously pursued a business degree with the idea of helping American companies sell their wares to the Japanese.

Surely there was an opportunity to show small and medium-sized companies how to modify their products and marketing approaches to appeal to Asian consumers. In this way, I believed I would be doing my part to help the trade imbalance disappear. I wrote a thesis that was in effect a marketing plan for the Richmond Baking Company in Richmond, Indiana. It laid out a strategy to sell cookies and graham crackers to people raised on rice cakes and fish-flavored crackers.

To be successful, I knew I'd have to persuade U.S. companies that they had to adapt their businesses to the Asian market, and not the other way around. The whole idea was for a company to modify the way it had always done business in order to compete successfully in a totally foreign market. Now, I realize that before I'd even heard of consulting, consulting was what I wanted to do. I wanted to help businesses by taking a hard, careful look at their products and practices and, when it made sense, to help them redesign those practices to better serve their customers, managers, and ultimately their shareholders. That's what I do now, but the Asian market doesn't figure into it—except to the extent that some of our client companies are competing with Asian businesses.

What I now do is focused on keeping companies strong by managing their employees with intent and compensating them in ways that would control labor costs, attract the best employees, motivate them to meet the company's expectations, and drive accountability and customer satisfaction. I'm constantly looking for new ways to meet a company's strategic, financial, and operational goals. What I do is help companies find ways to deploy and finance their most important resource—human capital—in ways that will bring the maximum return.

Perhaps it's not surprising that payroll provided my launching pad into my present career. After all, how many seasoned and well-established business executives do you suppose were going to listen to a fresh-faced 22-year-old, obviously very non-Asian, young woman from the Midwest tell them how to sell to the Japanese? Not many.

At that time, I was also fighting complacency among American business leadership. The imminent threat and the implications of the global economy hadn't yet sunk in, and the Asian market seemed incredibly distant and strange. Most American businesses expected their international customers to adapt to our ways of doing business. Although Japan was doing very well, we weren't doing that badly in America, and competitive forces weren't compelling managers to think or act differently.

It didn't take long for me to realize there weren't many opportunities to engage companies in modifying their products to appeal to and penetrate Asian markets. After a frustrating job search, I decided to follow another passion—airplanes—and took a job with one of the largest charter airlines in the United States.

Of course, I wasn't actually flying. Nevertheless, it was invigorating just to be working in the industry. I suppose my enthusiasm for flying motivated me to learn as much as I could about the company and how an airline works. My "in" was a pretty lowly job in payroll, and it was there that I realized what a big disconnect existed between payroll and operations. Operations and payroll rarely interacted with one another other than sending paperwork back and forth. The result was that each knew very little about what the other did. They both provided only what the other side "needed to know" and busied themselves with their own responsibilities.

The Importance of Shadowing

I've become a believer in what some call "shadowing," or temporary staff rotations. Organizations come out ahead when workers understand what the various business units within the company do and how they relate. Not only does this strategy provide an appreciation for the work being done outside an employee's immediate area, but once the uses of and reasons for deliverables and deadlines become known or how one's own area is perceived, workers are more likely to apply their understanding of what they do to the business as a whole. They begin to think beyond the immediate four walls and become aware of the inherent dependencies between departments. Shadowing helps to break down walls that separate people and how they view problem solving within the organization. This builds a spirit of collaboration and appreciation. Having a fundamental understanding of what kinds of information are important to decision makers throughout the organization and what drives success is crucial to a fully engaged workforce.

I was the sort of person who would take the long way to the copy center—back before there was a photocopy machine in every department—so that I could stop by the Chief Pilot or Chief Flight Attendant's offices and chat with any crew members who might be in the area. Or I might walk through the flight-scheduling area and peek in on any developments that were in progress. I learned about crew protocol, Captain's checks, and a

Captain's decision-making authority during flight in an emergency situation. I learned about the safety training that the flight attendants had to master, and how much they knew about each airplane's equipment and emergency procedures—for example, that crew members are routinely being "checked" by another senior crew member to ensure they are going through all the proper safety procedures during flight. I learned about deadheading—flying a plane with no passengers—and how airlines cautiously ferry a plane when it is partially disabled and operating on only one engine. I discovered that this airline paid the airport a fee for every minute the plane is on the ground, or tarmac.

I even ventured out into the maintenance hangar at every opportunity to get a glimpse of the aircraft and to find out what the A&P (airframe and power plant) mechanics had to do when a jet came in for routine maintenance. (Did you know an aircraft is almost completely disassembled at regular intervals? It is thoroughly checked, meaning that its engines, seats, and tires are replaced and then reassembled to ensure that the plane is structurally sound, mechanically fit, and safe to fly? These checks are required after a certain number of takeoffs and landings.) As with most businesses, there were many activities going on behind the scenes to get the product off the ground, and I was certainly familiarizing myself with all of them.

In retrospect, I realize the important thing about my wanderings was that I didn't limit my curiosity to what other people were doing. I related it as much as I could to what I was responsible for—and that was "just payroll." But to me it was all connected, and I saw opportunities to bridge the gaps and enable the different areas to benefit one another.

It occurred to me that much was being overlooked that could be done to manage a company's workers and labor expenses to improve sales, boost quality and efficiency, increase employee satisfaction, and above all have a positive impact on the bottom line. In addition, it would significantly improve the processes and outputs of the payroll area. All it would take was a little effort and the right technology.

Then one day, an opportunity came. The payroll department had a "disaster" that perhaps only a payroll person can imagine or appreciate. A check for $50,000, made out to a single employee, got pretty far along—well out payroll's door—before it was caught. A misplaced decimal became a short-lived lottery ticket for one individual when $500.00 became $50,000.00. It was an error that should not have gone unnoticed. Within a short time, the supervisor position of this dozen-or-so-person payroll department became open. It occurred to me that I might land the position, but common sense told me I didn't have much chance. After all, I was the youngest and least experienced person in the department. A number of others had been in place for many years. But I was young and fearless, and I wanted to show my confidence and ambition. So I applied for the job.

A new managerial position was created, and someone was brought in to fill it; the department was restructured, and to my surprise, I got the job of supervisor, reporting to the new manager. I had the good fortune of working for a truly wonderful lady who recognized and understood how to use my talents. Her name is Kathy Barras, and she is perhaps the best boss I have ever had. Not only was she extremely competent and easy to work with, she knew how to position and leverage an individual's skills and interests. You might say she had a talent for understanding where people would best fit, and she knew how to employ their special aptitudes for the benefit of the department and the company. Employees with technical skills were promoted, but not into supervisory roles. Others with great people skills and the respect of their peers were put in leadership positions.

As a relative greenie in the corporate world, I considered Kathy my mentor. Kathy made certain my assignments fit my strengths. My talents had less to do with the nitty-gritty processing of payroll and more to do with analysis and improving processes. As time went by and I mastered my routine areas of responsibility, I took on special projects along with my supervisory duties.

It didn't take a very hard look to see that our department had outgrown its processes. For example, there was a serious lack of auditing procedures; the $50,000 check had brought that to light. We also did much of our work on paper, and believe me, a lot of paper was generated. We had approximately 200 cockpit crew members consisting of captains, first officers, and flight engineers, and about 800 flight attendants, which varied depending on the time of year. All of them submitted manual time sheets monthly. Obviously our department's tactical approach to getting its job done needed improvement.

The Offspring of Observation

By getting out and networking with people in other areas and attempting to learn as much as I could about the business, I discovered that a database loaded with information existed on the other side of the building. This was a gold mine that could make the manual time sheets we had to deal with obsolete. The FAA required the airline to include all kinds of information on the flight log of each aircraft every time it took off. The company maintained a computerized flight-scheduling system that recorded all scheduled flight activity. After every flight, a log sheet was submitted that included the names and positions of the crew members, their duties on the flight, and the actual flight time recorded in what is called "block in" and "block out" time. A flight doesn't officially start until the blocks are removed from around the airplane's tires. Similarly, for payroll purposes, accounting for the crew's time didn't start until the flight was rolling.

This was nothing less than incredible. The information we required these employees to report on paper—which we collected on time sheets—was already being gathered and entered into a computer system. All that needed to be done to get the data for payroll was to tap into a flight operation system already in place. This would eliminate an enormous amount of paperwork and the potential problems that went along with it.

Imagine, for example, how prone to error and delays a paper system is. Time sheets are processed by passing them along from one person to the next as different information is reviewed, calculations are made, and data is collected. On average three to four people handle the timesheet, representing four opportunities for error. People in manufacturing, particularly those familiar with Six Sigma, know how difficult it is to deliver quality when a product goes through several steps in a process. What Six Sigma black belts call the "rolled throughput yield" is the final outcome. "Yield" refers to the percentage of good outcomes produced by an operation. For example, if there are four operations each with a 99 percent yield, the rolled throughput yield is $(0.99) \times (0.99) \times (0.99) \times (0.99) = 96$ percent. Imagine having four wrong checks distributed for every hundred employees. It can happen in a manual setup, but the potential for human error is eliminated if the data is processed electronically. Computers simply don't make processing errors the way people do.

Other benefits to this automated process were apparent as well. Crew member activity was no longer reported twice—once on the log sheet and again for each employee on a time report. So this redundancy was eliminated. Omissions decreased because the information used for payroll was data that had been collected at the actual time it happened, not at the end of the month. Paper reports no longer had to be routed around for verification and supervisory evaluation and then gathered and mailed to the corporate office. The use of a single source of data meant payroll would be entirely in sync with operation's data.

These were benefits anyone could quickly and easily grasp. What perhaps was more remarkable were ways the company could benefit beyond those that were immediately obvious.

The Efficiency of Technology

I quickly realized more was to be gained from this than just the benefits to employees and payroll. As is the case with practically every organization, the airline had to package, price, and sell its product. This meant it had to estimate costs and market forces and build a pricing model. Many overhead factors exist for an airline, and pricing factors are constantly changing. Fuel costs are a big one. Seasonal demand and the pricing of competitors are others. And of course, it takes people to fly the plane and to service the passengers. Quoting a competitive price was one of these things that had to be done. You see, the company was a charter airline that did ad hoc flying. For example, a pro football team might win the division title and have a game next week in Green Bay. Teams contracted with the company for travel needs. The front office would make a last-minute call and want to know the cost to fly the team to a particular city.

The need to project actual costs accurately was extremely important, because doing so could determine whether the flight was profitable. The company had little trouble calculating the fuel cost and the landing fees. But no method existed to accurately estimate the cost of labor when a flight was added to the schedule because the amount could vary considerably. Once a crew member was in overtime, which was triggered by passing a certain number of flight hours in a month, he or she would be paid up to $60.00 an hour on top of base pay. Overtime at a crew member's rate is no small amount. The company used averages and historical data, but no forecasting tool was in place that delivered reliable labor cost information.

The pricing process was fascinating to me. I imagined myself in the cost accounting area putting that pricing model together and being exactly on target—how gratifying that would be. But I wondered, how the heck could I do it? I was in the payroll department and I couldn't even predict what the total crew payroll amount would be at the end of the month.

Then it came to me. We had labor data in our computer that was real-time. Tapping into it would solve this problem.

So I went to management and said, "Not only can we eliminate the manual processing of payroll—the need to collect time sheets, add them up, combine and total them, then compile the data into reports—and not only will all that work and the manual effort be history: Everything we need to predict the labor cost of a flight in advance will be in the computer." Not surprisingly, they wanted to know what in the world I was talking about.

I explained they wouldn't have to wait until the end of a payroll cycle to get information about who had worked how many hours, because the data in the computer was always up to date. Assuming the computer was programmed to do so, it would show whether overtime would be triggered by adding a flight to any crew member's flight schedule. No longer would it be necessary to wet a finger and stick it in the air. We'd be able to calculate exactly what the cost of labor would be whenever a flight was added.

Real-Time Labor Data Gives Visibility

The old saying goes, "You can't manage what you can't see." This applies to just about any industry. The activities of workers drive operational efficiency and cost. Managers need to see in real time what is happening, why, and how much they are spending out on the production or sales floor, the nursing unit, or even at 25,000 feet during a scheduled flight. Today you don't have to conceive, design, and build these tools from scratch. Obtaining real-time visibility into the organization can be achieved from software that's easy to install or offered as a subscription service. The products range from basic timekeeping records to sophisticated performance dashboards that alert a company's management to production problems, budget issues, or open slots on the schedule. Labor effectiveness, cost, and quality are all reported relative to targets as they occur during the work day. These dashboards give visual graphs and charts, use colors and symbols, and provide drills down into related reports for further detail. It's all designed to focus a manager's attention on cost and activity and to give that manager the critical decision-making information needed.

These dashboards weren't around when I was trying to help the airline manage its labor costs—but I wish they had been. The software vendors have developed powerful analytical tools with scores of key performance indicators and the ability to hone in on problem areas and generate forecasts based on analyzing time and attendance data. The applications also allow customers to define for the system their own unique indicators and targets. When you start to look at these gauges it can be surprising how clearly they show targets for improvement. At one hospital, for example, the workforce analytics system evaluated two years of time and attendance data. Based on an analysis that included more than 350 departments in the organization, it became apparent that with better management of just the top 25 outlier departments that would bring them in line with the median, 80 percent of the total overtime cost could be saved, an amount totaling approximately $2.5 million. This analytical tool made the process of finding the biggest problems less of a "hunt and peck" process. It isolated the problem areas and quantified the impact of the worst offenders. Visibility took this organization from driving in the dark to X-ray vision.

The Impact of Efficiency and an Intelligent System on Staffing

It was time to add some visibility into this airline's labor management. Working with a management information systems (MIS) developer, a flight crew payroll system that generated payroll costs onto the Crew member Activity Notification sheets, or C.A.N. Reports as we called them, was put in place. This gave the airline the ability to forecast labor utilization and cost and adjust schedules and pricing accordingly.

A side benefit was that as the company grew, adding more aircraft and the crews to support them, we wouldn't have to add people in hub offices or the payroll department to handle the added volume. This had been required in the past because manual systems entail a fairly fixed ratio of payroll processors to employees.

Generally, workers are hired and managed so that they are tasked to capacity. Obviously, there's a limit to the additional work that can be put on existing workers. The difference, however, between processing 1,000 C.A.N. reports or 2,000 is not much for a computer. This provided the airline with what's called "scalability." In other words, as the workload increased, the solution still met the demand. A bigger problem didn't require more people or systems. I've worked with companies that have 200 employees and with companies that have tens of thousands of employees, both using the same basic technology. It takes considerably more manpower to process 100,000 records than it does 200 using calculators and adding machines, but when a computer is doing the work, it doesn't take many more people, it just takes more servers and bandwidth—more computer power.

This is a nice advantage to have for a company in a growth or an acquisition mode. It will assure economies of scale for the merged company, which won't need two payroll departments; in addition, the challenge of adding new people from the acquired company to the timekeeping process will have been greatly simplified. As an organization grows in personnel or complexity, the fixed costs may remain somewhat stable when automation is effectively deployed.

In fact, well-planned use of automation can help reduce the number of people needed to support certain business processes. The most significant reductions come when time-consuming manual tasks are performed using good technology. Jobs can be eliminated or the growth of payroll staff curtailed, depending on the volume of manual work. This happened at the airline that employed me as a result of automating payroll functions. But in many cases, the bulk of work involved with manual time cards is performed outside of payroll by people who are administrators or supervisors of a department. They perform this function in addition to their regular primary job, usually monitoring, updating, and identifying problems on a daily, weekly, or pay-period basis. Perhaps they have been spending a half day each pay period attending to this. When a system is automated, the time devoted to this task will be reduced. The mundane tasks of validating the data, looking for missing information, checking entries, and manually tabulating time are thereby eliminated.

Sophisticated time and attendance systems verify an employee's identity and location. They can even restrict when an employee is able to report into the system. Problems are flagged, and the system filters out the clean data so that only the questionable records must be personally reviewed. So the most important impact in terms of hours saved is usually out in the field. Supervisors in a retail store, for example, can now spend more time on the floor, interacting with customers, keeping an eye on sales reps and cashiers, and making a positive impact on sales. Supervisors or production cell leaders in a manufacturing plant can spend more time training new workers, solving problems, clearing bottlenecks, and pitching in to make production quotas. Working smarter is how we describe the time managers spend in today's timekeeping software; time saving efficiencies are just the beginning.

A New Time and Attendance Opportunity Presents Itself

My career at the airline left a huge imprint on me and set my future course in ways I could not imagine at the time. The lessons learned and the opportunities I was given to remodel processes and expectations gave me insight and business skills I use every day. Although I enjoyed those years and the excitement of working in a young, dynamic company, when motherhood came along I took a hiatus from working to focus on our family.

After being a full-time mom for a few years, I returned to the workforce taking a job at one of the nation's largest providers of care for the mentally and physically handicapped. This company needed someone to help in making the transition from localized, manual time and labor management processes to a centralized, automated timekeeping system. It was a great opportunity to leverage what I had learned at the airline and apply that to the latest available technology.

My Time and Labor Management Technology Journey Begins Again

The company I went to work for had about 29,000 employees in 32 states at that time. They operated 1,500 group homes across the country. The company was operating on a totally paper-based time and attendance system, and a centralized payroll department at its headquarters processed the incoming information. Management knew an upgrade to this operation was needed and believed savings and better labor cost control could be realized by implementing an automated time and attendance system. So the mandate for this project was to install an enterprise-wide system that would create visibility, standardization, controls, and cost savings.

This project was actually preceded by another project—standardizing some of the fundamental components of the timekeeping system. Wisely, this organization undertook to align their pay practices and naming conventions. This effort created a common language and established standards that made it easier to understand what went on at each of those 1,500 business locations and efficiently put them into play inside one system. So while the standardization efforts were being finalized, the new team, of which I was a member, began to take training on the new time and labor management system that had been purchased. We also began our discovery process with the regional headquarters and documented our findings.

Eliminating Payroll Errors and Beyond—Exposing the Iceberg

Discovery is such an important part of preparing to implement a new or upgraded system that it cannot be underemphasized. Any good project manager will tell you that an hour spent planning and collecting information saves up to eight hours of time down the road. Given my background in payroll and human resources at the airline, I knew we had to do an excellent job of capturing every detail about time and labor activity and expense before we touched the new system. As I'll explain later on, it's important not just to take note of what people say they do, you must also validate what they actually do. You must dig below the surface. This project gave me the opportunity to begin to develop a discovery documentation process for time and labor management systems that is now nearly bulletproof.

Without going into the entire story of that project, I do want to highlight a couple of examples of how these systems had a positive impact for this organization. As mentioned earlier, a tremendous opportunity for error exists in a large manual system; a method of checks and balances must be put into place, because adjustments and corrections are costly. Depending on state requirements or company policy, the immediate generation of a manual check is often mandated. At this organization, the estimated cost of issuing a hand check was $50, which is how much could be charged back to the local business unit. This company had 500 or 600 such checks on average per month. That's nearly $30,000 dollars in processing expense per month. Using the system to improve accuracy and reduce the number of checks would create an immediate benefit.

Beyond this, management was even more concerned about its lack of control over labor expenditures. A centralized, automated system was viewed as a way to get a handle on this. This company was very successful and had grown largely by acquisition. Most of the revenue was directly related to labor activity. Management knew that automating their processes was not enough to achieve their overall goals for this system. The greatest benefits came from instituting policies and activities that *drove* expenses and revenue potential into a workspace that could be managed and lever-aged. And as the implementation matured, those policies and activities did just that.

One goal was to reduce overtime. This is a simple, straightforward objective that nearly every implementation aims for. It's a very real and easily quantifiable improvement to achieve. What was remarkable was that this organization specifically named that goal, put a benchmark on it, and began to make people accountable. I have to admit that leadership was a little naïve at first and thought just having the system would garner the results. After a minor stumble in the beginning and a loud cry from the field that asked "How are we supposed to do this?" the project team put together a package of materials that made reducing overtime a new process for managers to follow. We turned on features within the system to alert managers to employees who were approaching overtime and we put together job aides to show them when and how to use these system features. With relative ease, no custom programming, and no intensive training effort, we gave the organization a tool, a new way to manage expenses.

Automated workforce management systems can eliminate a host of problems and lead to all kinds of benefits. Efficiency and accuracy are obvious improvements to expect. What is more exciting is the ability of these systems to deliver meaningful information for decision management. During this time, my appreciation grew for how far "off-the-shelf" technology had evolved in this area. Instead of homegrown solutions such as those that were developed at the airline, companies could now purchase advanced systems that had been developed to meet business needs. The evolution for this company from a manual system to a sophisticated and automated application was tremendous. Without having to invent it for ourselves, we were able to institute greater oversight, influence, efficiency, and accuracy across a large and remote workforce with the systems that are now readily available. As you read the next chapter, you will begin to see just how much can be done with this technology.

Chapter Summary

- It's important to learn as much as you can about your organization.
- There are areas of the traditional business organization that offer an untapped wealth of information—not enough is expected from time and labor (payroll) management processes.
- Efficiency is the most basic outcome of automation and the easiest to understand.
- Visibility into workforce activity and spending results in better decision making and planning as well as increased accountability and savings.
- Operations can benefit strategically and financially from data that is gathered in the routine business of collecting time and labor activity data.
- Time and labor management system solutions have evolved into sophisticated, configurable products that are available right off the shelf.
- Time and labor technology is transforming timekeeping from a basic transactional process to a strategic decision management tool.

CHAPTER 2

Using Labor Data Technology to Better Run Organizations

Every organization is unique in size, complexity, and maturity. It's important to understand the organization's readiness and requirements. Many outfits are still operating the way they used to before much of today's technology was available. In this chapter, we'll explore how the business world has changed and what needs to change within the business to keep up. Time and labor management systems are spreading throughout every industry, meeting needs and solving problems far beyond simply processing payroll. Case studies focus on success stories and provide insight into how companies are benefiting from these systems. We'll even look at global operations and the challenges that these systems overcome to help overseas organizations run better.

What Is the Perfect Setup for Managing Your Business?

If you could read this book and walk away with the ideal frame of mind for managing your business, what would that look like? That's really the key to this book. What is it you need to know?

It's been said that an organization's most important asset goes home at the end of every work day. If that's true, then your second-biggest asset could very well be the technology you use to track your employees' activities. Your time and labor management technology should be saving you significant amounts of money related to your labor expenses, and it should be an important tool for reaching your organization's strategic, operational, and financial goals. But is it?

You're probably aware of the four levels of knowing as illustrated in Exhibit 2.1. The lowest level is, "You don't know what you don't know." The second is, "You don't know what you know." This is followed by, "You know what you don't know," and at the top, "You know what you know."

```
The four levels of knowing

            4. You know what you know.
         3. You know what you don't know.
      2. You don't know what you know.
   1. You don't know what you don't know.
```

EXHIBIT 2.1 The Four Levels of Knowing

When it comes to time and labor management technology today, many chief executives simply don't know what they don't know. Perhaps one of the biggest obstacles to that perfect mind-set is lack of visibility.

Until recently, management has not had a clear line of sight into hidden costs and internal success stories. There has been no mechanism until now to bring the activities and expenditures related to workers and activity into view in a meaningful way. Many managers are detached from truly understanding how work is being managed. *It is being managed today, but how? And at what cost financially, operationally, and strategically?*

It is no longer acceptable to passively manage the workforce. If your business is not fully engaging the available technology to manage its business and human capital, you are abdicating control over time and labor decisions to influences that are not concerned about the productivity and profitability of your organization. Without a tool to intelligently direct the workforce, to channel decisions and actions toward the highest-level strategic goals from even the lowest-level work effort, and to watch as the outputs from that work effort move your business, you are working in the dark.

The optimal place from which to work is to be engaged in a holistic approach to your human capital. You may have become interested in this topic because of economic pressures on your business or some other catalyst driving the organization to improve. Take a thorough look at your processes from end to end. **Break down any boundaries that exist that have historically defined "what can't be changed" or "what is of little importance" in those processes.** Hold each problem up and look at it from the absolute inception of that issue to the final outcome regardless of where it takes you. Don't focus only on the tangible evidence. Take the time to investigate the virtual and human processes that coalesce only inside workforce management systems.

What many managers don't realize is that the biggest dangers, as well as the greatest opportunities, exist at the point where data, decisions, and execution are handed off to another person, team, or process. This is where things break down and become inefficient and poorly managed. This is where the hidden factories lie (i.e., workarounds, rework, side work, or unintended processes, byproducts, and cost) in the dark crevices of operations. Fortunately, this is also where time and labor management technology gets its power. By providing a convergence of information about work activity, the cost of that activity, and the people involved in the process within a transparent system, time and labor management technology offers the optimal solution for managing your business.

Notice I didn't say "manage your payroll." Nor did I limit the declaration to "manage your labor productivity and expense." **The ideal mind-set for managers looking to improve their business is to look at workforce management technology as having no boundaries.** Yes, it can help manage payroll expense and productivity. Easily. But that's not all. What you need is a vision of success for your organization and the understanding of how to map that success to the tools within this technology. That is how this technology is being used to run companies better.

The Workforce Management Maturity Curve

You may very well agree with the preceding statements and have already purchased a time and labor management system. The next questions to ask are "Do you have the right system for your business?" and "Has it been fully and properly deployed?" and "Do you know what your return on investment (ROI) is?"

There is a broad continuum of stages of development—everything from managing the workforce entirely manually and without any defined processes or goals to deploying a time and labor system with the KISS (Keep It Simple, Stupid) principle. When KISS is the mantra, much of the ROI is discounted. Some organizations roll out a sophisticated system with little or no training and expect the "system" to magically change the organization. Fortunately, some do manage to achieve a well-orchestrated, strategic implementation that uses business intelligence from its workforce management technology (WMT) system to measure and extend success throughout the organization. What does it take to be on the mature end of that spectrum?

First, there must be a vision for success. Where the technology will take the organization must be clearly defined and measurable. **Second**, planning for a successful deployment takes time and money. A willingness to invest in planning and to purchase based not on price but on value is key. Many managers think they know how to procure IT systems, including WMT. Don't make the mistake of thinking the only requirements for this technology are to replicate today's processes more efficiently. **Everyone in the purchasing process must understand this is not a commodity item and price alone should not be the deciding factor.** That vision

Where Is My Organization on the Maturity Curve?

Here are some fundamental questions to consider. The answers will help explain how well developed the organization's time and labor management systems are and how they are being used.

- Are current time and labor management processes designed to help control costs?
- Have existing time and labor management processes proven to deliver ROI?
- Are processes designed to increase employee and manager engagement, satisfaction, and productivity?
- Have the systems in place been proven to create a stronger workforce?
- Do you have line-item visibility into costly operational issues such as unapproved overtime, premium stacking (i.e., the concurrent payment of multiple additional hourly rates on top of base pay), absenteeism, and leave management?
- Is there real-time visibility into excessive overtime, nonproductive time, or the manipulation of work and pay?
- Has the system been shown to improve customer satisfaction or product quality?
- Is the system being used daily to deepen follow-through on C-level strategic goals at all levels?
- Were design reviews conducted during and after implementation to ensure that the vision for the time and labor system will be achieved through specific features and uses of the system?
- Is the technology used for manual tasks or knowledge tasks? Do you know what and where your workforce-related knowledge tasks are?
- Do you know how much payback you expect from your investment and how long it will take to achieve?
- Do you measure for ongoing payback? Do you look for new ways to get payback?
- Is the system used to enhance the return from other business systems?
- When you train employees on the system, do you focus equally on business expertise and technical competency?
- Is the system a part of daily decision making at every level?
- Do users know not only what and how to use the system but also why and when?
- Have you deployed everywhere?

of success will describe and prioritize the value proposition that different systems offer.

Third, take a daily interest in your key performance indicators relative to labor. This will keep your organization focused on the strategic benefits. Using the right performance indicators will make sure you get the most "bang for your buck" as you manage your workforce according to those signals. And **finally**, listen to the people in operations and finance and make certain their needs are met. Take it from an expert at researching ROI from WMT systems, David O'Connell: "If you are not doing a lot of cost accounting analysis as a result of your time and attendance system, then you're leaving money on the table." The evolved end of the maturity curve includes tracking activities, managing leave, optimizing schedules, and using labor analytics in the day-to-day operations.

Developing the perfect frame of mind may involve breaking some old habits and stepping into some tricky political ground. Making certain that the needs of operations and finance are fully met may conflict with the game plan that IT and Payroll have in mind. For a long time, these two business units provided infrastructure to the organization without much outside input. They may indeed initiate the latest improvements to your workforce management systems. However, they may have an overly narrow view of the front-line audience for these systems and see their requirements as unnecessary demands or a threat to their sphere of control. Operations is where the work gets done, the products are made, and the services are delivered. **While efficiencies in IT and Payroll processes will be an improvement, the greatest opportunity for ROI is in operational and revenue-generating areas.** The administrators of the system should not be allowed to dictate the boundaries of how the system is applied to the business. Again, having no boundaries on the system means understanding that in order to deliver value there may be new demands, new stakeholders, and new relationships within the organization. Those organizations that understand that are getting the most benefit.

Paving the Cow Path

Some organizations have all the best intentions but still manage to get little more than the basic benefits. I'm not saying that is entirely bad. I would rather see an organization see a small improvement than nothing at all. I ask my friends in the time and labor technology industry all the time, What holds an organization back? Why didn't they see more ROI? I get a lot of answers: a system not deployed fully, failure to integrate well with other systems, no internal champions to fight strong resistance to change, not enough input from operational experts, among other things. But one of the most interesting explanations is that organizations spend a lot of time and resources and end up doing little more than "paving the cow path."

Now, if you are like me and didn't grow up on a farm you may not understand exactly how walking trails for cows relates to workforce management systems. I have to give credit for this humorous analogy to Jerry Nepon-Sixt. Before Jerry became an expert in time and labor systems, he spent his childhood growing up on a farm. As he explains it, cows will walk the same path day after day. But if a tree falls across the path they will blaze a new trail around the barrier. Later, when the tree is removed, the cows will continue to take the long way around the spot where the tree fell, even though the obstacle is no longer there.

Humans, apparently, aren't much different. Processes meander for one reason or another through the organization. These processes were constructed because of technology (or a lack of it) and various operational barriers that forced movement in a certain direction. When new technology is introduced and the obstacles are removed, people stick to their old way of doing things. The reasons for those processes are now gone, but the indirect route is still being followed. The cow path has remained the same, except now it is nicely paved with asphalt or concrete. In WMT systems, the concrete might consist of shiny new time clocks and a cool Web interface. But the organization failed to leverage the technology to redirect the processes along a more logical, efficient, and effective route.

Organizations that pave their cow paths actually make things worse, because putting them inside a formal system actually makes them more permanent, more universal, and more destructive. When you think about your time and labor systems, investigate carefully what you model. Make certain the systems aren't aimlessly following a course around obstacles that have been removed. For example, finding a lot of very particular reports in a system requirement is where this syndrome often reveals itself. Challenge these requests to make certain a stubborn behavior isn't the true source of the need.

The manager with the perfect mind-set realizes that it is very likely that WMT is an untapped engine for improving their processes and financials. He can quickly read case studies and vendor pamphlets to find out who has done it and what their results were. But *how* they did it is more important; and *how we can* do it is an even more valuable discussion.

If I had to sum it up succinctly, I would say that there are four workforce management technology best practices:

1. **Pay people accurately and appropriately.**
2. **Use labor wisely.** Know what you've got, how to use it, and what it costs. Understand the workforce completely. This entails using the full suite of applications where appropriate.

3. **Actively steer the workforce toward your strategic goals.** Align decisions and activity with corporate objectives by using business indicators; move away from risks and toward opportunities minute by minute.
4. **Integrate and accelerate.** Use the technology to merge business intelligence from other systems with workforce management to gain the efficiencies and aptitude needed to run the business better. Create "organizational workforce intelligence" experts at every level.

Everything timekeeping, scheduling, attendance, analytics, and hiring systems have to offer falls into one or more of these areas.

What Is Workforce Management Technology?

With any emerging technology, the language used to describe that technology must evolve as well. You may know exactly what Time and Labor Management Technology is and you're eager to find out more about the rapid and powerful developments in this sector and how to apply them to your business problems.

For those of you who are new to Time and Labor Management and unfamiliar with the terms, welcome. You are not alone. In this practice, we struggle with vocabulary every day. How do we effectively describe what these systems do? How do people find what they need if they don't know what to call it? How do we gain better visibility and understanding in the marketplace if we don't agree on the labels we put on these applications? Unfortunately, adoption of a common, stable verbiage within the industry has not yet happened.

What is Time and Labor (or Workforce) Management Technology? Is it about "time and motion" studies? No. Does "Labor" refer to union issues? Indirectly, yes, but that is not a primary focus in this book. Exactly what kind of technology are we talking about—hardware, software, or networking? All of the above.

Time and Labor Management Technology is the evolving focal point of managing workers, activity, and cost. It is the best tool for treating human capital as a valuable asset. WMT systems encompass many different technologies and business solutions designed to help organizations effectively administer their labor-related processes. From talent acquisition, training, compensation, time and attendance, and scheduling to automated workflow, productivity analysis, and retention, these systems help companies more effectively manage their workforce.

Automated workforce management systems can be the vehicle for the collection of extremely valuable data and information about worker activities and the costs associated with these activities. This can, in turn, become the source of a new way to manage worker activity. WMT can become the very centerpiece of managing workers. The information can be used to evaluate all kinds of business issues. Data about what goes on in a business every day is gathered and stored in one central repository. Key business indicators from a variety of sources are linked to people, their decisions, and their activities. The database allows managers to make a direct connection between their workers, resources (e.g., material, equipment, and money), and their customers. The tools enable them to make decisions using that information while also conforming to the rules and constraints the business demands that they follow.

WMT systems deposit information into their memory banks, creating an ongoing history of the business and its workers. Best of all, when the data captures a pattern of success, it can be shared throughout the organization, thus "institutionalizing" the success. On the other hand, if analysis of the data reveals patterns that are problematic, the technology can be used to provide solutions. For instance, if data shows that employee turnover is highest in people who work long shifts, the system can limit the scheduling of excessive-duty periods. If a certain phase of a production is consistently creating delays and resulting in overtime, this may call for reevaluating the staffing assignments. Thus, the system can be used to develop solutions or to model alternatives.

As you can see in Exhibit 2.2, WMT provides a natural platform for integrating all sorts of business intelligence. The more WMT information that's gathered, the more the WMT knows about the business and the more meaningful the data will become. Data from external and internal systems can be plugged in. Scheduling software provides the background logic, and

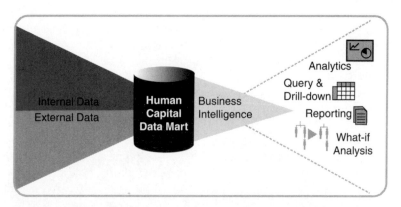

EXHIBIT 2.2 Develop a Platform for Workforce Analytics

This is a diagram showing where workforce data originates and how it produces business intelligence to the organization through various WMT features: analytics, query and drill-down, reporting, and what-if analysis.

Source: Used with permission.

the human resources database supplies employee demographics and job information. The enterprise resource planning (ERP) system provides tracking labels and production volumes. Labor analytic tools can draw upon WMT data and analyze the outputs. Training—or learning management systems (LMS)—can be integrated with job data, employee skill sets, schedules, and payroll. Access control systems use WMT systems to control entry into the facility and track the flow of people onsite. Billing systems use the data to eliminate redundancy and insure consistency between paid hours and billable hours. **The WMT system becomes a human capital data mart of knowledge for further use.** The business can draw upon the repository for query, drill-down, and roll-up of details, reporting and modeling, and what-if analysis.

Moreover, WMT is extremely efficient. Exhibit 2.3 illustrates how detailed information at the lowest levels is collected and summed up as it moves higher in the organization's hierarchy. Each piece of data needs to be entered just one time, and then it can be shared among the various systems and totaled, making the data more meaningful. Instant access is possible because information is distributed immediately. Additionally, everyone will be analyzing the same data—that is, everyone will have the same version of knowledge so that business units can better communicate and all will know that various decisions will be based on the same information. When disparate units attempt to converse without integrated systems and a central repository of common human capital data, the organization can become

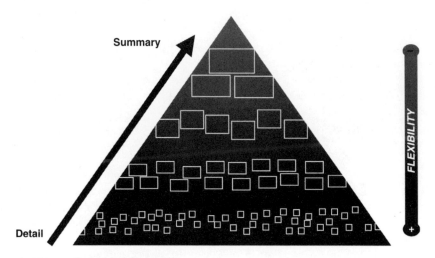

EXHIBIT 2.3 Collect the Details

This exhibit illustrates how detailed data that is collected across the organization is rolled up within WMT to give visibility to all levels within the company.

Source: Used with permission.

like the Tower of Babel, each entity speaking its own language with its own facts and figures. WMT eliminates this barrier to communication and gets everyone speaking the same business language.

Making Certain Your Organization Is Data Literate

Not only is language important relative to how we communicate about the workforce, it's essential to make certain that people in the organization understand how to read and interpret data and translate it into meaningful information. Although the technology has advanced rapidly in delivering integration and presenting data relative to various business indicators, the people using these systems most often have not kept up; they are not number literate. Except in areas such as accounting and engineering that use numbers in their work, business people who deal with workforce issues typically aren't trained to comprehend labor data. They are often more socially oriented than business oriented; quantification and objective data analysis aren't areas with which they are comfortable. Because tools haven't previously existed to measure and evaluate the workforce scientifically, business people have long been operating on intuition and habit (trial and error) and simplistic notions of change.

When business people describe changes as "better" but can't come up with an answer to "how much better?" or reply "Well, a lot better," they are operating on simplistic, gut reaction "data." Worse than that is the absence of a logical approach to the collection, interpretation of, and response to data. Knowing what should be measured and how, when, and what is the information related to are all part of a valid method for using data. **The ethos should be to make the important stuff measurable, not what is easy to measure important.**

WMT systems deliver a wealth of information in a variety of formats, such as alerts when certain milestones are met; totals and percents; and even dashboards with charts, graphs, and trend indicators. These can be very powerful signals, but the users must understand what they mean and how to use them. It's easy to look at a line chart and tell whether the numbers are going up or down. What's difficult is to know whether the movement is significant and, if so, what can and should be done about it? Should I care about a bar chart that consistently goes up over several hours, days, weeks, or months? If a particular line graph goes up and down constantly, how much volatility should be tolerated? Is there a peak, valley, or trend line to watch out for?

If the data being gathered is irrelevant, then no matter how fancy the dashboard is or how well people react, it won't make much of a difference. If the information is relevant but the user fails to interpret the information correctly, the organization could be steered off course.

It's not really that difficult for employees to get a handle on what important data is; it just takes time, intent, and training. Be aware that the systems are easy to navigate, but not completely intuitive to use. And it's not uncommon to see a report or a screen with a lot of data in several formats (lists, charts, graphs, highlights, etc.). Information overload or "analysis paralysis" can ensue. Reading charts and reacting to indicators are skills. Unfortunately, perhaps because the indicators are visual or color-coded, we think somehow they are tools people instinctually understand. If the new WMT system is going to deliver information to users, it must be implemented with adequate training and practice. People have to understand where the information comes from and where it maps to out on the shop floor, in the store, in the office, or in the ward. The system and training should filter out the chaos and bring what is important to the surface, and that is applicable yet unique to every business.

Taking this discussion beyond the practitioner level and into the boardroom, the problem with data literacy is not ineptitude but perhaps more a reluctance to embrace analytics relative to the workforce. Leadership in the organization may need some convincing that the function of human capital management is no longer just an expense issue; it is a value issue and a revenue-generating opportunity.

Time and attendance management is about managing expenses and WMT systems are the best tools to accomplish that. Reducing overtime, employee turnover, and absenteeism; improving processes; and reducing supervisor time spent dealing with schedules is where 90 percent of the mind-set is for business leaders. This is according to Dr. Jac Fitz-enz, a notable author and the first person to develop human resource metrics, in the 1970s. Business leaders should also look at the other side of the balance sheet and understand how WMT information can become a revenue-generating mechanism.

Cost is perhaps the easiest measurement to quantify related to labor and the constraint it puts on the organization's ability to produce more or enjoy more profit. It's easy to track and understand. Timing is also fairly easy to comprehend—the faster workers can get the job done and respond to the demand, the better. A workforce operating in a timely manner maps directly to higher production and greater profits. Efficiency has value; it increases the opportunity to sell more for less. When WMT systems are used to measure cost and timeliness, there can be a direct impact on the bottom line. This discussion, however, still falls within the cost-reduction mentality. Not that there is anything wrong with that, but it doesn't represent the entire value of improvements in cost and timing.

Costs and timing can be reduced while revenue still remains the same (spend less and make the same amount of money), but they can also be reduced and income increased (spend less *and* make *more* money), and that's even better. The total value of these kinds of changes occurs on both sides of the balance sheet, meaning that the ROI is even greater.

Output is another area that can be captured with relative ease, recording how much a worker produces and the quality of that work effort. What if output is improved but timing and cost are not changed? In other words, the company gets better at producing with the same number of workers paid the same amount (spend the same, create more, and make more money). Does that have value? Expenses have not been reduced overall, but the per-worker output or the amount of revenue per employee has increased. So managing workers better creates more revenue from that given set of human capital.

Key Idea

Data about Worker Output Must Be Understood

High-performance workforce requirements have significantly increased as a result of a skills gap as well as the challenge of competing in a global economy, according to nearly 75 percent of survey respondents.

Source: Deloitte's 2005 Skills Gap Report

Data literacy relative to these scenarios means knowing how the data relates and what matters. Little improvement in overtime dollars spent might be all right if production and revenue are headed in the right direction. Effective workforce management is about both sides of the balance sheet. People have to understand what to look at, when it matters, and what to do about it. When WMT is limited to managing only one side of the balance sheet, that could be a costly mistake. When it isn't done at all, the organization is living in the dark ages.

The Evolution of Business Technology

When was the last time a secretary took a memo in shorthand?

Okay, maybe there's someone out there still working that way, probably pushing 90 years old. But people who have been around longer than I have tell me it's been 30 years at least. Communications and technology in the workplace have come a long way.

How did payroll get done back then? How did companies collect information on workers' time and tabulate it? Manually, and on paper, right?

How is it done in your company today? Perhaps your company is now collecting the information electronically, but even so, chances are *what is done* with all the information that's being collected hasn't changed much. It could well represent a gold mine of data that management could use in ways you will soon learn about that can make things run more smoothly and efficiently.

Paper time cards may have been replaced, and your company may now be using electronic time clocks. This may be a "mechanical improvement," but the only real difference is the way data is being moved from point A to point B. Such small incremental developments in collection methodology have delivered only limited benefits compared to what is actually possible.

The extinction of secretaries who took dictation, answered phones, and took messages between typing letters, filing, and getting coffee came about as technology evolved. Desktop computers with word processing and list management programs began to proliferate. Telephone systems with voice mail made the companies that printed pink telephone message slips look for a new line of business. The *coup de grace* came when nearly every office worker had a computer on his or her desk, linked to the Internet. Integrated, multimedia, real-time communication was now available to all. A whole new way of communicating emerged, and this sent secretaries the way of the dinosaur. It was a dramatic change that occurred in just a few short years.

One development just as dramatic is now in the making. Exhibit 2.4 illustrates the dramatic changes in timekeeping technology that have occurred during the past 30 years. Time clocks remained essentially unchanged for almost a century until the late 1970s. Since then, the clocks have evolved into a variety of collection devices, and communication with related systems is instantaneous.

The Way We Used to Work

My friend told a story about going to work for an advertising agency right out of college. Like others, his firm developed and produced ads for its clients, some of which ran on TV, others in magazines or newspapers, some ran on radio, and of course there was the occasional outdoor billboard. Each job, whether it was a TV or radio spot or a print ad or billboard, had a job docket that traveled from one person who worked on it to the next. Everything to do with a job (which might have included briefing documents, background material, the copy, and the layout, once these were developed) traveled with this job docket. Also inside was a time sheet in triplicate, complete with carbon paper.

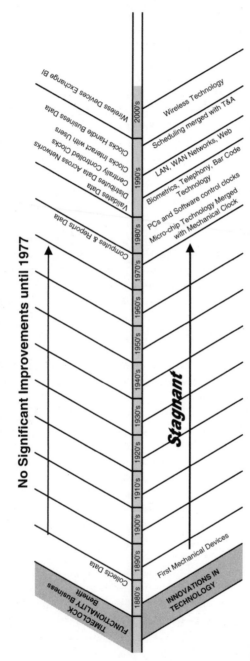

EXHIBIT 2.4 Time Clock Evolution

The timeline shows how time clock technology remained relatively stagnant for almost a century until 1977, when Mark S. Ain of Kronos Inc. first merged microchip technology with mechanical time clocks. This created the first intelligent device that could capture, record, and add employee time.

Remember carbon paper? Perhaps you recall the admonition "Press hard, you're making three copies." Or maybe not.

It was up to each person who worked on a job in the ad agency to record his or her time on that card, along with what was done and the date. This meant people had to record time twice. Once for the job and again on a time sheet that was turned into accounting and used to calculate a person's pay. That's because the time card in the job docket remained in the docket until the job was completed and closed. Eventually, layout time would be billed at one rate, copy time at another, and production time at yet another, even though the same person might be responsible for all three and would be getting paid at one hourly rate.

This is a good example of how payroll is often compartmentalized and viewed as being unrelated to actual work. It's also an example of duplication of effort since employees had to do the same thing twice. Now, it's possible to call up what in effect are time sheets on a Web-based system that allows employees to post their time against specific jobs and tasks. The same posting also records their time for payroll purposes. The system will calculate client billing and employees' paychecks; it also provides real-time data, so that if someone in management wants to know how much time has been posted to a particular job, he or she can find out up to the minute with a few clicks of a mouse.

In that ad agency of yesteryear, there were probably hundreds of these job dockets floating around the agency at any given time. They represented what in manufacturing would be called work in progress (WIP). As would also be the case in a factory, this WIP was worth many thousands, if not hundreds of thousands, of dollars. The accounting system at this firm considered time that had been posted to a job to be earned income even though it hadn't yet been billed. The work had been done, and it had been earned. It would be billed and would become money in the bank unless some part of it had to be written off. Of course, no one really knew how much WIP there was at any given time. The best anyone could do was guess.

This being the case, what do you suppose happened at the end of each year? The controller of the company needed a tally of this work in progress in order to put it on the balance sheet as an asset. So a mad and frantic dash would take place to round up all the job dockets and total up all the time cards.

My friend hasn't been in advertising for a number of years, but he says that for all he knows this yearly ritual is still taking place during the last two weeks of December. Maybe so, but let's hope not. Just imagine how much easier it would be to have all that data entered into a central database. Not only would there be less chance of loss or error, all the totaling and all the billing could be automated and immediately available. In addition, the controller of the firm would be able to know how much work in progress existed at any given moment simply by consulting the computer on his desk.

The Way We Work Now

What would you think of a company that still had secretaries taking down memos in shorthand and typing them up on an IBM Selectric? Okay, what would you think of a company that still processed payroll and looked at its data the way it did 30, 15, or even 5 years ago?

You might think a lot of people in such a company would be doing work that could easily be eliminated, given the technology that exists today—effort that could be spent in more productive ways. You might also think the people who run that company were probably missing out on a great deal of valuable information they could put to work if only they brought the way the company processes time and attendance and manages labor activity into the twenty-first century. This has happened in other departments, even in advertising agencies. Art directors no longer use T-squares and drawing tables; they use computers. And it's a pretty good bet the general ledger isn't handwritten in ink and totaled by an adding machine. Human Resources probably uses up-to-date software and computer power to store and access the records it needs. And computers have done more than just make typing or compiling and storing records easier. They have assumed other functions as well that used to be done by hand or with a slide rule or an adding machine.

For example, engineers don't simply draw on a computer, they input variables and extrapolate results and make projections about viability and performance. CAD (computer aided design) software replaced the draftsman and the manual process of making mechanical drawings, but engineering technology went further, putting the computerized drawing into intelligent design applications where stresses, temperature, and materials are analyzed, enabling engineers to determine where a plan could be prone to failure or exceed expectations.

Finance departments and investors use data not as simply data points plotted on a line but as analytical tools that demonstrate trends and deliver buy or sell signals. Procurement and logistics departments use systems that evaluate production data and supply needs and enable companies to operate "just in time," increasing efficiency and reducing costs.

Why should payroll be different? Instead of just getting checks written, why shouldn't a time and attendance system deliver valuable information management can use to run things better? Why shouldn't it be analyzing and providing actionable data? Could it be that an integrated timekeeping and scheduling system could generate forecasts that enable managers to make informed decisions about staff, workload, and compensation? The fact of the matter is, it can.

Establishing an Effective Human Capital Management Strategy

Time and activity data can be invaluable. Company management needs to take a hard look at the issues being faced to see where the costs are and what's driving the business and to link that to labor activity and compensation. Studies have shown that not everyone in the typical company is working to move the ball forward. According to a Gallup survey shared at an industry conference, about 25 percent of the workforce is actively engaged and working the way management would like and hope, and approximately 50 percent are what is termed "neutrally" engaged. They come to work. They warm their chairs. They muddle along and don't hurt the company. The remaining 25 percent of the workforce is actively working *against* the company that employs them. You might label them "disgruntled." That's an enormous number, and a very scary one if true. These people might be stealing from their employers; they might be involved in fraud or in some other counterproductive activity. Is your company doing anything to combat this threat? The disparity in employee engagement is illustrated in Exhibit 2.5.

Perhaps you can't believe you have employees who are actively working against you. But think about this: Another study, a survey done in 2005, indicates most American workers could fit a lot more work into each day. Conducted by America Online and Salary.com, it says **the average worker wastes 2.09 hours a day** chatting with coworkers, running errands, surfing the Internet, or making personal phone calls. That lost time costs U.S. employers about $759 billion a year in unproductive labor expense.

To tackle the problem of employees spending too much time on things other than their work, it's important to understand what makes workers

24%	51%	25%
Actively Engaged	Not Engaged	Disengaged

EXHIBIT 2.5 Workforce Engagement

This exhibit illustrates the extent of nonproductive time. Only 24 percent of the workforce is actively engaged in productive activity; 51 percent of the workforce is not engaged, and 25 percent of workers are actively disengaged and working to the detriment of the organization.

Source: Gallup Organization

perform. But not only are the drivers of performance important; so too is the uniqueness of your organization and the need to know what work is most important. As seen in Exhibit 2.6, there are four basic tenets of establishing an effective human capital management (HCM) strategy.

1. **Every company's workforce structure, attributes, and culture are unique.** We all know our company is special; no two organizations are exactly the same, and the response made to the differences is critical. Use your understanding of your company to design what will work best for your organization.
2. **Measure human capital according to the three principles.**
   A. **Operate from a top-down approach when developing a plan.** Identify what you want to achieve; what you have, in terms of people, to get it done; and what has the greatest potential value. Designing from high-level objectives down to the detail of specific tasks will ensure there is a connection between how employees are tasked, who is tasked, and the outcomes of their efforts. Make certain you are operating from the top level of the "four levels of knowing."
   B. **Find out who is engaged.** Focus on the activities, skills, and preferences that are yielding results, not on job titles.
   C. **Get in touch with the things that make your business successful. Understand what is needed and when—such as the retailer we discuss later in this chapter.**

Four Basic Tenets	
1	Every company's workforce structure, attributes, and culture are unique.
2	Three principles of Human Capital Measurement: ▪ Think and operate systemically (connect the dots) ▪ Get the right facts (you have them) ▪ Focus on value (creation and destruction)
3	Go beyond perception (*what people "say"*) and focus on actual behavior (*what they "do"*).
4	It is possible to identify and understand the real human capital drivers of business performance.

EXHIBIT 2.6 Human Capital Management

The four basic tenets of human capital management outline areas to focus on for an effective workforce management strategy.

3. **Don't be misled by what people tell you; discover what is actually getting done.**
4. **Remain confident that thorough discovery and validation will enable the organization to improve employee behavior.**

Data Collection: A Source of Motivation and Reward

I hate to admit it but some very smart people have actually been rather skeptical when I tell them about the principles of human capital management and workforce technology. They say, "Those systems don't offer anything new" or "We've already implemented BPO (business process improvements)." The use of labor activity data to drive business productivity and profits makes so much sense they simply cannot believe that companies aren't already using it. In fact, many companies have tried, and many continue to put effort into this area. Walk any manufacturing floor and you'll see they are evaluating production levels, parts complete, and all sorts of business data. However, one industry analyst told me that 75 to 80 percent of that data is out of date within two weeks to a month or more. The systems and processes used to collect and analyze the data aren't yielding much value to the organization when the data is that stale. The tools for collection are cumbersome, the data originates from disparate systems, and participants in the process don't have much motivation to keep things 100 percent complete and up to date.

Go into any organization and ask workers to walk around with a clipboard and collect data. After a period of time, the participants begin to lag in their duties and the entire process declines in value. What's new with workforce management technology entering into the mix is that **workers care** about the data, and they are able to report data *and* **see the results in real time.** Why does that matter?

Workers care about the data in WMT systems because it is used to compute their paychecks. Money matters, plain and simple. They are highly motivated to continually input the right data at the right time.

Key Idea

Time and labor data is important to workers and therefore must be accurate and credible. Workers care about the data in WMT systems because it is used to compute their paychecks. Money matters, plain and simple. They are highly motivated to continually input the right data at the right time.

They will even check for omitted data because ultimately that may result in less pay. Data will *not* degrade over time, because workers will always care about their paychecks. Managers care about the data too and help to validate accuracy to ensure their budgets are met.

Workers also see the effect of the data they are collecting today. Let's return to our discussion about worker behavior and attitudes. Workers who have been around a while have seen more than one young whippersnapper come along asking for information. They know they are going to outlive the latest fad in productivity studies. It may be that no one has ever *done* anything with the information that's made their life any better.

Most people, at some point—usually early on in a job—want to be successful. What happens is that older systems asked workers to collect and report information, but the effort did little to quantify the challenges they are facing on the shop floor to help reduce cycle times, to reveal both problems and high producers, and to make reaching their goals easier. When employees know the information is being tracked and measured, that non–value added activities are being identified (i.e., the daily challenges and obstacles they encounter are being illuminated) they are more willing to participate. More important, the technology can give them a visualization of exactly what is happening, the cumulative effect or outputs, in real time. **What's noteworthy is that the technology gives them a way to see how they are moving the needle.** Workers can see, for example, that "it's Wednesday and I'm behind on reaching my target, I'd better report the problems I'm having and see what can be done to help."

In a real-world example, a manufacturer used workforce analytics to identify a "hidden factory" within its production process. A wiring harness was being shipped with wires crossed, and line workers were fixing this problem. This non–value added time (unintended rework that was not part of the planned operation) was affecting their productivity. When the activity was reported, the problem was identified in real time and a value engineer was called to the floor to evaluate the low outputs. The problem was quickly resolved. Another discovery at the same plant was that when work orders were released to the floor without 100 percent parts complete, the job took twice as long. The analytics tool played a major role in uncovering this non-intuitive problem and allowed the manufacturer to resolve this impediment to productivity. The result was that the company exceeded its cycle time goal for that product by reducing it by over half.

What's new is that **the technology empowers the employees to reach their goals, to be successful at an individual level.** They can monitor their performance and know their supervisor is monitoring it as well in real time. Instant feedback, instant recognition, spotlights on obstacles and challenges—add those individual benefits up and the company benefits as well. **What's different is that unlike the lean and quality**

initiatives that satisfy the needs and interests of workers higher up on the management ladder, these systems impact the front-line worker. The advantages for *them* compel them to support the system, to continue to give the system the information everyone needs, and to react to the data, changing their behavior to reach their goals. That's different.

It's also important to keep in mind the changing dynamics of worker attitudes as more and more Generation X and Y employees join the workforce. This generation has been groomed to expect feedback and to offer input. They have grown up in the information generation, and working with a technology that provides them the instant gratification they are accustomed to will satisfy their expectations. For those companies that stubbornly resist upgrading their technology, it may be the Gen X and Y employees who rise into management that finally turn their companies on to these systems.

Incentive Plan Cost-Efficiency Analysis

One thing is true in just about any business. You get what you measure and pay for. When people's jobs and livelihoods depend on something getting done, it is more likely to be done. This means it's important to keep score to know precisely how the business is doing in each key area and to hand out rewards to employees when the goals they've been given are met. That's why management might also consider tying a percentage of workers' compensation to achieving company goals.

A good incentive plan can have a major impact on a company's bottom line, and the right WMT system can be helpful in developing a plan, because modeling can be used to determine the financial impact. Suppose someone comes up with an incentive plan to get people to work weekends. Before instituting it, management would be wise to see how much it's going to cost. This won't be difficult with an automated system. Take last year's weekend time and attendance data, for example; overlay the proposed incentive program on top of it; and presto, the cost of the new incentive program can be compared to the current compensation plan.

Key Idea

Modeling can test compensation plans. The technology is, for the first time, introducing simulations into front-line human capital management.

This is particularly helpful when the plan involves qualifiers such as minimum number of hours, overall attendance, or limits on stacking the new plan on top of other premium programs. These qualified plans are useful when the incentive is designed to provide a consistent labor supply.

They are weighted to discourage employees who might consider working something less than 100 percent of what is required. They become "vested" and risk losing all of their "bonus" if they fail to work as they promised. Overlaying a new commitment plan against employee work patterns yields a more realistic estimate of the cost than any educated guess or "calculation." The question can then be asked (assuming the plan produces the hoped-for behavior modification): If employees do begin to work weekend shifts consistently, can the company afford the additional expense? Or does the additional expense offset the avoided costs of what happened when workers could not be persuaded to work the weekend?

The converse can also be determined. Say there is already a weekend differential, but management senses there is an ample supply of workers willing to work the weekend. By removing or reducing the incentive pay and running the numbers, it's possible to see what the potential savings would be.

It's not always necessary to use historical data. These systems are designed to help management determine how they should operate in real time or in the future. **It's the integration of the business knowledge, creating correlations between operational demand and labor supply, that provides the manager with a forecast and a barometer of his or her labor situation.** In health care, for example, a certain number of each category of health care worker, based on skills and roles, must be present during a hospital shift, depending on the number of patients on a particular floor, or in a unit, and the patients' acuity level (i.e., how sick the patients are and how much care they require). Set ratios can be programmed into the software so that "what if" scenarios can be run. If the cost of the incentive program seems too high, the conditions can be tweaked. Instead of a 24-hour minimum before the incentive is earned, bump it up to 30 hours and see what happens. How many employees would still meet the minimum and be eligible for the bonus? How much would be saved? This ability to tweak and adjust is one of the things that make this feature so useful.

Software vendors offer scheduling solutions for use by manufacturers that help them optimize output based on the variables of workload and staff. They use optimization routines with sophisticated algorithms to run and compare scenarios in order to calculate the best possible schedule in terms of the work to be done and the employees needed to perform it. An employer can define the parameters and the priorities so that the system takes into account desired limits and goals. This brings scheduling to an entirely new level—to demand-driven labor forecasting.

■ **CASE STUDY: A MANUFACTURER USES ITS TIMEKEEPING SYSTEM TO TRACK PROJECTS AND PRODUCTIVITY AND MEET ORGANIZATIONAL GOALS** One company client of ours builds water towers—those big things that look like giant mushrooms rising up around communities and industrial parks across America. The company uses WMT to track the status of its projects. As you can imagine, one of these huge tanks takes weeks to fabricate. Managers from engineering, supervisors, and sales personnel now track the time spent on each project and its progress toward completion. Employees enter into the system the amount of time it takes to complete certain tasks—for example, coating a large assembly. On any given day, this enables the company to see how many hours have been put into a particular tank and what steps in the build have been performed. It identifies who is working on a project right now and who is going to work on it tomorrow.

Let's say a customer wants to know the status of a particular water tower under construction, and he calls his service rep. The people at the company can tell him exactly where it stands up to the minute by calling up real-time information in the computer. Yep, it's on time and on budget. Hallelujah! And that's not just a "best guess" based on last month's reports.

You see, the company's president had a vision. He realized how outdated the company's systems were when he heard about the new technology. He imagined and he planned what it could do at *his* company. This was not a huge corporation. At the time the new time and labor system was installed, the HR department was still doing things on paper for the more than 400 employees on the payroll. But the obvious lack of investment in information technology to that point didn't deter him from seizing the opportunities he saw.

For this particular business, **the technology can also be used to create incentives for workers to get things done faster and more efficiently.** Let's take a welder. Say Steve is scheduled to weld one of the panels today. He clocks in when he starts on the welding work order by swiping a bar code representing the specific task he's about to perform. This task is part of the purchase order and the project plan. The time and labor system now tracks his time on that task. Then he swipes again when he finishes. If he completes the job before the standard time, he might get points toward a bonus. Operational objectives and time and labor data have now been linked.

What are the business objectives in this process?

- The work is more likely to be completed on time.
- The project is completed at the lowest cost and shortest timeframe.
- Steve is motivated.
- Management can see labor activity and cost in real time and measure progress against budgets and milestones.
- Steve's performance is tracked.

How did the time and attendance system help reach these five goals?

The manufacturing schedule became the employee's work schedule. The assembly process put the work order on Steve's task list. Of course, that process probably hasn't changed and has been ongoing for the company. What has changed was that instead of Steve just reporting that he is at work today—"Hi, time and attendance system, Steve here. It's 8:00 A.M. and I'm at work"—Steve now tells the system, "I will be working on Work Order 4566 starting at 8:00 A.M." The Supervisor can even put the work order in Steve's work schedule in the WMT system along with the next work order he has to complete—and the next. When Steve goes to the time clock or swipes a bar code, the work order becomes "in progress." The computer system can now compare what was scheduled to occur against what is actually occurring or has already occurred.

Anyone who needs to monitor this project can now see, in real time, what is being worked on, what is complete, how much time it took, and what is scheduled to be worked on next. And the person doesn't have to be in Farmville, where the water tower is being built, or out on the shop floor. He doesn't have to be in the same building, or even on the same continent. He doesn't have to call Steve's supervisor.

Is the work being done at the lowest cost? The WMT system can help manage that, too. The system contains Steve's pay information. Time multiplied by hourly rate equals the cost. The system may even have suggested assigning this work order to Steve because he is the welder with the lowest hourly rate. Once Steve is finished with the task, the system can compute the cost of that particular work order by adding in all the welders, fabricators, painters, and so forth who logged time against that project.

Steve knows the system is tracking the time it takes him to complete the job and that if he finishes quickly, he may qualify for a bonus. This bonus may add to the cost, but it also will move Steve along faster to the next work order and help keep the project on schedule. This may make sense, given that not meeting the schedule could cost the company more than a small bonus. Further, if Steve's manager reviews the schedule and notices that he is about to exceed 40 hours this week if Steve picks up the next work order, the manager has the opportunity to change Steve's schedule and to assign another worker to that task, keeping Steve's total hours in check and avoiding an overtime payment.

In this case, **the WMT system helped meet three objectives—on-time completion, cost control, and visibility**—and it did so by putting front-line management in control.

Employee Score Cards

Sports teams and fans have long understood the value of performance data. Look at baseball cards. Players are rated, traded, and idolized for their "stats."

Who goes up to bat is decidedly scientific—based on batting averages, runs batted in (RBI), and on-base percentage. The player's performance determines how and when he is used in the game. Imagine employers keeping scorecards for employees (see Exhibit 2.7).

Integrating performance data such as stats on workers or teams or business units with workforce systems can provide valuable information. It can tell the employer who does what and when they do it best—at the individual, group, or organizational levels.

Key Idea

Workforce analytics is based on taking the labor data, measuring it, analyzing it, comparing it to key business targets, and using it to improve performance.

It's the coupling of the data from the various areas that reveal correlations and show where the company is "batting a thousand" and where some pinch hitters are needed.

It may reveal that more training is needed or where the presence of too many pitchers on the mound actually slows down production. What's important is that it will enable companies to distinguish between what managers "think or say their people do" and what they "actually do." Data provides the story, a history. Analytical studies and dashboards reveal causes and relationships and provide forecasts. Baseball managers don't just look at RBI numbers. Pro golfers don't just study their past scores; they understand

EXHIBIT 2.7 Employee Performance Cards

This exhibit illustrates how time and labor data can be transformed into employee performance scorecards, representing key players to the organization.

what makes them great players and they constantly work to keep their eyes on the ball and improve their swing.

■ CASE STUDY: A RETAILER USES LABOR DATA TO INCREASE SALES AND PROFITS   An outdoor equipment retailer in the northwestern United States, with dozens of stores located across the county, sells recreational and extreme sports equipment. Perhaps you've been in one of these stores. The stores look like lodges, and the salespeople are all 20-something with buff bodies and good tans. They sell hang gliding, skiing, cycling, camping, hiking, backpacking, and mountain climbing gear, along with other, extreme outdoor recreational equipment.

The company's management team recognized a connection between individual store sales and staffing. So the team decided to go to an automated time and attendance system. In other words, WMT would be used to increase sales. Part of the strategy was to make the operation and implementation of WMT by store managers a mandatory core competency.

Key Idea

Management recognized a connection between individual store sales and staffing. WMT would be used to increase sales. Managers would be required to gain competency on using the new system to drive sales.

The management team of this outfit "knew what they knew." They knew their numbers and understood their customer traffic patterns and sales trends. They also had a good feel for the "soft side" of the sales process. Their marketing approach included employing sales people who enjoyed and participated in the outdoor sporting activities for which the equipment being sold was designed. So they hired guys and gals who like to rock climb and rappel and hang-glide and put them in the department that sold these goods. They knew their customers were enthusiastic about such purchases and reacted positively to the workers who shared their interests. A certain "match" existed between sales staff, the products, and the customers. When everything was aligned, the perfect "sales chemistry" was created. The goal was to create this chemistry and to staff at a level that would return the maximum ROI. They also knew that customers eventually get tired of waiting for someone to help them and will go somewhere else if they don't get service within a reasonable length of time, which made having the right number of sales personnel for the amount of traffic on a given day a must.

Along with knowledge about what made the cash registers ring was an appreciation for how difficult it was to create this perfect chemistry without assistance. The team also realized that not every store manager was a natural "chemist." Some were better than others at conjuring up this staffing magic. So they studied what the best managers did and figured out why and how they were successful.

In this way, the management team came up with its own "best practices" based on what had worked in the past. Coupling statistical data on customer traffic along with sales and best practices, they knew their employees' "score card stats" and were able to build a model for staffing. They knew what types of workers to schedule during specific seasons and during special sales events.

Key Idea

Employee Scorecards Drive Revenue

Coupling statistical data on customer traffic along with sales and best practices, the management team knew their employees' "score card stats" and were able to build a model for staffing. They knew what types of workers to schedule during specific seasons and during special sales events.

You might say they viewed the workday as a sports team would on game day. The team could predict with a fair degree of accuracy what store traffic would be at different times of year and on different days of the week. They knew what could be expected during a sales event such as a ski equipment sale, or a mountain-climbing bonanza. They developed a game plan, knew their players, and set out to break records. All they needed was the mechanism to make it happen.

The retailer selected a workforce management technology vendor that understood the relationship between time and attendance and business objectives (e.g., maximizing sales) and offered a software product that fit the bill. Management was purchasing a new tool, not simply installing a new timekeeping and scheduling system. Knowing what the expected outcomes were mandated that the system be rolled out with a means for ensuring results.

There's a saying, "You cannot expect what you are not willing to inspect." The new owners of the time and attendance system must have come across this expression, because they decided early on to institute new job expectations for managers along with the new system. Not only would they train the managers on how to use the system, they planned to change how managers were evaluated at their annual performance reviews. Using set goals and best practices, a measurement for competency was determined. Management provided the targets (increasing store sales) along with the methods for reaching the targets (best practice tasks configured into the time and attendance system) and the timetable for evaluating their aim at the annual review.

What this employer instituted was measurable accountability with tangible processes and tracking tools. Much more was involved than establishing a sales target. Ways were developed to evaluate how the managers worked within the system by considering actual inputs, decisions, deployments, mitigating factors, and results. The managers knew their planning and reactions to the system indicators would be tracked and compared with the effect they had on store income. A hands-on tool was given to them to use every day in the pursuit of company targets. They knew it provided their leaders with visibility into how they were doing. As a result, this business tool became a part of the daily routine—a front-end business driver. It became a tuning instrument to channel each store manger's use of labor through a system with built-in standards, allowing the company to institutionalize best practices and to produce the desired sales results.

Not only did the company achieve success and reach its sales goals, the technology also resulted in smarter, more cost-effective use of labor resources. If they scheduled the "kayaking king" to work even though he was paid a higher wage than the local novice, they expected better results. Better results meant more money, and more money meant more value from the labor dollars expended—in other words, a better return on investment.

The management of this chain had its store managers match the right people in the right numbers to anticipated store traffic at the right time. They also wanted to get the supervisors and managers out of the back office, away from the tasks of scheduling and checking time cards, and out on the floor where they, too, could sell. Come game time, when the doors open at stores across the country, the strategy works.

The Need for WMT Exists in Every Market Sector

Time and labor management systems answer the needs and solve problems for employers in every market sector. While some segments of the market have already integrated human capital principles and WMT systems to replace outdated processes and improve operational success, others have been slow to recognize the relevance to their industry. In the next sections we'll explore a few of the sectors that have interesting stories to tell about how WMT systems make a difference in their organizations. We've already pointed out examples in retail, manufacturing, and health care. You'll find discussions throughout this book on almost every major market sector.

Government and Education Sectors

There are two segments of the economy that are relatively new to time and labor management technology: government and education. These employers typically exist in the public sector and operate under a unique set of mandates. While WMT has been rapidly evolving, times have been relatively good in this sector, and growth and spending were more predominant than lean or quality initiatives. However, times are changing. According to David O'Connell, senior research analyst with Nucleus Research, "higher ed has the most to gain and government is the most behind."

The pain resulting from the absence of systems to manage the workforce effectively is becoming acute, as 70 to 80 percent of operational budgets are tied to labor in higher education, 80 percent or more in K–12 school systems, and approximately 45 to 50 percent of expenses are related to labor in state and local government budgets. These figures are reported by Christine Carmichael, an industry specialist with one of the leading WMT vendors. For these employers, gaining operational efficiency soon is critical.

Universities and college campuses often look like miniature cities with a wide variety of worker groups. Safety, facility and plant maintenance, food services, staff and administration, and student workers create a high degree of complexity. Ten to twenty percent of the workforce is made up of student workers who work a variety of jobs on anything but a routine schedule. Collecting the data can be a challenge, given that workers are assigned to scads of buildings and offices and report to numerous supervisors. The real value proposition is in WMT's ability to rein in labor costs, do more with less, and maintain continuity of service despite all of the complexity and proximity issues. Overpaying or overstaffing causes higher-ed employers to spend money they can't afford to waste. With revenue constrained by state allocations, endowments, and tuition, the only income they have much control over is tuition. In a competitive market such as higher ed, pricing themselves out of the market is not an option for these institutions. The only option is to pay correctly and use labor wisely. WMT is the best way to ensure that gets done.

Key Idea

For higher ed, the real value proposition lies in WMT's ability to rein in labor costs, do more with less, and maintain continuity of service despite all of the complexity and proximity issues.

For educators in the K–12 market there are similar pressures to better manage labor budgets. What is key for these employers is to be transparent and consistent and to ensure that workers are at the right place at the right time. School systems employ many workers in mission-critical roles. If a bus driver fails to show up, a teacher becomes ill in the middle of the day and has to leave the classroom, or even a cafeteria worker is called to jury duty, each one of these positions must be filled immediately and with the right person before things get very ugly. WMT can provide real-time visibility into these situations and their resolution before a crisis is at hand.

Further complicating the K–12 workplace are unions that are vigilant in supporting employees with grievances. The cost of not managing labor issues to ensure accuracy and fairness can be substantial. The problem is that the management is local but the headaches are centralized. A principal who administers policy to the letter of the law, angering employees and setting in motion union complaints, creates a downstream cost where school corporations employ high-priced lawyers to respond to these costly distractions. WMT enforces consistency and accountability. Subsequently, we'll explore one school corporation that literally saved millions just in the first year with its WMT solution.

Key Idea

The K–12 segment is significantly behind in adopting WMT. Therefore, benefits from adopting it will be swift and sizable.

Unfortunately, according to Carmichael, too many school systems are way behind the private sector in their adoption of time and labor management technologies. Luckily, the benefits will be swift and sizable, making the investment a sound financial decision.

From a strategic standpoint, WMT may be able to assist schools facing the difficult decision of where to cut costs. Carmichael suggests that the technology can be used to help them decide where to shut things down for a period of time. In conversations with members of CUPA (College and University Professional Association), they indicated that they are monitoring real estate costs with few workers in buildings during certain times. Integration with enterprise resource planning (ERP) systems that can create this kind of intelligence can be very important.

Like the private sector, schools can benefit from more sophisticated ways to handle scheduling and attendance. Carmichael also maintains that the systems help support their efforts to comply with No Child Left Behind mandates and security concerns in this era of precaution for school safety.

The major touch points for school decision makers are often some of the features that bring the fastest time to value, or ROI, on their investments in WMT. They care about eliminating paper and manual processes, along with all of the problems inherent in those methods; reducing overpayments; and monitoring the number of staff tasked with those processes. **Broward County (Florida) Schools, the nation's sixth-largest school district, had a 52 percent ROI and payback of only 1.88 years from their purchase.** This school system realized significant administrative productivity gains and was able to eliminate overpayments and manual processes. (*Source*: Nucleus Research I 34, April 2008.)

In the government sector, decision makers are concerned with transparency and accountability. Their activity must be accessible to their governing boards and taxpayers. Government workers are also unionized, and compliance with contract requirements is another concern. Carmichael stressed that overtime is "astronomical" in state and local governments, and the negative press treatment of this is gaining more attention. As we mentioned earlier, overtime control represents one of the easiest and surest ways to save, using WMT.

Key Idea

Government sector employers benefit from greater transparency, accountability, security, and cost control. WMT enables this sector to succeed in its mission and become excellent stewards of limited resources.

In court systems, school buildings and any public building, WMT provides immediate reporting of "on premises"—that is, accounting for who is onsite. In many of these workplaces, managers are required to have safety plans in place, and WMT supports these initiatives. The ability to quickly read where leadership is and how many employees need to be accounted for could be a matter of life and death.

Public safety isn't just the purview of principals and security guards. It also applies to public safety professionals such as fire, police, and corrections. In these areas, WMT can be used to track the assignment of equipment (squad cars, tasers, laptops, etc.). Again, WMT supersedes boundaries that other resource systems conform to.

Because these segments of the workplace have been slow to adopt technology, a surprising benefit is that introducing a WMT system may present a welcome opportunity for workers to ramp up on their computer skills. Carmichael shared the story of a sheriff's office in Georgia that experienced some tragic upheaval within the ranks. When a new sheriff took over and implemented a time and attendance solution, the system actually brought people together around the new technology. "It was a wonderful win for everyone. For some of the workers it was the first time they had touched some aspects of the technology," she added. It's not uncommon for employee self-service features (e.g., access to benefit balances and time card records or self-scheduling, in particular) to be viewed as significant fringe benefits. The indirect benefits can include greater employee satisfaction, lower turnover, and fewer errors and adjustments.

Government and education workers have a strong sense of mission. WMT systems that help them succeed in their mission and service their constituents are certain to be a welcome addition. Supporting good stewardship of limited funds and resources while meeting the needs of their "customers"—whether taxpayers, school boards, students, citizens, or faculty—is a mission they must achieve.

■ CASE STUDY: CHICAGO PUBLIC SCHOOLS   One big user of time and attendance technology is the Chicago Public School System. Chicago has one of the largest school districts in the country, and it is the largest employer in Chicago, with approximately 44,000 employees, over 600 locations, 420,000 students, and an annual payroll budget of over $2 billion. The Chicago schools have been using automated time and attendance for more than 15 years as of this writing. I spoke with Mike Edwards, Deputy Chief Fiscal Officer, about the WMT system. He says the technology has been helpful in a number of instances, but one in particular is its handling of the different ways Chicago teachers get paid. Edwards estimates there are about 8,000 types of "buckets" or positions they can work in. Which one a worker falls into depends on whether he or she is an hourly worker or salaried, what subjects she may teach, union rules, and so on. This was not easy to administer in a manual setup, but a computerized system keeps it all straight without missing a beat.

But there's more. Before Chicago's system was put in place, each employee at each of the more than 600 schools had to fill out paper time sheets. At that time, the system had about 42,000 employees. Clerks would collect these and transcribe them to summary sheets. All this paper had to be transported to a central location and be key punched by data entry clerks. In a paper system of this magnitude, mistakes were bound to occur. Edwards estimates there were about 48,000 adjustments annually because of errors and omissions. Not surprisingly, people got upset when they were not paid correctly. In a highly unionized situation such as this one, workers and teachers would complain to their unions, and the unions would file complaints. Edwards says you cannot imagine the disruption.

The school system's labor agreements allowed employees who experienced a payroll error to leave the classroom—during school—and go to the downtown office on company time and dispute their pay. For that "missing in action" teacher a substitute had to be called in—and paid—while the teacher was out of the building. Now *that's* an expensive payroll adjustment!

Another factor that led to complaints under the old system was that people were treated differently at different schools. One clerk might allow a five-minute grace period for tardy workers. Another might give ten minutes. Or it might depend on how the clerk felt about a particular employee. One she liked might get a pass. Another might be held accountable to the letter of the rule book. Of course, teachers and school workers frequently moved from one school to another and would notice these inconsistencies. The result was hundreds of grievances filed each year by the union. Every complaint required a hearing and testimony to be given as to what had occurred. The school system employed four full-time individuals in labor relations devoted to handling these complaints, and top management spent a large amount of time and effort on this sort of thing.

But a computerized time and attendance system does not make human errors and it does not play favorites. It administers the rules fairly and consistently as they are written and programmed into it. **Edwards says that in 2005, under the newly automated system, a total of only 37 grievances were filed. The number of labor relations agents handling these cases has dwindled to only one staff member. The burden of these cases has been virtually eliminated. Imagine the time and money this has saved.**

Mike told me that when the system was just being implemented, the employees were dead set against it. The union filed a legal grievance, and the case went to arbitration; the union lost its case. *The Chicago Sun* newspaper wrote a scathing article about the folly he was getting the school system into ("Untimely Clocks" was the name of the editorial) with this new technology. The unions and employees were upset. He wasn't popular by any means. But Mike had big plans.

Mike convinced the unions and employees that things were going to get better. People would be paid fairly and consistently and the error rate would improve. **In fact, the errors went from 48,000 to around 10,000.** Not bad for an organization this large and with employees moving about and having varying schedules.

Mike looked beyond payroll for additional opportunities for improvement. The education world is commonly funded through grant money. These funds are made available to individual schools for specific programs and administered largely at the local (school) level. Teachers are compensated out of these, but it requires tracking, reporting, and reconciling the hours spent on the program against the pool of grant money. In Chicago, it was common for school administrators to struggle to keep track of teacher activities, and they often exceeded their grant budgets. Spending money you don't have is a big problem.

But Mike understood the power behind the workforce management system he'd purchased. He implemented the system in a way that enabled local school officials to track and schedule their teachers and programs so that they spent only their allotted amount of grant money. When the system registered that budget spending reached 75 percent, a caution was issued; at 85 percent a warning; and at 95 percent all activity was cut off. In the first year alone, the system saved $15 million dollars for the school system.

On the flip side, the school system didn't want to leave grant money on the table. Analytics looked at spending over the grant period and checked how program managers planned to spend all the money. Instead of discovering at the last minute that programs had a lot of money and then going on a spending spree that involved attending workshops and the like, administrators found that the dollars could be spent more effectively as they were intended. Quality was being managed as well as the financial side.

Key Idea

Significant Savings Can Happen Early

In the first year alone, the system saved $15 million dollars for the school system.

Mike soon got an award from the Mayor of Chicago. The city was now touting his success. The Mayor remarked to him, "Mike, you've gone from being on the hit list to the hit parade." **Mike made the connection between a business problem and a workforce technology solution.**

Professional Service Sector

Some organizations don't have hourly laborers, but even so, they don't have to miss out on benefits that stem from the advances in automation. This is true for the professional service sector. Employers in this sector often employ professionals who work on a project basis. Several vendors specialize in providing solutions for project-oriented organizations. The market for products that satisfy the challenges in the government sector, internal service organizations, consulting organizations, and advanced technology firms is growing. These organizations face three primary challenges:

- Paper-based accounting processes
- Legal requirements
- Ensuring top operational performance

It's easy to understand how automation would improve the inefficiencies, inaccuracies, and untimeliness of processes that have historically been done manually. **Once an organization grows beyond 25 or more employees, business leaders dealing with paper or even electronic spreadsheet–based processes can become overwhelmed with managing the "paper" instead of the core business.** Errors in processing in these business models can mean not only overpaying employees but undercollecting earned revenue from customers.

The regulations imposed on this industry are also a major concern. Here is a list of but a few of the alphabet soup of agencies and laws that can have an impact:

- Defense Contract Audit Agency (DCAA)—DCAAP 7641.90
- Per diem rates dictated by the Department of Defense (DoD), General Services Administration (GSA), and the Department of State (DoS)
- Sarbanes-Oxley (SOX)—internal controls
- Office of Management and Budget (OMB) Circular No. A.11—Planning, Budgeting, Acquisition, and Management of Capital Assets
- ANSI Standard 748—mandating earned value management reporting

For anyone who may not be familiar with or is considering government work, the DCAA governs the rules for the charging of any government contractor for labor. Some of the key rules include:

- Proper accounting of direct costs is required by contract.
- Time must be recorded on a daily basis, and changes in time must be appended with comments.
- "Total Time Accounting" (a.k.a. adjusted rate, time dilution) is enforced.
- All hours worked must be recorded.
- Signatures and approvals are required from employees and supervisors.
- DCAA dictates how policies must be written concerning time card responsibilities.
- Penalties for incorrectly charging labor are enforced.

The strict guidelines, reporting requirements, and the likelihood of being audited necessitate having an intelligent system to enforce policy and consistency and to ensure proper reporting. Without automation, imagine the manpower that would be required and the attendant cost an organization would incur just to stay in compliance.

Finally, like any other business, these organizations have to stay on top of performance. Resource scheduling is crucial in the project world. What may be unique is that workers may be assigned to multiple projects concurrently, and the mix of how they spend their time can vary widely. Complicating project work is that resources can be overbooked or under-booked if labor isn't managed effectively. This can lead to project delays or underutilized resources. These specialized solutions not only manage this, but they also provide forecasting tools to predict and evaluate revenue and project completion targets.

One feature needed in a professional service labor tracking is the ability to keep tabs on hours worked relative to project completion. For agencies servicing government entities, requirements exist for *how* hours are to be tracked. The technology allows users to append comments and "Estimated Time to Completion" to the labor hours, adding another level to the useful-ness of the data. Project expenses must also be tracked along with project hours. Unlike internal project expenses generally absorbed by overhead ac-counts or built-in rate margins, these may be billed directly to the customer and must be tracked alongside the work. Having one place to store all of this data is immensely helpful. The systems also integrate to project track-ing format such as Gantt charting so that data transfers seamlessly between different schedule mechanisms.

Project profitability for service organizations can be managed us-ing dashboards and tools that can track profitability by project, per-son, and task. It's important to know when companies are working under cost and truly making money. Summary reports offer high-level overviews and drill-down so that managers at every level can understand, at whatever level of detail is required, how the work is getting done. **Revenue man-agement is also key in project-oriented companies.** Finally, the best systems provide *"Earned Value Management"* (EVM) tools to analyze this component of the work.

Workforce management technology is growing in the professional ser-vices industry. Companies in this segment concerned with efficiency, com-pliance, and long-term profitability cannot afford to overlook the importance of automating their processes and integrating the areas of payroll, account-ing, and project management.

Benefits of a software tool include the following:

- Rapid invoicing and payables—typically improves from 20 to 2 days.
- Profitable projects—overruns are avoided early on.
- Optimal use of human resource deployment and capacity.
- Better decision making—real-time reports provide data for making de-cisions when it matters, not after it is too late.
- Improved compliance—rules are enforced so that compliance nears 100 percent.
- Enforcement of corporate policies—corporate rules are enforced across the organization.

- Reduced costs (eliminates paper, fax, storage), typically 90 percent improvement in costs—companies have saved $100.00 to $150.00 per employee in each year for time reporting and $30.00 per expense report.
- Reduced errors (typically 90 percent of the errors are eliminated)—companies have been able to bill hundreds of thousands of dollars formerly unbillable or unrecorded.
- Employee satisfaction—many companies report that their accounting staffs no longer have to work weekends to record the time and expenses to a project.

International Sector

We've discussed sectors that are primarily domestic, but many industries cross into the territory of international business. Companies operating abroad have many of the same challenges, along with a few curve balls to deal with. Participating in a global economy means that some managers will be faced with issues surrounding their workforce overseas. Multinational firms must find vendors that can meet their needs in distant markets where they are subject to foreign regulations, industry standards, and worker expectations. David Mitchell is Director of International Operations for a major WMT vendor. We talked about the various challenges facing employers who venture into foreign lands.

The biggest challenge in markets such as the European Union (EU) or Australia may be converting our concept of paid time. In Europe, the focus is on paying people accurately for the time they work, with the added complexity of accurately paying for time they don't work. We didn't get into the genesis of these workplace differences, but I do want to provide some insight into the various levels of complexity.

Employers in these countries have myriad governing bodies dictating rules and regulations concerning employee activity. At the highest level, the (EU) Working Time Directive regulates the number of days off per year, rest time between shifts, and how employees get paid. Below that, each country sets up guidelines that must be enforced, such as France's "modulation" formulas for calculating overtime or Belgium's rules for maternity leave. France's averaging method can require an employer to compute the pay and ensure compliance with work-hour regulations (e.g. 35-hour workweek) based on a rolling average of time worked over several weeks or months.

Within each industry there may be rules as well. The transportation industry sets limits on the number of consecutive hours employees are allowed to work before taking a mandated rest period. At every level there are violations just as there are in the United States, with heavy fines and penalties for noncompliance. The European workplace is heavily unionized—more so than in the United States—with unions permeating even white-collar jobs and carrying on in what we might consider an aggressive, confrontational manner. Mitchell shared that "you're constantly reading about workers going out on strike." This means compliance and employee satisfaction are important issues a workforce management solution can support.

The reverse concept of paying for time off with premiums and bonus payments could be a challenge for many WMT systems. The level of complexity in the European rules equates to a requirement to have the same degree of regulatory complexity on the attendance side of the application as there is for the worked time. Add to that the fact that there are few vendors who do it all; most specialize by country. Therefore, an employer with sites in more than one European nation might have to manage several different systems just to administer time and attendance. According to Mitchell, hardly any vendor takes a "Pan-European" approach to its product, providing sufficient flexibility and complexity to handle every layer in one system. But at least one vendor is beefing up its product to meet these needs, and customers with this degree of diversity will benefit greatly from owning such a system.

WMT HANDLES OVERSEAS BUSINESS RULES   The business requirements for WMT systems outside of the United States are quite different from industry standards familiar to most of us. For European operations the key benefits of WMT systems designed for these markets are in the advanced rostering (Europe's term for scheduling) tools. These tools allow employers to manage employee activity according to complex and expensive rules. An additional benefit is absence management; paying for time off correctly and consistently is critical to effectively controlling profit margins in these overseas operations. Workers in Europe apparently don't come cheaply, and staying competitive in the global marketplace is made more difficult by these intricate practices. The good news is that European workers are some of the most productive on the planet, says Mitchell. (*Source*: UN Study http://www.cbsnews.com/stories/2007/09/03/business/main3228735.shtml. Note that U.S. employees are the most productive in the world, followed by workers in Ireland, Belgium, and France.) So managing productivity is less of an issue. It appears that all of that paid time off creates some very good workers.

Closer to home, Canada is a hybrid. In the case of health care, Mitchell says Canada's half-socialized system creates some drivers to greater efficiency, which means health care employers in this region will benefit from the productivity benefits within WMT systems as well as the value from gaining efficiencies and accuracy in their workforce processes.

On the other side of the globe, companies are finding that countries such as China, India, and leading Southeast Asian nations are in their infancy in terms of workforce management technology. In these countries, the sheer volume of people is enormous, wages are extremely low, enforcement of overtime is not consistent, and paid time off is not of great concern, at least up until the past five years.

More recently, growth has been creating constraints in the labor supply, as manufacturers compete for skilled workers and business expands at a breakneck pace. Pay rates have considerably appreciated during the past few years, adds Mitchell, to the extent that "in India if you looked at an engineer in Bangalore vs. an engineer in Silicon Valley you are paying them the same rate." Turnover rates can be as high as 50 percent as workers chase higher and higher wages. At the same time, China is watching as its own manufacturing jobs "go south" to lower-wage markets such as Cambodia and Vietnam.

With these rising wage rates overseas, employers must start thinking about how to control labor costs. Second, the rule of law begins to kick in as these countries enter into the modern economic system and join the World Trade Organization, where they must begin to put in place labor laws and ensure compliance. In January 2008, China passed new labor laws around unions, overtime, and numerous other work regulations. Competitive forces are at work as well, as multinational firms with global workplace standards demand that their domestic counterparts, competing with them locally for workers and margins, must institute the same practices to level the playing field. Taking on these new constraints while dealing with a challenging marketplace necessitates having a system that helps these companies ramp up quickly on effective management processes and valuable business intelligence. (For more information see "China's Contract Law, Something for Everyone," *Workforce Management Magazine*, Sept. 6, 2007.)

GETTING "TIME TO PAY CYCLES" RIGHT   There is an awakening demand for the benefits of workforce management systems in relatively immature markets such as China, India, and Southeast Asia. These economies are flush with people, but as a whole they are well behind Western markets in their use of labor-related technology. But things are changing. Following the adoption of ERP and HR and payroll systems, time and labor systems are increasingly being sought by companies that need to automate the collection of time, pay correctly, and roster effectively. China and India are both hyper-growth markets, and what took 30 years to mature in the United States (from the first microchip in a time clock in 1977 to today) will take less than 5 to 10 years. First, these companies will begin to get the basic "time to pay cycle" right. Managing absence and scheduling represents the second stage. Once managing people is under control, these employers will begin to optimize.

However, this compacted timeline for advancement is not without problems. Many workers in these countries lack sufficient knowledge about technology as well as about the fundamental business processes they support. This is where the experience vendors have gained during the past 30 years in this country in creating products that are easy to use, intelligently designed, and inexpensive to operate is paying off.

Some of the key differences between these foreign markets and the United States are that Europeans tend to like "slick and stylish." What is a sturdy, functional time clock to us "looks like a microwave" to the fashion-conscious European worker. But vendors are working to make their products more appealing. In both the EU and Asian markets, Web and wireless technologies are less popular than clocks, whereas biometrics, while generally accepted, are subject to local privacy laws that can sharply constrain their use. Access control is a huge data collection driver overseas. These markets view security and time and attendance as an integrated solution. WMT systems have a long history of integrating tightly with access control devices.

In India the hyper growth is incredible. When visiting there, Mitchell talked with a company, Infosys, that was hiring 25,000 people each quarter. Nokia, another company, went from approximately 2,000 to 14,000 employees within a two-year period. Onboarding 800 to 900 people a day is not something that can be done with paper and pencil. It's almost impossible to imagine the headaches generated by that kind of growth. Labor processes, such as complex rules governing shift premiums and breaks, are not very prevalent; the biggest advantages arise from economies of scale and process efficiencies. Self-service is also very attractive across all markets.

TAKE-AWAYS FOR THE INTERNATIONAL MARKET   The value of instituting WMT to manage a multinational, foreign-based workforce is that the complexities, processes, and decisions involved in deployment and compensation cannot be adequately managed without these tools. In the international arena, the most important benefits are

- **Single source of truth.** A globally deployed application allows management to use the power of information to evaluate, manage, and predict. For example, productivity intelligence might help a multinational business leader decide whether to move a foreign operation to a lower-cost, higher-productivity location. In addition, having the ability to gain insight into the total cost of operations in a foreign market with so many different compensation practices is extremely valuable. Real-time visibility into the detailed costs (creating line-item financial data) of doing business in a particular location is the only way to fully understand the price of those operations.

- **Risk management.** This is a major area of concern; it involves allowing companies to apply global standards for workplace practices throughout their operations.
- **Maximizing production.** This is accomplished in the cheapest and most efficient locations.

The fundamental challenges are the same although the issues are unique and the competitive forces are accentuated. Being an early adopter may be the advantage that spells success.

Chapter Summary

- Workforce management success is achieved by breaking down the boundaries that separate the owners of the problems and solutions to redefine what can be changed, what is important, and where to go for help.
- Companies should be moving themselves up the technology maturity curve to reap the full benefits of workforce management systems.
- WMT institutes "organizational workforce intelligence" when the technology merges business intelligence from other systems with workforce management to gain the efficiencies and aptitude needed to run the business better.
- Human capital is now a predominant asset within the organization. Failure to manage this resource is a costly mistake.
- Organizations that neglect to empower themselves with WMT technology are leaving dollars on the table in terms of overspending on labor and lost revenue.
- In order to deliver value there may be new demands, new stakeholders, and new relationships within the organization relative to your WMT system.
- WMT makes the important data measurable.
- Make certain employees are "data literate" if you expect positive results from systems that deliver information in the form of charts, graphs, and technical indicators.
- Every industry has its own compelling reason to adopt WMT.
- Government and education have been slow to adopt and thus have more to gain.
- Overseas operations can benefit from WMT's efficiencies, ability to handle a diverse array of rules, real-time visibility into a single source of data, and its ability to improve productivity and profit.

CHAPTER 3

Labor Data—A Device Used to Achieve Financial Goals and Maximize Profits

E very organization is in business to make money or to be a good steward of the resources with which it is entrusted. Leaders should be concerned with the ongoing financial viability of their organizations. Yet an atmosphere persists in which labor data is underappreciated and overlooked. The tide is changing, however, as more and more companies realize how time and labor management systems can create transparency, help manage budgets, control costs, and manage complex policies. The savings can be immediate and dramatic.

In addition, a new way of looking at labor is evolving, as these systems provide a tool to introduce economic principles such as real-time supply and demand and employee-centric features such as self-service into the mix.

Many organizations struggle to understand whether or when these systems are right for them. We'll explore how to assess whether it makes sense to pursue a new system for the first time or replace an old one.

The Power of WMT Will Change Expectations

People who have witnessed the transformation that follows a well-orchestrated WMT implementation have a new perspective on workforce management processes. They see activities within the organization in a new light and recognize a new team of allies in their race for more productivity, lower costs, greater control, and larger profits. When they cross that divide between their traditional notions of who has the means to impact the organization and the reality of a new technological model of how to manage, they reinvent themselves and their organization. WMT systems are the mechanism of that transformation. They are the framework of the new paradigm of business management.

If you're ready to embrace this new world, I will show you what it will take and how it's being done.

Five Important Guidelines Ensure ROI

"When properly deployed these [Workforce Management Technology] applications can be like finding a bag of money in the attic." That's according to David O'Connell of Nucleus Research. He's analyzed software deployments at companies in virtually every industry and his findings have revealed that people underestimate how much slack there is in workflow processes and accuracy. "Properly deployed it [WMT] will make you money," says O'Connell. The absence of ROI indicates an implementation that is either insufficiently mature or not broadly applied throughout the organization.

O'Connell is a Senior Analyst at one of the leading technology investigative research firms. His research into how companies achieve success from their investment in WMT reveals some **important guidelines for ensuring the most ROI.**

- **Deploy everywhere.** Don't leave chunks of your organization untouched by the technology. Work to overcome the political and cultural obstacles to applying your WMT to the entire workforce population.
- **Change your workflow.** Don't permit pockets of target end users to resist the changes that will enable the greatest ROI.
- **Protect the benefits from the ravages of time and turnover.** At the beginning, significant improvements will occur. However, if these are managed by only one WMT specialist, over time this specialist may leave and with him goes the likelihood that the benefit will continue. He will take with him expertise in the best practices that are key to cost savings. Have backups in place, and continually refresh your specialists. These resources accumulate a wealth of knowledge and history about the application. If that expertise is lost, so is the ROI. The same goes for front-line specialists. Make certain you periodically refresh your end users and validate their competency level.
- **Conduct periodic audits.** After deployment, purposefully go into the system on a recurring basis to measure the numbers of corrections, edits, and manual processes. This will tell you where the automation didn't stick. This sort of ongoing quality management will reveal benefits that have been lost or degraded over time as the organization and personnel have changed.

■ **Gather the right data at the very beginning.** Find out what labor-related cost data is important to the organization. Plan to collect not only time and attendance information but key information about how the organization is performing.

The size of that bag of money will be greater by magnitudes for companies that have more work sites, more hourly workers, collective bargaining agreements, and greater rule complexity; operate in more states; and have more data origination sites (e.g., work locations, databases, etc.). The rewards will also be larger for organizations that reach into their time and labor systems and understand their workforces so they can price more aggressively.

They Don't Know and They Don't Believe

As I continued my conversation with David O'Connell, we talked about the obstacles in the way of full adoption of workforce management technology (WMT). In his experience, the biggest gap is that business leaders don't know how much payroll error is out there. (Remember: They don't know what they don't know.) The ROI can be so high that even when the business case for a WMT deployment is well made, it can be greeted with skepticism. But simple application of the phenomenon of large numbers is valid here. A few pennies saved on a large payroll can add up to very large savings.

Key Idea

On average, companies spend 36 percent of their revenues on human capital expenses but only 16 percent say they have anything more than a moderate understanding of the return on their human capital expenditures.

Source: Mercer Human Resources Consulting and CFO Research Services, 2003

Take, for example, an employer with an annual payroll of $10 million. The average payroll error rate is 1.2 percent. That's not a very large percentage. WMT systems will reduce payroll errors by as much as 70 percent; a well-deployed system will reduce errors by 80 to 90 percent; that equates to an error rate as low as 0.12 percent. The company realizes a reduction in the cost of errors that saves $108,000. Figure in some of the additional savings from automating with WMT; they would amount to anything from

2 to 9 percent of total payroll, and that would be an ROI of $200,000 to $900,000. Those are very large numbers to get your arms around.

Another way to estimate the amount of potential financial savings is to examine the manual checks being processed each pay period. Count the number of adjustments, and then take note of the average amount of each manual check. By and large, adjustments are for underpayments. Employees are much more likely to notify management when they have been underpaid. O'Connell tells his clients that their employees are giving them a way to estimate the amount of overpayments. He proposes that those adjustment figures are the mirror image of the unreported overpayments companies let slip away. If a company that is completely manual properly deploys WMT, it should be able to reduce that amount by 90 percent. Again, the financial gains to be realized are almost unbelievable.

Keep in mind, however, that Mr. O'Connell is not a WMT salesman. He is a research analyst, the guy out there spending every day, year after year, collecting and analyzing data. His job is to drill down and quantify the benefits. The potential savings from time and labor management technologies are illustrated in Exhibit 3.1. These are the "low hanging fruit" savings from automating with rule-driven systems that deliver significant improvements. Multiply the savings per cents times total payroll dollars. The figures speak for themselves.

Costly Attitudes Persist

Costly attitudes persist among many in management because of unspoken perceptions. These long-held, somewhat subconscious attitudes create invisible barriers to change. Simply because you present new ideas and

EXHIBIT 3.1   Total Payroll Savings

Reduction in total payroll cost:

▪ Payroll error rate:	1.2%
▪ Payroll processing time:	0.47%
▪ Labor reporting:	0.75%
▪ Payroll inflation:	0.72%
▪ Biometrics:	2.2%
▪ Absence management:	3.8%
Total Payroll Savings:	**> 9.0%**

Industry analysts estimate that up to 9 percent of total payroll can be saved using time and labor management technology.
Source: Nucleus Research Papers

material to your audience of decision makers will not automatically make the issues important to them. There are deeply rooted, strongly held beliefs about the business that will be hard to overcome. This is where education is not enough; persuasion is the instrument you must use. If you encounter this barrier, you will not be able to simply lead your audience to a better place—you'll have to prod them. (Remember the cow path discussed earlier.)

Jerry Nepon-Sixt has been in the industry for years, participating in the decision-making process surrounding WMT systems for scores of customers. He points out several notions about workforce management that impede otherwise open minds from changing they way they look at their businesses.

- Time and attendance are not that complicated; we stick them (*the people who take care of it today*) in the basement. We never hear from them, we don't pay them that much, and it can't be that tough.
- Buying a WMT system is not strategic; we've never involved these people in strategic planning before, so how can automating their processes be strategic?
- Failure to recognize that the messiness is in the "wetwear."
- We aren't being sued today; therefore, it must not be that risky.
- These "costs" or "savings" are not on our balance sheet, so how can these numbers be trusted?

The first in this list is perhaps the most dangerous of these misconceptions and the most difficult to overcome. Failing to acknowledge that time and attendance touches the core of operations and offers a direct conduit into operational excellence is a costly attitude to hold onto. I call it the baggage of the "P" word—payroll. WMT cannot be discussed without bringing up the functions that reside in the payroll department.

This word, payroll, conjures up an immediate resistance, because decision makers see this function as perhaps the most rudimentary and impotent business unit in their organization. If the janitors went on strike there would probably be a more immediate reaction than hearing the payroll department walked off the job (except two weeks later when no one got paid). Payroll is an important function, but few within the organization see it as driving change. The archaic perception that payroll processes offer little opportunity to impact the direction and success of the organization can be difficult to overcome, because it is so widely accepted and was, for the most part, true up until now.

However, failing to convert management to the belief that payroll processes can play a strategic role could be one of the costliest mistakes an organization makes. Why? The money that payroll and a WMT system manage is often the single largest expense a company has. Failing to move beyond the traditional notion that work percolating down in the proverbial basement of the business is of no consequence is the equivalent of replacing all of the computers, networks, printers, and copiers in the company with manual typewriters and carbon paper and thinking that not much will change.

Not upgrading the technology that supports the management of workforce activity and cost is like taking your company on a ride with Michael J. Fox in the movie *Back to the Future* and returning to the mid-1900s. Being stuck in a time warp is definitely not strategic.

Key Idea

Failing to move beyond the traditional notion that work percolating down in the proverbial basement of the business is of no consequence is the equivalent of replacing all of the computers, networks, printers, and copiers in the company with manual typewriters and carbon paper and thinking that not much will change.

Creating Transparency

Jerry had a great way of explaining why WMT makes the functions it manages strategic: **"The messiness is where the wetwear controls the processes."** Think hardware, software, and so on. *Wetwear* is people; people are what create the opportunity for strategic improvements. And workforce management cannot be entirely mechanized; people will always be involved to some extent. But without the right tools, it's almost impossible to do things completely right. Without tools, processes can't be influenced or audited, and the human variable is not managed. This is where things begin to break down. As a front-line manager, if I'm responsible for administering absence policy and production **I need to know how I do that and get the job done. How is the manager to know if his decisions follow all of the policies and laws and meet demand? Without a tool, how can that manager consistently avoid risky behavior?** Humans aren't inherently evil or bad; we all do great things, bring our own point of view, make mistakes, and so on. But in WFM, consistency, compliance, and good decisions are critically important to the welfare of the organization and its employees. The perception often is that it's working today so it must not be broken. Ask a race car driver if his car limps around the track while the competition speeds by at 175 miles per hour, does his car need repair? It still runs, doesn't it? Is performance important to the business?

Performance isn't the only hidden issue. Not getting caught at something doesn't mean you aren't at risk. Jerry adds that the greatest risks are where humans are involved in the handoff of information. The wetwear is what is most likely to break down. This is an area where you hope there is no direct evidence of a problem in your own house. In that case, the barrier is getting people to believe that what's happened to other companies could also happen to them. Or there may indeed be evidence that noncompliance is an issue. The problem then is convincing managers that even though wetwear problems have always slipped under the radar up until now, it's worth the investment to make certain the problems don't become court cases. Some people are bigger risk takers than others. Put the numbers in front of them quantifying the cost and you'll be able to gauge how much of a gamble they've been making so far.

Those hidden bets that the company has been making—gambling they won't be caught—can be as hard to convey as the unmeasured costs of numerous things a new WMT system will begin to control. The following are costs companies don't put on the balance sheet:

- Unreported time off
- Buddy punching and fraud
- Human error
- Intentional manipulation of scheduled and reported activity
- Overtime as a result of unexcused absences
- True labor costs of projects, products, and services
- The total cost of partial absences, planned absences, and unplanned time off
- Inadequate visibility into real-time production costs and performance
- FMLA abuse
- Employee turnover
- Poor morale and disengaged workers
- Working the clock (e.g., gaming the rounding rules, guarantees, minimums, bonus programs, etc.)
- Unapproved overtime
- Missed meal breaks
- Abuse of shift breaks
- Pyramiding premiums and extra pay—earning two, three, four, or more times the base rate
- Overpaying nonworked time
- Lost productivity due to no-shows or to scheduling employees with the wrong skills
- Poor customer satisfaction

- Incentive programs that no longer motivate
- Bonus programs that do not produce desired results
- Responding to employee grievances
- Cost of processing payroll adjustments
- Unreported overpayments
- Management time preparing and adjusting schedules
- Work effort that is not aligned with strategic goals
- Decisions and activity that do not conform to policy
- Inconsistent management practices
- Hidden report factories churning reports
- Duplication of work efforts

The list could go on and on. The good news is that WMT brings transparency to these issues. Costs that have gone unnoticed are measured, quantified, "dollarized" (put into dollar amounts), and made known in real time to anyone who needs to know.

APPROVALS FORCE ACCOUNTABILITY   Requiring supervisors, managers, and even employees to register approvals throughout the pay cycle, instead of only after the period ends, gives everyone the responsibility to evaluate, adjust, and confirm the activity and payments before they go over the budget or exceed limits.

Depending on the product, approvals can be set up as being required, or they can be optional. Users can enter them daily or weekly or at periodic intervals. Multiple users can be allowed to approve the same employee time card when this is appropriate. Approvals can be tagged with comments, adding more description and value to the data. WMT systems can put payments into pending status until the record is stamped approved for payment.

Be aware, however, that it is not legal to disapprove and thus deny payment for actual hours worked, as in the case of "unapproved overtime." Hourly employees who actually work hours in excess of the overtime limits (40 hours weekly) must be paid for their time according to wage-and-hour guidelines. Employers cannot refuse to pay overtime because the employee did not get approval for the hours worked. But they can track an employee's time and label overtime payments as "unapproved" as a disciplinary matter. It's best to consult your state's department of labor, a labor consultant, or your legal counsel for classifications of possible overtime exemptions for workers by industry, trade, and position. There are exceptions. What is useful is that tracking unapproved OT distinguishes this cost from approved (i.e., operationally required) and draws attention to unnecessary costs that ought to be controlled. In other words, management will know who is answerable for these costs and can take action as necessary.

RECORDING APPROVALS PROVIDES A VALUABLE AUDIT TRAIL   Eliminating the paper trail requires that we have a place to record approvals, so it makes sense that this should be a feature of the technology. This isn't just about replacing the supervisor's signature at the bottom of the time sheet at the end of the pay period. That happens when the supervisor communicates that his time cards are ready for payroll, whatever the process. Electronic approvals can be a form of "checking in" on activity throughout the pay cycle. They can be used to verify that "I have observed this record of activity and have made adjustments where needed." It can be a method of hand-off. Each layer of management can input approvals so that the final approving authority is certain all managers have completed a review of the data before it's finalized for payment.

What if a policy is in place that says a manager's approval must be obtained before certain types of extra pay or thresholds are awarded? Before a check is cut, the system can flag this for the manager to approve. The activity then gains visibility as the records are examined at each level. The supervisor will feel a greater sense of accountability as the data migrates electronically up the chain of command and he or she realizes that the discretionary use of labor is being monitored by a number of stakeholders.

You may not fully anticipate the impact such approvals can have. The exceptions and filters that database logic and queries generate become "red flags" to managers who can usually identify the problems and outliers easily. Would you continue to shop at a store with no price tags if your spouse got an e-mail alert that you were exceeding your credit limit as you loaded your cart? Rest assured the disparity between budget and actual labor costs will shrink when supervisors feel the spotlight's glare on their use of labor. No longer will it be possible to ask forgiveness after the fact.

Key Idea

The supervisor will feel a greater sense of accountability as the data migrates electronically up the chain of command and he or she realizes that the discretionary use of labor is being monitored by a number of stakeholders.

GHOST EMPLOYEES BECOME VISIBLE   A ghost employee is one who is on the books but does not exist. This can and does happen in organizations, regardless of size. It may be that a fictitious employee has been "hired" and someone is fraudulently collecting his pay. It can also come into play when an employee is terminated and an internal person hijacks the record of termination before it is recorded, diverting the ex-employee's pay to their own personal account. New regulations, such as **Sarbanes-Oxley**, are designed in part to make certain that companies institute checks and balances to reduce the potential for such fraud, among other things.

To meet these requirements, a company ought to be able to demonstrate that the person who sets up new hires in the payroll system is not also someone who can approve time cards and distribute checks. The more hands involved the better. Even so, some companies do have locations where everything to do with payroll is performed by one individual because there may not be enough people at the required level. The problem is, what's to keep that individual from creating a person, filling out time cards for her, getting a check every week made out to that nonexistent person, and depositing it into a fake account? There's little in manual systems to enforce the necessary checks and balances. Technology offers a more secure way by involving more people in the process, validating a person's identity and existence, and monitoring his or her productivity. It's hard to create a productive ghost.

There's also a scam called "shadow employment" whereby the person really did exist at one point but has since quit or been terminated. Through simple collusion, the individual may still be getting paid. Let's say Darla Goins quit, for example, but her supervisor, Anita Raze, didn't let anyone in payroll know. Anita gets Darla's checks and splits the money with her. It's difficult if not impossible to pull this off in an automated system, particularly when timekeeping is tied into the scheduling of employees based on work to be performed.

Another method of fleshing out ghost employment is that a system workspace can be set up to automatically list terminated employees as well as those on leave of absence who are still getting paid. Time cards with photo IDs can also help, but the goal of totally eliminating the possibility of ghost and shadow employees may be sufficient justification to use biometrics such as finger, palm, or retina scans, or to install a voice validation system, any of which will make this sort of fraud much more difficult to pull off.

Key Idea

Ghost employment can be eliminated through the use of employee verification (e.g., biometrics, PINs, voice validation, etc.), user profiles that limit access and create checks and balances, schedules that spotlight unassigned workers, and filters that identify inactive employees clocking time and getting paid.

ROLLED-UP INFORMATION IS REVEALING   A WMT system can roll up information in practically any way management may find helpful or revealing. It can take the data from a group of employees and combine it into a department. Departments can be combined into divisions, divisions into districts, and so on. This is important so that actual expenses can be compared with budgets at every level. Employees who work in multiple roles or departments or facilities can be accounted for in the cost center where they actually work. Regular, holiday, weekend, overtime, even nonproductive time can be segmented and then rolled up across job, department, and facility lines as an expense type instead of as an aggregate by business unit. Such roll-ups give the organization a total picture of the cost of compensation programs. What's different about WMT roll-ups compared to payroll registers is that the data can be totaled for any time frame (not just payroll cycles) and related to actual business events and activity performed. Nonproductive time can be parsed or classified into travel time, training time, administrative, and so forth. These categories, which may be considered overhead, can be rolled up across the organization and evaluated as well.

Key Idea

Totals for nonproductive time relative to output may reveal things about staffing levels that were otherwise undetectable.

If there are internal sources of excellence that ought to be emulated within your organization, roll-ups and comparisons may spotlight these performers. With data that can be parsed in any segment or time frame and related to key performance indicators for the business and delivered in real time, the proliferation of this excellence doesn't have to wait until the annual report.

MONITORING OFF-SHORE OPERATIONS   On a commercial airline flight not too long ago, I sat next to a fellow who manages plants around the globe, including China. He and I chatted for some time about his experience with Chinese management. As a student of Asian business practices, I was naturally curious. One of the truly frustrating things he related was how resistant the Chinese are to change. Initially, the management and workers would consume the information about this company's standard operating procedures and replicate these practices quite nicely during the initial operations. At this point in the relationship, U.S. oversight of the Chinese operations was intense. He would be onsite for extended periods, monitoring progress and achieving relatively good production output. His company in the United

States was a lean manufacturer with streamlined operations and state-of-the-art equipment that kept labor needs to a minimum. U.S. management was proud of its accomplishments in these areas and felt the lean approach had served the company well.

In all lean environments, demand-driven scheduling is a key component. During the initial operations, the Chinese plants staffed similarly to the U.S. operations. My seatmate said that as soon as that phase had ended, however, and the intense on-premises American management presence ended, the Chinese plant managers altered their staffing significantly. In China, where the population has reached 1.3 billion, employment is an issue. There's an abundance of labor, and full employment is the goal. So the Chinese abandoned the U.S. owners' staffing models and tripled the staff, significantly increasing the labor-to-production ratio. Suddenly, the advantage of low-cost Chinese labor was offset by the number of employees now working in the plant. Cultural expectations had overridden the business's standards, and my seatmate was tearing his hair out. Little could be done to manage the situation remotely from U.S. headquarters.

I let this man know that with a WMT system in place, he would have had the ability to observe and control these issues from afar, even from his office in the States. What was going on may have been halfway around the world, but the system could have been his window into what was happening in real time. The costs associated with the Chinese managers' actions would have been readily accessible over the Web. Instead of finding out about this "alternative" labor model weeks into production, his company would have found out about it in real time, well before the situation got out of hand. It's something important to consider when a company is operating across a cultural and geographic divide that inhibits having a representative from headquarters on premises. This is a perfect illustration of the value of this new way to enforce policies and practices regardless of physical or attitudinal barriers.

Use WMT to Manage Budgets Today

What tools have managers above the front-line supervisory level had in the past to manage their budgets? Typically, they received after-the-fact payroll reports. This group is not inclined to sit down and sift through a stack of time cards and payroll reports. They may have had a budgetary monitoring process and some standalone scheduling software. These tools were probably not integrated, however, and the targets were primarily at the department level. Until now, organizations as a whole have generally lacked a consistent approach or standardized productivity measurements.

Some companies use well known Human Resources related applications or reporting budgetary software programs. But these solutions are geared to midlevel management in businesses where labor usage and costs fluctuate little. Furthermore, they offer no dynamic evaluation of skill mix and activity in the labor-to-budget picture

The latest WMT analytical modules work closely with the timekeeping and scheduling components, thereby allowing both the front-line and higher levels of management to blend data from operations, HR, time and attendance, and finance to evaluate the different types of labor being employed across the organization. This tool also helps shorten the evaluation cycle, and for companies in which billable hours must be submitted within time limits, this heightened accuracy increases revenue potential. A study by Nucleus Research revealed a facility that recovered hundreds of thousands of dollars by putting this WMT analytical tool to work.

WMT analytical modules come with templates for dashboards that are configurable to the customer's specific needs. Customers can watch—in real time on their computer screen—as the indicator arrows and charts change. These arrows—green and red "indicator lights"—alert managers to issues that may result in overspending. The budget targets are continually measured. Managing the budget becomes a real-time process. This is actionable data, not a spreadsheet stuffed in a drawer.

Key Idea

Managing the budget becomes a real-time process. This is actionable data, not a spreadsheet stuffed in a drawer.

There is up-to-the-minute visibility into how front-line managers are deploying labor as well as the cumulative effect of that activity on the bottom line. This gives managers at any level the opportunity *today* to investigate and take action to align expenditures and budgets to current business needs.

Businesses that experience frequent or unforeseen peaks in labor demand and that rely on supplemental labor, such as contract or agency workers, are well positioned to benefit from this kind of budget process. Significant cost savings and ROI can be realized. In studies conducted by Nucleus, employers were able to "improve labor productivity and control costs by increasing accountability for labor usage and driving adherence to productivity standards." (Nucleus Research, Inc. Research Report D69 2003.)

In the government sector, organizations are beginning to manage budgets in the same way business has traditionally approached the process.

Chicago Public Schools, for example, created a new position of CFO in an attempt to improve in this regard. The new CFO quickly noticed the district was continually over budget on many projects, probably due to a lack of timely information. School administrators may have wanted to stay on budget, but they had no idea at any given time where they stood because reports often were not available until weeks or even months after the fact.

To operate the system as a well-run business and to make administrators accountable, the CFO and his staff began using the analytics tools available in the system the Chicago Public Schools already had in place. Budgets were tracked by grant or project and reports were distributed to the owners daily. The CFO's office then took the bold move of shutting down projects that went over budget. This demonstrated to everyone that budgets had to be managed and that the old way of operating would not be tolerated. As you might imagine, not many projects had to be shut down before everyone got the message.

Why weren't Excel spreadsheets used to manage these budgets? It's best if the tools to manage budgets are resident in the work life of the users and the users are familiar with the applications employed. These users already were using a time and attendance system on a daily basis, so it made sense to deliver the budget information in the same environment. Employees were compelled to go into the time and attendance daily so they would be paid correctly. This made it easy to take care of other business in the same workspace. And from an administrative perspective, **integrating this type of budgetary information with time and attendance made reconciliation between the two systems automatic,** which made sense because any audit of grant money spent for hours worked would require a match between payroll's numbers and the grant report.

Eliminating Blank-Check Budgeting

The first concern of a front-line supervisor is usually to get the work done. Higher-level managers want the work done, too, of course, but they are also perhaps more concerned about doing so within the confines of a budget. Sometimes this disparity—the disconnect between the guy getting the job done and the big guy worrying about money—results in budgets that look nothing like the actual dollars showing up on the payroll reports.

Key Idea

Managing a department within budget while meeting production demands can be a challenge. It can also be a blank check if not managed effectively.

The divergence between what has been allocated and what eventually is spent is an aspect of labor management that should not be overlooked. Two things contribute that can be alleviated by workforce management technology: visibility and accountability.

In order to know what's going on, a manager has to "see" it. He must be cognizant of what's happening. That's what's meant by visibility. Managers need to observe and assess labor activity and spending. They cannot be expected to manage things that are invisible. No one would go to the store and shop for items that have no price tags, pay for them at checkout, and simply live with whatever amount arrived on the monthly credit card bill. No one would hire a contractor to remodel a home without reviewing the design and the bid. No one in his right mind would leave for six months and return later to simply pay whatever it cost to get the job done. Anyone who's ever dealt with a contractor knows there is always *something* unexpected that arises that demands *more*.

To manage, we have to know what's going on, such as how much things cost as the shopping cart fills up and items are checked off the list. We want to decide if fixing that old furnace is worth it, or if we should buy a new one. Managing money means knowing how it is about to be spent and giving approvals along the way. If costs get too high, it may mean changing plans and making other choices.

It should be the same with employees and payroll. Managers need to know what is going on and how much is owed for the work that's being done. What happens all too often in the workplace, however, is that supervisors and schedulers, who are intently focused on getting the job done, are managing the work with little scrutiny by management when it comes to the costs they are racking up. Today, they'll be judged by whether the activity was completed. It won't be until tomorrow that anyone looks at the cost, and then it's "a done deal," justified by the fact that the work *did* get done.

What WMT provides is transparency and accountability vis-à-vis the accumulation of labor costs. It gives managers an opportunity to review and approve or not approve the way labor dollars are being spent. It may be that supervisors and schedulers will welcome a system that provides a justification for and stamp of approval on the scheduling decisions they make. Forgiveness for poor decision making should be replaced by priority-driven management.

Basic WMT systems provide transparency via roll-up sums of numbers from any population a manager needs to view. Those numbers can be compared to their budgetary targets for any timeframe. The systems can also be configured to generate flags when certain thresholds are met or high premium payments are triggered. Inside the WMT system the policies and rules converge with the labor activity even before it hits payroll so that management can visualize the cost of doing business at any moment.

More advanced WMT systems provide mechanisms for going a step further and forecasting the cost of scheduled labor activity in the future (whether it's in an hour, tomorrow, next week, or six months from now). The system can be set up to notify managers when planned work assignments go against spending limits. If overtime is to be reduced, managers can quickly see where that is going to happen, for example.

The most sophisticated systems offer dashboards that enable managers to watch as labor activity pushes the needle relative to performance targets. Instead of viewing spreadsheets full of rows and columns of numbers and dollar figures, the manager is informed about how his numbers are trending. These dashboards are configurable to the specific needs of the business displaying any combination of measurements. The dashboards can be formatted to show graphs, charts, and trend indicators. They include employee-specific information and totals by groups. Some systems even provide related reports and "drill down" capability so that a manager can click and search for more discreet information about an indicator that he wants to know more about. He can quickly see how factors such as attendance or scheduling are impacting operations or which subgroup is falling behind. When performance doesn't meet expected thresholds, indicators light up warning the manager to take action. These dashboards are also accessible to the manager's boss. This kind of multi-level visibility lets managers know they are being watched and held accountable.

■ **CASE STUDY: ANNUAL BUDGETING AT 3M**   Bill Monahan, a top 3M executive, was put in charge of a newly formed company that came into being as the result of the spinoff of six business units from that company. All at once, Bill was in charge of those six units. In listening for the first time to reports from leaders of the spun-off businesses, he says he probably believed 50 to 75 percent of what he heard. Even though he took much of what was said with a grain of salt, he did not examine the details of the plans they presented as aggressively as he now realizes he should have, according to his book *Billion Dollar Turnaround*. In retrospect, he believes he should have started by believing nothing and to have required all the business unit leaders to prove every aspect of their portion of the plan. He should have applied the third tenet of human capital management (see Exhibit 2.6). "Go beyond perception (what people say) and focus on actual behavior (what people do)."

This budgeting methodology is called zero-base budgeting. In other words, the six unit managers should have been instructed to work budgets up from zero revenue rather than adjusting from the other direction, which Bill says often included unrealistic growth projections. Executives who have come out of GE say that company does a good job at this. Bill says he learned his lesson the hard way, and this delayed the turnaround he orchestrated by at least a year. As Bill moved forward, he used companies like GE as benchmarks, but not doing so sooner cost him time, energy, and a lot of indigestion. With the proper labor data, the first look Bill took at those new business units would have been transparent. Also, having workforce management technology in place would have made it easier for each business unit leader to build a budget from the ground up.

Many companies take a broad look at the business during the budget process. They determine what it cost to run the business for the year that is ending, take note of the inflation rate or annual revenue growth, and budget an increase of 2 percent, 3 percent, 10 percent, or whatever the case may be for the upcoming year. You might say payroll budgeting is done in much the same way that profit sharing is determined. The amount is then divvied out to department heads. Department heads in turn take a subjective look at staff and try to figure how much it will take to keep each person happy. The entire salary budget is often allocated among the staff as an annual or hourly base rate increase. Often, no margin is set aside for staffing changes, overtime, or incentives. The budget is merely a bonus payment spread out over time. This is hardly the way to plan labor expenditures.

I continue to be amazed at how labor is treated compared to other business resources and assets. If the purchasing department decided on New Year's Day that it was going to pay each vendor a set amount on a weekly basis for the rest of the year, the company would be turning itself over to "autopilot," unable to react to any turbulence or headwind, unable to avoid catastrophe or to seize opportunities for improvement. The company would have lost any power those funds could have wielded as unexpected needs arose or services failed to meet expectations. The budgetary process for labor needs to be more intelligent and more closely related to productivity.

Doesn't it make a sense to budget for payroll based on the amount of work anticipated? Budgets haven't been put together this way in the past, perhaps, because useful data wasn't available. Now it can be. Sales trends and company goals need to be taken into account, of course, but with the right WMT system it's much easier to know how much work can be turned out, how many widgets can be produced, how many can be patients served, based on historical data.

Using WMT in the Labor Budget Analysis Process

If you've been around a while, you may remember the television show *Kung Fu* with David Carradine. For some reason certain scenes from that show have stuck with me. I remember Kung Fu's instructor casting a long glance at him and knowingly prodding him to "choose wisely, young Grasshopper." As I recall, it was when novice Kung Fu was trapped in a cave and had to figure out how to escape. He had only one option. Move a scalding caldron with his bare arms so he could get out. This resulted in a brand on his forearms. It seemed so ominous. I just ached for him to make the right decision because if he didn't, well, I didn't want to imagine the result.

It can seem that way in business, too. I see businesses struggling with problems and unable to come up with new solutions, unable to see the future. The choices can be painful. The budget process is somewhat like that. Where should dollars be put to best serve the company going forward? Who should the company invest in, and how much should we expect to pay? That goes for labor budgets, project budgets, capital budgets, and marketing budgets. Any time money is spent, a choice has been made.

It's best to analyze every budget plan thoroughly and to pay attention to the details. As part of the process, it's important to study the alternatives, including the possibility of keeping things the same. This is where WMT modeling can really come in handy by identifying the amount and cost of labor required to produce a certain amount of goods or to generate a particular level of revenue. It will allow you to quantify and qualify the rationale for budget expenditures.

Proposals based on data and analysis and presented in a familiar format are easy to produce and hard to refute. Making workforce management technology data part of the process will remove personality issues, give the data credibility, and level the playing field. It's a flashlight, a magnifying glass, and a scale all rolled into one and applied to the decision process.

My advice is to position the budgeting process as an investment activity and go about it diligently, as though the objective were to fund your own retirement. This goes for labor costs and salary budgets, as well as operating expenses and capital expenditures. Resources are almost always limited, and some ventures are potentially risky. It's important to determine whether something is "nice to have," such as a store greeter or an ergonomic engineer, or whether it will bring a return on the investment. If so, what will the return be? How does that compare to other ways that money might be used?

American industry has advanced in its understanding of commodities and purchasing. It has adopted and developed lean manufacturing and sophisticated supply chain management techniques. It seems apparent, however, that efficiency programs have not gone far enough in the area of human capital. Knowing the true value of human output enables management to put labor dollars to work in areas where they will generate the greatest return. Regarding labor as a manageable commodity opens up new possibilities for acquiring this resource at more cost-competitive rates.

WMT Controls Costs and Manages the Complex

Timekeeping, scheduling, absence management, and analytics modules work because they help control what has otherwise *not* been proactively managed. Applying these tools to the everyday issues that keep labor expenses high will result in greater influence over payroll expenditures.

Reducing Overtime with WMT Is a Sprint to the Finish Line

When business objectives, human capital strategies, and technology are integrated into a single workspace for managers, achieving financial goals not only becomes possible, it becomes inevitable. For example, an intelligent, automated system can help reduce overtime hours. This is probably one of the most clear-cut ways WMT can provide a positive return on investment, and it is one of the easiest to implement. In fact, **overtime reduction produces one of the fastest "time-to-value" results out of WMT.**

Overtime is a premium paid on hours worked in excess of a set periodic limit of total hours worked. The Fair Labor Standards Act (FLSA) stipulates a weekly overtime threshold of 40 hours in a seven-day workweek. The pay week can start on any day of the week but it must remain consistent. An employer cannot decide that the pay week starts on Sunday this week and Monday next week—particularly if this is done in an effort to avoid paying overtime. Employees who work more than 40 hours in a week must be paid time and a half (1.5 x their base rate) for the time worked that exceeds 40 hours. The actual rate of pay should be calculated on the average hourly wage earned during the workweek in question. This is commonly referred to as the *"blended overtime* rate." Many employers fail to accurately calculate the overtime rate. Before making a selection, it's important to make certain the time and attendance system and the payroll program can accommodate the mechanism used to derive this blended rate for the overtime payment, and whether that mechanism is internal or external to the system. Otherwise, someone will be forced to come up with creative ways to calculate this rate.

In addition to the FLSA regulations, which are considered the minimum statutes for overtime pay, many states add their own rules regarding overtime payments. Some states, such as California, have instituted daily and consecutive day overtime guidelines. Unions often stipulate special overtime rules for their members, requiring overtime payments on certain days of the week, such as Sunday, or double time beyond a certain number of hours worked in a shift.

The good news is that these overtime limits are well known and easily defined. Better yet, WMT systems can forecast when an employee is likely to work beyond the point when overtime will begin to accrue and create a warning signal to alert the appropriate supervisor or manager. The system does this by constantly compiling data, minute by minute, hour by hour, day by day. Unlike old technology that used clocks or paper time cards, it doesn't wait until the end of the week or the pay period to tally a report. As a result, **the point at which an employee will exceed an overtime limit can easily be determined, and the system can detect this and produce an alert, thus allowing management to take action to prevent overtime from occurring.**

Managing the "Icing" on Top of Base Pay

Roll-ups and forecasts are just two ways this new technology helps executives "see" what's really going on. All kinds of things can now be tracked, such as attendance and referral bonuses and other incentives. Tracking allows leadership to evaluate the effect of these programs. WMT provides a realistic picture of whether these programs actually contribute to attendance or retention.

The ability to track *total* compensation packages vis-à-vis the competition is often overlooked. Think of all the ways employees might be compensated. Overtime, incentives to work on holidays, weekend incentives, travel pay, new hire bonuses, overnight pay, and call-in pay are just a few examples. There are also bonuses that are not directly tied to work activity such as student loan repayment programs, home loan assistance, and shoppers' clubs. An employee whose base salary is $50,000 per year can make $80,000 plus the fringe benefits if he's figured out the system and works it. Suppose he gets overtime after 40 hours, plus an incentive to work weekends. If he's reached 40 hours by Friday he is likely to sign up for the weekend too. If a potential employer across the street offers a better bonus plan it won't be long before the employee knows all about it, and it could be enough to draw him away. **Have a look at the difference between base earnings and total compensation for your employees. That "icing" on top of the base pay is often entirely unmanaged. Typically, no one evaluates the total cost, the impact, and the return on investment.**

Another category of additional compensation includes plans such as sign-on bonuses and loan repayments. As of this writing, RNs can easily get a $5,000 incentive to take an open position. This usually comes with the stipulation that the nurse will work for the organization for at least a year.

Commitments like these are often not tracked or enforced, particularly in a manual system.. Are these bonuses impacting recruitment, retention, and overall quality? WMT enables the business to take the cost, the actual labor contributions, and the business results (quality, revenue, retention rates, and so forth) and analyze the program, as is done in other parts of the business.

Preventing Overdrafts of Time Off

Banks are good at preventing customers from withdrawing more money from their accounts than they have on deposit. Unfortunately, companies don't always control time off benefits as carefully. But putting an automated system in place can prevent people from taking PTO (paid time off) they haven't earned. The system can also enforce that minimums be taken. Exempt employees, for example, usually are required to take PTO in full eight hour increments representing a "day." Hourly workers will often have to take time off in quarter-, half-, or full-hour increments. Otherwise, what's to keep someone from leaving ten or fifteen minutes early and charging it to PTO? That kind of erratic disruption to staffing is not what PTO time was intended to provide. This way the company disburses the benefit in an orderly, manageable manner that diminishes the impact on operations and administration.

Key Idea

On average, employees take 1.25 extra days of leave time per year. This is equal to 0.48 percent of total payroll.

Source: Nucleus Research, G45, July 2006

Tough Times Trigger Closer Tracking of White-Collar Leave

Sometimes problems are brewing and management doesn't smell the coffee. When reductions in the workforce occur, the employer must pay out the accrued leave that salaried managers have on the books. How accurate is that payout? It quickly becomes a serious cost concern if the organization has not captured the usage of that benefit time over the past year or years. If poor tracking goes back very far the problem compounds especially where unused benefit time rolls-over from year to year.

When an economic crisis hits the organization and large groups of employees are let go, a massive amount of financial liability comes due. This is the time when management begins to sweat over the financial cost.

Key Idea

Seventy-three percent of CFOs don't know what the company's PTO liability is; when calculated, 82 percent were surprised the actual liability was higher than expected.

Source: Circadian Technologies: "Absenteeism—The Bottom Line Killer," 2005 white paper

---

If the processes have not been in place to manage paid benefit time (e.g. vacation, sick, personal, PTO, etc.) consistently and correctly, the cost will be tremendous. Now, when the company can least afford it, a huge debt must be paid. Employers who use workforce management technology to track white-collar worker attendance and leave and enforce the accurate reporting of time off will have a much smaller bill to pay.

Preventing Piling Up Premium Pay

Next time you are in the grocery store take notice of the frugal shoppers— people with coupon pouches or pockets stuffed with discount coupons and two-for-one ads. They study advertisements in the Sunday paper. They time their trips to the store to optimize savings by shopping just when the sales start, or the freshness date markdowns hit, or the double-coupon deals go into effect. They are there to get double or triple deals.

Many employees approach work the same way. They read up on the compensation policies. Their union contract is their compensation Bible. They talk to other workers about how much they get paid. They scope out the schedule. They know that when Jupiter aligns with Mars they can work that shift and qualify for overtime and shift premium and holiday pay. They'll earn double or even triple time for a single shift. An associate of mine mentioned a newspaper article, for example, that told about a nurse who was earning six figures despite a base salary in the neighborhood of $50,000. She was making more than some senior-level managers.

This kind of large disparity between base and actual pay occurs for several reasons. First we need to look at these compensation programs and how they came about. Most have been offered to satisfy a demand in the labor market for incentive compensation for certain classes of workers, or during especially difficult-to-staff periods such as holidays and weekends. Unfortunately, these well-intended programs are rarely considered as part of an overall package. They are created and managed in what might be called silos. The programs become entitlements in the minds of employees, meaning that once one is in place, it's difficult for an employer to retire it.

Then, when another influence on labor creates a demand for a new pay policy, an additional program is written and implemented as though it were just one more item in a buffet line. Instead of replacing the red Jell-O with a healthy spinach salad, employers simply add the salad to the menu.

Even though these targeted programs are often not, pay programs should be designed in concert with one another. If a particular situation qualifies an employee for a financial incentive, the program should define exactly what is required to qualify and how that program pays if the employee also qualifies for one or more *other* programs at the same time. If, for example, employees can earn a shift premium for working second shift, and a weekend premium for working the weekend, what happens when the employee works the second shift on the weekend? Does the employee qualify for both? What happens if the employee is also working overtime during the second weekend shift? That shift might also fall on a holiday making the employee eligible for the second premium + the weekend premium + overtime + holiday pay.

Count the number of programs in any company's compensation policy book. That may possibly be how many programs that can be "stacked" on top of one another to exponentially pay one fat and happily overcompensated employee. Is this really what it would take to get an employee to work that shift?

Workforce management technology systems can apply a hierarchy structure to compensation programs, capping the amount an employee can earn for working any shift. The employee just described may have been earning $2.00/hr extra for shift two, $3.50 more for weekend, and 1.5 x the base rate for overtime and double time for holiday. At a base rate of $10.00 per hour that's now a rate of $30.50 per hour or more when blended OT is also taken into account. Automating this process could allow management to enforce a cap on this combined rate limiting the rate to a certain multiple of the base, say two times the base rate.

Or there's another option. The hierarchy could institute a matrix structure where employees who qualify for multiple programs are paid the premiums in a certain order until a set limit is reached. The matrix can be used to enforce a policy that stipulates how payment is to be handled when two or more programs coincide. In this scenario, perhaps only OT and holiday are paid, to limit the excessive payment to double time (2x base). That limit having been reached, nothing more would be paid. Suffice it to say technology offers a way to build equitable compensation to meet business needs without obligating the company to pay excessive compounding of premiums.

Another practice we see is the unintended continuation, or misuse of a premium within another premium zone. Call back pay is a good example. Often call back is paid at 1.5 x base rate. Several mistakes are very common.

In the first scenario the person setting up the automated call back neglects to factor in an overtime zone into the configuration, thinking that the employee is already earning "time and a half" (i.e. "overtime") and therefore an overtime zone is not needed. What this administrator forgets is that overtime must use the blended rate, which is not always simply 1.5 x the base rate as is used with a call back pay code. In addition, without an overtime zone in the setup, some systems will not include the call back hours worked in the computation of total hours worked for weekly or daily overtime. In other words, the setup is likely to result in an underpayment based on the percentage rate paid and the total hours counted.

The second scenario is to set up the system with an overtime zone and to pay both, call back and overtime, when they both occur. This also happens frequently in manual systems because the process of figuring call back and overtime are two different computations. However, depending on how the policy is written and pay codes are set up, this could actually be *overpaying* the employee because that employee may be earning 1.5 + 1.5 = 3 times base pay for the same hours. This is another example of "pyramiding," or stacking one premium on top of another, resulting in multiples of the base rate. WMT systems, at the very least, bring these to light and provide an opportunity to avoid these unintended pay situations.

The WMT system can also be set up to help avoid double paying of overtime. In some states, California being one, daily overtime is mandatory. In that state, overtime also must be paid to someone who works more than 40 hours in a week. If someone works more than eight hours in a day, that person is entitled to overtime on the extra hours worked that day. If someone works more than 12 hours in a day, the person starts earning double time. If a person works seven consecutive days, even though they may only work one hour on each day, the seventh day is automatically paid at the overtime rate. After eight hours on the seventh day, double time kicks in. Confused? When manually administered, these payments can easily be overdone. Imagine being able to set up a system that understands the intricacies of these regulations, avoids noncompliance, and better yet eliminates double payments.

It's easy to see why programs in existence for many years are often vaguely written and lack limits and qualifiers. They would have required considerable manual intervention to compute. But time and attendance systems can automate those processes and allow the programs to mature in complexity. Compensation programs and stacking guidelines should be written clearly in every compensation document, union contract, and employee handbook. The write-up should support and concur with the configuration of the program in the time and attendance system. It makes sense to assemble a binder with a printed copy of each compensation policy and place it where it is accessible to employees, supervisors, and payroll personnel. It should be kept up to date at all times. If an employee questions her pay, the binder will become the backup to support how a payment amount was calculated. In segments of the health care industry this is required.

Keeping Track of Complex Compensation Programs

In today's large, enterprise organizations especially those doing business in a number of states, often many different overtime rules and compensation programs exist. Not only does California mandate more than weekly overtime, so do Colorado and Kentucky, among others. Later, we will touch on the different holidays that vary by region and locality. I know of many companies that have dozens of overtime rules to keep track of, and even more premium rules. Prior to installing a sophisticated time and attendance system, these programs had to be administered at the local level. Without centralized administration, the corporation had even less control and visibility into these programs than would be advisable. In some companies there could be so much "leakage" (i.e., excessive compensation), I wonder how anyone who recognizes the situation can sleep at night.

Companies can be struggling with a lot of rules and regulations as well as policies that are complex, poorly written, or simply unclear in their intent. Who is going to consistently manage and enforce these policies and rules? Who is out there watching with the proverbial "payroll radar gun"? Like speeding down the road, failing to follow the rules can be dangerous and costly. Certainly employees are not going to be the ones who report overpayments or pyramiding excesses. And they quickly find out where the few "speed traps" are and where they can get away with putting the pedal to the metal.

Compliance could be the simplest solution to controlling labor costs. Some pay programs are written very clearly and spell out the exact conditions under which payment can be earned. For example, there are programs we refer to as "bonus programs" whereby employees work a specified number of hours to earn a special bonus payment. In manual systems, compliance with these strict requirements becomes a relative matter, exercised at the discretion of managers. Automated systems don't know what a "good excuse" is, and they don't play favorites. Their enforcement isn't random either; they are on duty 24/7. The rule is hard-coded, and exceptions need not apply. The system can play the bad guy, because managers are loath to be payroll police.

Key Idea

Compliance and avoiding pyramiding could be the easiest solutions to controlling costs.

In some cases, a person working on a particular day of the week has to be paid at the overtime rate. Sunday work, for example, may have to be paid at double time or time and a half. Another twist on overtime is known as "8 and 80." In this case, a person becomes eligible for overtime under multiple conditions. For workers, there is not just one way to qualify, there are two. If the employee works more than 80 hours in two weeks he gets OT, or if he works more than eight hours in a single day he starts earning OT. In big, complex organizations, especially those doing business in a number of states, many different categories of labor compensation can exist. One company I know of has 50 or more different overtime rules. Keeping up with this can be complicated and difficult in a manual setup. But no matter how complex the rules and regulations may be—they might be different in different locations or change because of the time of day or the shift worked—they will be taken care of once programmed into an automated system.

Gaining Accurate Cost Accounting and Reducing Manual Checks

WMT can help manage financial affairs in other ways as well. Management may not realize the impact, for example, on cost accounting when payroll corrections are not factored into the reporting. Eliminating or reducing manual check adjustments is the first step to ensure payments (labor expense) can accurately be related to productivity. The next is attributing the payments to the proper time frame and labor events so that payroll records reflect the total accumulated cost of those activities. Systems that report costs based on payment dates alone are not an accurate tool to use in understanding true business costs. Payroll calendars do not relate well to business cycles, and manual check payments are rarely matched up to business activity time frames.

To get a handle on this, let's say a department suffers from poor reporting, a high incidence of payroll adjustments, and no ability to record those adjustments properly. Last week, most of those in the department worked overtime to complete an important project on time. Due to long hours the tired workers put in, and Payroll's willingness to fix employee mistakes, several employees forgot to report all of their additional time by the regular deadline. When paychecks were distributed, these employees instantly realized their mistakes and presented Payroll with corrected time sheets. The added hours substantially increase overtime hours and costs to the department. Let's say Payroll processes hand checks the following week, which also happened to fall in the following month.

When the department manager receives his monthly payroll report, he will probably not realize that much of the cost for that crunch week will in fact be on *next* month's report. With what he has been given, relating his production numbers to labor expenses and the cost of pushing to get the order completed is not possible. If a historical edit capability were a part of that company's WMT system, however, the monthly report would accurately reflect the additional costs incurred during the peak level of activity. Historical edit functionality allows Payroll to attribute the manual checks, along with their inherent labor expenses, to the appropriate time frame and activity.

Delayed reporting can also be an avoidance technique or a true attempt to defraud the company. An employee's request for payment after time has passed may mean her manager, who must approve the additional expense, will be less resistant because he can't remember what actually went on that week, so long ago. Historical data and recalculation functionality gives the manager the ability to rewrite the history himself and determine, just as he would have at the time, whether an additional request was justified or has already been paid.

Such rewrite features give visibility into what happened, what should have happened, how it was fixed, and what the correction does to the budget numbers. Historical edits update the accrued expenses relative to the activity they represent. Overlaying payroll amounts that include corrections from prior periods and omissions from the current cycle (to be paid out later) to a production-based budget doesn't lend itself to much accountability. Putting historical updates into this tally helps keep managers on target.

Key Idea

Accurate cost accounting relies on accurate data (fewer corrected paychecks), attributing costs to the proper cost center and time frame, and timely reporting. WMT accomplishes all of these and, when adjustments are required, allows users to adjust historical data as needed so that cost accounting records truly reflect actual expenses.

Automated Workflow Offers Direct and Indirect Financial Benefits

WMT systems increasingly come with features that automate processes and give employees and managers self-service capabilities. The direct cost savings come in the form of improved payroll accuracy and significant reductions in the cost of managing these processes manually. The indirect savings are in the form of greater employee satisfaction, less interruption and manager time spent on administrative duties, and lower employee turnover.

These savings are achieved through a number of system capabilities, including:

- Automated time-off requests
- Access to employee time off balances
- Automated attendance and leave management processes
- Electronic alerts and notifications
- Self-scheduling, including shift swapping and shift bidding
- Scheduled reports

Not only do these automated systems make life easier and allow employees to focus more on productive efforts, they enforce consistency and compliance, because the systems limit the options. The more sophisticated systems offer highly configurable workflow options to meet the unique and complex requirements of each customer. A time-off request process can be easily initiated by an employee, automatically sent to the supervisors, quickly validated and approved, reported back to the employee, and updated in the system, This is accomplished with very few human inputs. An absence policy violation can be identified, validated, and processed—including preparing a written warning, sent to the manager for signature and a counseling session—all without a person doing anything except opening a system-generated e-mail and printing the prepopulated form. People are usually eager to be relieved of mundane phone calls, research, data entry, and paperwork. WMT systems divert that energy toward activities that will help customers and the bottom line.

Key Idea

According to a 2006 benchmark survey conducted by the American Payroll Association, companies that deploy employee self-service models on average realize cost savings as high as $250.00 per employee per year.

Self-service options can have a positive impact on unplanned absences, which in turn reduces reliance on overtime to fill the void. As you follow the influence of these systems further downstream, idle time is reduced and safety is increased. Planning to have the right workers in place means having trained, rested employees who are apt to be more satisfied in their jobs and less likely to quit or be absent themselves. It's almost a cycle of good or bad behaviors and outcomes. Automated workflow can have compounding results downstream within the organization. Which whirlpool would you rather swim in—one where good things typically result in more good things, or the opposite?

Key Idea

"Circadian's Shiftwork Practices 2005 study, in particular, found that in facilities where employees select the schedule pattern, the absenteeism rate is 8.3 percent compared to 9.4 percent when a schedule is mandated without employee input. In a company of 5,000 employees, even a half of the 1.1 percent difference in absenteeism resulting from an employee-selected schedule could save over $1.6 million."

From "Absence Management: Making the Critical Shift from Transactional to Strategic," white paper by the Bureau of National Affairs, Inc. 2006

Introducing Supply and Demand to Labor Management

I love television commercials that make me look at life differently. Often, they are designed to make us, the consumer, feel as though we're in control, to take the proverbial driver's seat in the dog-eat-dog world we live in but are often victim to.

Take the advertisements for online mortgage brokers. A husband and wife sit at a table contemplating a document before them. An anxious salesman sits across the table awaiting their reply. They hand the paper back to him, show him the door, and say, "Next" to the waiting throng of eager brokers standing in line outside their door. What if mortgage lenders competed for your business? Wouldn't you be empowered? Wouldn't it be to your advantage?

In the world of WMT, something approaching that scenario is beginning to occur. Vendors have seized the supply and demand concept and put it to work for companies and employees.

Key Idea

Human Resources has traditionally been focused on making HR processes more efficient. WMT systems are making the workforce more effective.

What software vendors have produced is an intelligent tool to supply the appropriate type and amount of labor based on business needs. Shift bidding or, more aptly put, *competitive* shift bidding is at the doorstep.

In scheduling systems that allow employees to bid for shifts, a workload template is created indicating how many workers in each job category are needed, at what times they are needed, and at what locations. Employees can log onto the system, review the open slots on the schedule, and submit bids for particular shifts. This is different from basic self-scheduling, where employees either sign themselves up or request shifts without regard to pay. Shift bidding is able to add a money component. For highly desirable shifts, a company may be able to acquire its labor for the lowest cost by allowing employees to submit their best "price."

Adding Controls with Self-Scheduling

Such bidding systems can allow those with more seniority to request a shift before people with less seniority can do so. Union rules might even require that a certain class of employee gets first dibs. So the system can automatically let these employees in to make their requests for a set period of time before opening up for others to make requests. In this way, the technology eliminates the distraction that employee grievances and gripes cause when protocol isn't followed.

Alternatively, a system can also be programmed to take into account employee preferences. Employees enter the days and times they'd most like to work; conversely, they are able to notify the employer when they cannot work due to such things as child care, class schedules, or even transportation issues. Once their preferences and availability have been established, the scheduling program takes these into account. Why is that important? For two reasons: reduced absenteeism and improved job satisfaction. That equals lower costs and employees who are more engaged.

Of course, rules can be applied to all of this. For example, state or union regulations may require that only people with specific qualifications work a job or shift. A scheduling rule can be programmed to ensure that a worker with the right skill set is scheduled for a shift. The company sets up the criteria specific to its needs and the regulations to which it must adhere. In health care, for example, these needs are based on the patient population and acuity. The employer may need respiratory therapists or G-tube certified staff on the ward with the addition of new patients. Only a sophisticated, rule-driven system can facilitate ensuring such compliance in a self-scheduling process. The risks of delivering the wrong type of workers to the work site are almost nil.

Compliance with staffing requirements often makes employers subject to audits by outside regulatory agencies. In some industries, guidelines dictate rest periods between shifts or maximum number of hours that can be worked in a set period of time. If the employer has received an exemption from overtime or minimum wages, government agencies will periodically monitor compliance. Records are pored over to determine whether a facility has been staffing and paying personnel according to the rules and regulations. This makes it essential to have a system to help the company comply with the rules while still allowing supply and demand to work to the company's advantage.

Is a New Time and Labor Management System Right for Us?

The evidence is compelling that these workforce management tools really do have a significant impact on the bottom line. But you may be wondering whether they are dependent on economies of scale. Or you may ask whether the improvements are seen only when dramatic changes need to take place, such as replacing manual systems and initiating controls where there have been none before. The answer is that the benefits are there for everyone to some degree.

You Don't Have to Be Big to Benefit

I'm often asked how big a company needs to be to use workforce manage-ment technology. I answer that there's no minimum size, but it does make sense to evaluate how reasonable it is to expect benefits sufficient to justify the investment. There are companies with only a few dozen employees who are using time and attendance systems. The key is finding a vendor with the right product and pricing structure to fit an organization's needs, budget, and opportunity for savings. Small organizations typically have con-cerns about system administration, and they don't want to have to buy more complexity than they need. Of course, they are subject to the same needs for accuracy, compliance, and savings as big operations, but there may be areas where overly sophisticated technology simply isn't necessary.

There are vendors that offer time and attendance software to companies in the small to mid-sized market. DPT Laboratories, for example, selected a product for its ability to deliver greater accuracy to the company's processes, its easy-to-use training materials, and its system's growth potential (given that DPT plans to expand in the future). DPT anticipated the improvements to their processes that were realized. But management was pleasantly sur-prised when savings added up to $30,000 annually for this 500-employee company. Three years after implementation, savings are still apparent in overtime and the processing effort, and accuracy has been achieved that could not otherwise have been realized. In such a case, the question should not be, "How much will the system cost?" but rather, "How much will it cost if we *don't* purchase a system?"

When Is It Time to Take a Second Look?

Some of you reading this book may already have installed a time and la-bor management system months or even years ago. You may have been involved in the initial implementation or you may have inherited the applications that are running today. Ask your organization the following questions:

- Was the system in place today installed from a strategic perspective or a tactical one? In other words, was it simply a replacement of outdated processes, or did the organization purposefully intend to change the way it was doing business and benefit from the advanced technology?
- Is there an upcoming event that may impact your time and labor management processes? These include an upgrade to the HR, Payroll, or accounting system, a merger or acquisition bringing on new employees into the organization, or an internal reorganization?
- Has the organization achieved certain milestones and become ready to go to the next level? You may have made it to second base and recognize a readiness to get that home run.
- Based on feedback from management, front-line workers, or stories in the media, is there a growing awareness of problems or a sense that more could be done to improve work-related processes within the organization? Is the company struggling with issues such as growing payroll expenses, poor productivity, or shrinking margins or sales?
- Is the organization facing new financial pressures? When economic times are tough it's time to take a close look at areas that are undermanaged. If you haven't scrutinized labor spending and utilization in the past two years—especially relative to the latest software and collection devices—you are not taking advantage of every tool available to manage the cost of your workforce.

If the answers to these questions reveal that the KISS principle was in force during the initial roll-out and only the most basic features were turned on or very little has changed since the system was added, it's time to assess your current state.

If you know that another event within the organization is on the horizon you have a terrific opportunity—possibly a mandate—to discover how your WMT systems are performing and what needs to change.

If you knew you were going to phase in the full implementation of WMT capabilities and you've successfully completed the first phase, it's time to turn your attention to where this technology is going to take the organization next.

Finally, you may have only a suspicion that there is something missing based on a variety of clues. Watch for manual checks being processed in Payroll; these are flags that something is not working in the system. Listen for back chatter from end users that the system has a lot of latency or there is evidence of abuse. Executives might think the system is nothing more than a clock on a wall and they don't get anything out of it. Look at some key areas of improvement such as overtime, absenteeism, or turnover, before and after the system was put in place. Have these changed at all? When was the last time your compensation and benefit policies or contracts were reviewed or updated? If you haven't conducted a check-up on your system during the past two years, it's time to call the doctor.

When it's time to take a second look, the greatest areas for optimization are usually apparent. But let's pause a moment and discuss optimization. The term has been overused, and anyone in business is probably suffering at least a little from "optimization fatigue." Sometimes people think this means that systems are going to be hyper-tweaked to get results. For others it may just be fancy, wishful talk about magical ways to improve performance. Neither of these is true for WMT.

I can tell you from experience that, over time, organizations evolve, processes change, performance degrades, users come and go, and systems need tune-ups. For WMT optimizing means cleaning, maintaining quality control, and using the system with intent.

The primary areas to hunt for improvements include:

- **Having a good platform.** Is the IT infrastructure able to handle the demand, are rules and settings up to date, has the database outgrown the storage and processing capacity, what happens during peak loads of activity?
- **Education.** Do employees have adequate and ongoing training? Are their skills and competency routinely refreshed and verified? Do new employees get formal training? Did the initial training cover everything users have access to today? How many calls is the help desk having to handle? What are the primary problems being reported?
- **Schedules in the system.** Does everyone have a schedule that is kept up to date? Are managers using schedules to improve productivity? Are there features of scheduling that were never engaged?
- **Analytics.** Is anyone besides Payroll using the data from the WMT system? Is anyone comparing business information with WMT data? How many interfaces are operating and how often? Have new external business systems been integrated?
- **Improvements.** What is the system doing for your organization—what is its role in achieving success for this year?

There is a long list of items under each of these key areas to explore. This is just the tip of the iceberg. The best way to evaluate your current system is to involve people from Finance and Operations, as well as Payroll and IT, in evaluating how the organization is using its workforce data. Hire an outside consultant or the vendor to come in and conduct a thorough diagnostic evaluation of your system. That partner should help you put together focus groups and workshops to assess and strategize your WMT future. Make certain that the ultimate outcome is a clear and actionable plan covering hardware, software, networks, people, policies, and processes.

Companies that are serious about using their system to achieve financial goals and maximize profits will take that second look. They won't pass the opportunity to increase their profits and performance.

Chapter Summary

- The absence of ROI from WMT systems indicates an immature or narrowly deployed technology.
- There are five guidelines for ensuring the greatest ROI: (1) deploy everywhere, (2) change your workflow, (3) protect the benefits over time, (4) conduct audits, and (5) gather the right data at the beginning.
- Senior management must move beyond traditional notions about the relevance of time and labor management processes that prevent them from understanding their return on their human capital investments.
- A lack of transparency results in uncounted and poorly managed labor expenditures. The introduction of visibility produces accountability.
- WMT systems make managing budgets a daily activity. Even the most complex compensation practices can be administered within WMT.
- Automated workflow results not only in direct financial benefits but in indirect cost savings as well.
- Complexity and opportunity are more important than size when deciding whether a WMT makes sense for the organization.
- Current events and related system life cycles may indicate a financial reason to upgrade your systems.
- If you haven't evaluated your WMT systems and processes in the last two years, it's time for a checkup. You should be able to define exactly how WMT features are being used to drive organizational success—if you can't, it's not a system that is being used with intent.

CHAPTER 4

Using Workforce Management Technology to Enhance Operations, Quality, and Compliance

B eyond the direct financial reasons to engage WMT systems, a strong case can be made that time and labor technology is essential to efficient, high-quality, low-risk operations. In this chapter we investigate how the industry has matched the products to the demands of production and service. Like the lean initiatives of recent years, WMT is the latest driver of increased quality and efficiency. In addition, companies have found creative ways to apply the tools within WMT systems to their workplace problems.

The day-to-day operations also offer WMT the chance to really shine as they tackle the intricacies of managing absenteeism and leaves of absence. And while operations personnel are busy trying to get the work done, WMT effectively relieves them of a number of compliance, waste, fraud, and abuse issues.

Operations: The Greatest Impact

Finding financial gains from improvements in time and labor systems is fundamental. The opportunities are fairly straightforward, easy to capture, and quick to show a return. The most significant benefits, however, are in the next level of engagement where these systems touch the heart of the business.

Operational improvements are the ultimate goal, because they will drive productivity and revenue. While savings can be trimmed from labor costs and process efficiencies, the most significant benefits are derived when WMT systems are used to operate the business more intelligently, improve quality, and avoid risk. This is possible because the technology is a decision tool that aligns choices and activity with operational goals.

Addressing Labor Costs and Productivity in Manufacturing

Manufacturers are under constant pressure to minimize unit costs while meeting demand for high-quality products and on-time delivery. To achieve operational excellence, we've already pointed out that continuous improvement initiatives such as Six Sigma and Lean have been instituted to cut costs and maximize productivity. The target has been the two largest expense areas on the balance sheet: equipment and inventory. Labor, while a smaller expense, is controllable and provides a good opportunity to target waste and cost reduction.

Manufacturers should start with an awareness of where they are on the WMT maturity curve. In this environment, being at the early stages of maturity means that automation is being used to improve reporting accuracy and to perfect processes related to the workforce. Ensuring accurate and repeatable processes for tracking and paying people correctly is the first step. There are many who assume that accurate paycheck delivery "just happens," without realizing that there are many influences beyond Payroll's control that have an impact. Production delays that require overtime; absenteeism; new rules in a renegotiated bargaining agreement; and changing federal guidelines concerning leave can manifest in processes with as much daily volatility as the company's operational units experience.

Applying the tools within WMT systems helps eliminate the variability and institutes controls and mechanisms for adjustment that result in accurate paychecks and credible data. Once a manufacturer is collecting and paying correctly, it can move up the maturity curve to a more developed stage in which WMT is used to measure output and create the perfect product. The information gathered can be used to examine production variances caused by employees (e.g., absenteeism), payroll (e.g., work rules), and operations (e.g., material delays).

To understand the business impact of variability, you need a simple management framework such as overall labor effectiveness (OLE). For those familiar with overall equipment effectiveness (OEE), this is the same concept but applied to labor. OLE is a metric, based on the interdependency of labor utilization, labor performance, and quality. It measures the impact of the workforce on the business and helps to improve costing and labor utilization issues.

According to Gregg Gordon, a WMT expert relative to manufacturing organizations, Toyota's Production Systems have identified the Big 6 Losses when measuring Equipment Effectiveness and the contribution people make to each. (See Exhibit 4.1.)

EXHIBIT 4.1   The Big Six Losses

Top Reasons	Impact	Root Cause/Measurement	Example
Breakdowns	Availability	People and machine	Tool breakage, missing operator
Setup and adjustment	Availability	People, fixture design	Setup process, tooling is inefficient
Small stops	Performance	People and machine	Jams, cleaning
Reduced speed	Performance	People, machine, and materials	Machine wear, operator inefficiency
Start-up rejects	Quality	People, machine, and materials	Incorrect assembly, improper setup
Production rejects	Quality	People, machine, and materials	Process out of control

Under each of the six losses are causes for an OEE score to drop, the reasons for which often have to do with people. Workers are the variable, one that is often not taken into account because of the lack of good systems for measuring the people element. Is the assigned worker absent? Is the person working adequately trained? Is the company receiving eight hours of work for eight hours of pay?

To overcome the lack of measures, OLE has been introduced to provide manufacturers with a baseline measurement to understand the effectiveness of corrective actions. For instance, OLE will show whether employee training has an impact on quality.

To achieve operational excellence, equipment, inventory, and people have to be tightly integrated so that all three are doing their best at the same time.

A PRESCRIPTION FOR MANAGING OPERATIONAL HEALTH HOLISTICALLY   Operations measures delivery dates, production costs, machine down time, scrap, and the like. These are the metrics that enterprise resource planning (ERP) systems take on the shop floor. On the HR side, they look at average wages, retention, and demographic information and measure the workforce by these attributes. These measurements, however, are very compartmentalized. Operations and HR management are experts within their domains. But their expertise is really limited to examining what lies within their territory, because that is the only data their systems and measurements present. These domain-centric analyses fall short of any real evaluation of the causes and their impact on one another. Operations knows only that output on Line 1 declined last week. HR sees a spike in absenteeism and turnover. Their systems don't allow them to make any direct connections to assess the causes and make adjustments to mitigate the outcomes.

WMT is the system that ties these areas together. WMT operates beyond the compartmental boundaries, or perhaps in spite of them. The real issues become measurable and understandable within WMT because, like the real world, they make the issues tangible, visible, and workable.

How does this work? WMT supplements the value of ERP by extending its reach to the shop floor. WMT imports data from ERP systems and gives supervisors real-time visibility into their people, WIP, and machines. This real-time visibility would allow, for example, a supervisor to move an employee who is idle due to a material delay over to a work order that is behind schedule.

That same data can be used to generate actual labor costs by production line or work order, rather than relying on standard costs. The benefits are twofold. First, cost performance can be measured accurately to determine if there is too much overtime being used or that higher wages are being spent on a particular operation. Second, actual time can be used to verify the accuracy of labor standards.

Gordon points out that the actual costs measured by WMT system are essential to cost-plus pricing for government contracts. Overcharging in this model can lead to potential audits and damaged reputations.

Different types of manufacturers will use WMT differently and collect different amounts of data. Repetitive, high-volume manufacturers might manage by exception, whereby employees clock in and out only at the beginning and end of their day unless the line stops because a machine breaks or setup time is required. Discrete manufacturers that build unique products by job order, brand or customer may have employees record their time each time they start a new batch or reach a piece-rate milestone.

In summary, workforce management can help you to understand and control your costs and increase productivity, leading to higher overall labor effectiveness. If you aren't certain yet whether you'll benefit from a more mature WMT system, consider the following questions:

How does your company reconcile payroll to labor hours? Many manufacturers manually reconcile their direct labor hours to production to measure workforce productivity against a particular line or work order, leading to information that is either too summarized or not accurate.

Does reconciliation accurately capture indirect hours? Many companies do not capture indirect hours resulting from activities that do not directly affect production or are variances from expected times to execute an operation.

Can you measure your workforce not only by hours, but also by actual wages, to gain true cost performance? Different wages paid to accomplish the same work can have a significant impact on costs.

Are you measuring the status of your machines, WIP, and labor at the same frequency with which your demand signals are changing? The status of the shop floor should align with the ability to change according to the rate of change in your demand signals.

How flexible is your workforce, and are you able to take advantage of that flexibility? The ability to translate production demand signals into labor requirements, and then schedule and redeploy labor while still meeting company, union, and regulatory constraints is how leading manufacturers are able to evolve their operations into true make-to-order production environments.

MANAGING OPERATIONAL EXCELLENCE WHEN SERVICE IS THE PRODUCT WMT is a tool for managing more than just widgets. A friend of mine, who works for a large health care operation, was promoted to the position of Vice President of Patient Satisfaction. His organization has the goal of becoming the health care provider of choice in its region. A WMT system can provide data to help in achieving this goal. Set up the right way, it will allow the organization to track individual employees' contact with patients and relate this to patient satisfaction levels, provided satisfaction levels were measured through questionnaires or post-discharge interviews.

Here is an example. Let's say Mr. Amal Well was on a given floor in a particular room on specific days. A patient questionnaire designed to measure his level of satisfaction might be given to him when he leaves the hospital. It would be a matter of using the time and attendance system data to track "customers" and then relate Mr. Well's survey feedback to the employees who provided care during his stay. It might even track the specific dates and times of activities about which Mr. Well had particular concerns. The patient survey data and the employee activity data could be linked and compiled to assess whether satisfaction was related to specific employees or to events, and whether certain employees or activities generated higher patient ratings than others.

It could also overlay other aspects that may have impacted Mr. Well's level of satisfaction and the employees charged with his care. Were they unable to respond due to being short-staffed? Had the employees been working double shifts? Did other patients during the same time frame, dealing with the same staff members, register the same responses? Are trends evident in how employees are scheduled or are put together in teams that relate to the level of patient satisfaction? Do higher-paid employees deliver more satisfactory care? And so on.

It's likely some caregivers would prove to be more proficient than others at turning out satisfied patients. It might be that certain employees work better under particular supervisors or on certain shifts, and that this results in better patient satisfaction outcomes. The hospital might discover that ratings drop toward the end of a double shift worked by an employee or when an employee is called in from a day off. Linking time and attendance data to operational data, such as patient surveys, would add one more dimension to the organization's understanding of what patients experience and the way employees are scheduled to work and compensated. If there is a correlation between them, employee performance can be viewed as a key indicator of success in generating patient satisfaction. The same could be done in any customer-facing position in any industry.

Delivering the Right Tools and Data

Employees are the face of the organization, the deliverers of products and service. It makes sense to strive to identify the exceptional performers, as well as the poor performers. It would make sense to find out what each group is doing or not doing that others aren't. Specifically, what makes them different? Do nurse scheduling practices impact client satisfaction?

Supervisors can use this information on client satisfaction and relate it to their staff. Training is one obvious possibility. Modifying procedures is another. Applicants with certain traits might be targeted for future hires. It would also be possible to set up an incentive program based on satisfaction levels of clients. Manufacturers, retailers, and transportation and service sectors can all use the system to house skills, certifications, work activity, and performance records as well. With cause and effect identified, steps can be taken to improve performance. You need not take "client" too literally, either. The client might be the next department down the line internally in the chain of processes that the work goes through.

Knowing Who's Onsite and Remote Monitoring

Perhaps some remote sites in a company are not staffed with management personnel during late-night shifts. The technology discussed in the case history in Chapter 2 can be put to work in these situations. Since the new technology is real time, it's possible to know who is on premises at any given moment. If someone has punched the clock, called in from a phone, or logged into a PC at a work location, that person is there. This means a quick check on the computer, a text message, a cell phone page, or an e-mail can notify management if someone has failed to show up at each facility or workstation, who that person should have been, and who might replace him.

This feature is particularly important in certain segments of some industries. Home construction contractors, 24-hour convenience stores, and home health providers are examples. Employees travel on their own to these work locations, get there, and begin the day. Often, they are the only worker on-site. In a manual system, the employee reports work activity on a paper time sheet or an old time clock punch card that's rounded up and submitted at the end of the week or pay period. On a day-to-day or hourly basis, management has little or no ability to monitor whether an employee is actually on premises. Someone at headquarters needs to be sure a store is open. In the case of health care providers, employees sometimes travel to residential locations to deliver care. Often, the services provided are critical to a patient's well-being. Certain activities may literally be matters of life and death. Failure to provide such services could put both the patient and the health care provider at risk. It's critical that companies with such issues do the job they've been contracted to do, and a WMT system can help ensure this.

For retail businesses and contractors, not being open or having workers on a job site can mean lost revenue or delays. Managers must know when they have a kink in the human-resource supply chain so they can address it immediately. Like a production line shutting down, it simply can't be ignored. This is why visibility into what is going on in remote locations represents such a big improvement.

Controlling Exits and Entrances

Automated systems also can provide what's called gatekeeper technology. While clocking in to the time and attendance system, the employee simultaneously is granted entry into the facility. The matter of controlling who gains entry into a building, a hall, or even a room can be easily managed and monitored. You might call this killing two birds with one stone. In this case, the two birds translate into two separate technologies, essentially providing the same functionality.

The increasing need for such technology says a lot about our modern society. It reminds us that we are often anonymous, unidentified, presumed untrustworthy occupants of the places we go. We live with the expectation that daily life is full of activities in which we encounter "transients." We expect out-of-town coworkers to fly in for a meeting. We work "remotely" from our home offices doing our time on the "cyber shift," where our business associates are known by their user names and Web addresses instead of their faces. We actually see fewer and fewer people routinely except for our closest "cube mates." We are temporary patients in large institutions with specialist doctors we do not know well, so staff wear photo IDs. Unexpected "visitors" cannot enter our schools without signing in and sticking "visitor" labels on their lapels. As random customers at convenience stores, we are videotaped on the chance we may turn into shoplifters or robbers. All this lack of familiarity, along with a media culture that feeds our insecurities, has fostered the fear that people are not where they should be, doing what they ought to be doing. The bottom line is that identification is a big issue.

For some, security is mandated. This is for internal reasons—to keep the lid on top-secret processes in a production area or to keep unqualified personnel out of the pharmacy cabinets—or external—government contractors, airlines, and the owners of sensitive material as well as other businesses are required to restrict access as a matter of national security.

Fortunately, the technology exists to help us verify identity, to replace the need to know all of those around us, and to work in close proximity with a sure knowledge that we're interacting with the right person, that the right person is working for us, and that people are where they say they are, doing what they should be doing. Integrating WMT to door locks prevents unauthorized entry by person or by time of day and tracks movements of people in the workplace. When I worked at the airline—nearly 20 years ago—the Federal Aviation Administration (FAA) required security controls and ID badges in the airline's headquarters because of the sensitive nature of the business—the systems the building housed that controlled planes flying around the country. It seems the dangers are now even more commonplace. This aspect of WMT is referred to as gatekeeper technology or access control. It's worth considering.

Preventing Employee Theft

For one of my clients, the value of access control addressed a perplexing problem. Management suspected tools were "clocking out"—leaving the premises and walking off with workers at the end of the late-night shift. People who wanted to take tools with them could go out a rear side door where lighting was poor and no security guard was posted. Few workers used the door because it was some distance from the parking lot. Barring the door wasn't an option because it had to be accessible for emergency and fire evacuation.

The solution to this turned out to be fairly simple. What was the absolute last thing workers did before they left? They had to clock out. Restricting third-shift employees from using the clock by that back door during the third shift was the answer. This way, everyone would be forced to use the exit in a high-traffic area where workers could be observed leaving the premises. Further, the system could report anyone who attempted to use the clock near the rear door during third shift.

Making a change to how clocks were used was certainly cheaper than adding a security guard or bearing the cost of stolen equipment.

Managing Company Store Purchases: "I Owe My Soul to the Company Store"

Company stores exist in many businesses. Hopefully, they've come a long way since the time when coal miners and mill-town workers relied on them for daily needs. For today's worker in a health care institution, the gift shop in a hospital is an example. In retail, an example might be discounted in-store purchases. In others, the cafeteria is today's company store. Employees often are allowed to make purchases using their payroll ID number and badge as a debit card. In many cases, they receive a discount, and the purchase amount is deducted gradually in small increments from upcoming pay.

Systems are available that will integrate the sale at the cash register with the time and attendance system. This can head off potential problems many employers have experienced when employees run up large balances. Suppose, for example, a part-time employee makes purchases totaling $300 and this amount would take several pay periods to be repaid out of that individual's small earnings. The system can check the current credit balance this employee has and impose a limit on how much more the particular individual can charge or it can set other parameters.

An employee who quits his job and goes on a shopping spree at the gift shop on his way out the door can be problematic as well. He still has a badge. The cashier knows him. She has no reason to question him. First, the system might check to see how much the employee currently owes and compare this to a set threshold to determine whether the charge should be allowed. If Greta has just resigned or been let go, the system will not allow the transaction, and the cashier will be alerted that Greta is no longer an employee.

Measuring Travel Time and Mileage

Then there's the issue of travel time and mileage. Some companies pay employees at a different rate when they drive on company time between job sites. They may also reimburse for mileage. Managers need to know the mileage charge is reasonable. With a manual system they probably don't attempt to verify everything. But with an automated setup, metrics such as the distance between work site A, reported in the system when an employee clocks in for work, and work site B, his second stop, where he also clocks in, can be integrated with the WMT data.

Making Sure the Right Unit Is Charged

Which business unit is charged for travel time and mileage can be handled automatically as well. Should it be the location the employee was traveling from (site A), or the one he was traveling to (site B)? The employee can punch a clock or use a phone or PDA when he leaves location A, and then clock into the new location when he arrives, marking the start and stop time of the trip. The system will allocate this to the unit management has determined should be charged.

It's not uncommon for employees to earn a different rate of pay at each facility. He will certainly want the higher rate to apply. Putting this payment process within WMT will make the payments consistent. There may also be opportunities to reduce this expense. Is nonproductive travel time between sites required to be paid at the employee's normal base rate, or could a lower rate, say minimum wage, apply? If the employee takes his lunch break during the travel period, that may or may not be compensated time. Could travel be charged entirely to an overhead account and not the work locations? What if the answers are different based on the job or work location? The complexities might be practically endless, but they still are manageable and controllable within WMT systems.

Tracking Unproductive or Downtime

Unproductive time is another concern. If a person is doing something that's not his primary responsibility, such as cleaning up, that's still considered compensable time. Even so, a company might want to segment this time, since it didn't contribute directly to production or sales or providing service, and account for it differently, since it wasn't spent directly adding value to an end product.

WMT systems are designed to allow employers to keep track of any type of activity. For example, if workers have to dress in clean-room outfits before they actually get to a work area, they might be required to punch in when they arrive at the dressing room and punch in again when they arrive at their workstations. In this way, the time getting dressed and moving from the dressing room to the production area will be captured in a separate category. The best setup for data capture in this work environment would be to use two devices—one near the entrance or dressing area and one closer to the production area.

Note: Some industry experts predict that GPS technology will be integrated with timekeeping and used to track employee movements within the work location via wireless devices. This development will eliminate the need for fixed data collection devices at the work site.

■ CASE STUDY: A WAREHOUSE CLEARS A LOGJAM AND GAINS GREATER EFFICIENCY   One company found through its new automated system that forklift drivers were causing a tie-up around time clocks. One vendor developed a labor analytics product that evaluates the activity reported through time and attendance for operational issues. The company was engaged by a major manufacturer to apply this tool to the manufacturer's labor data and determine whether employees were "working the clock." What the WMT vendor uncovered was that the plant's drivers would pull their forklifts as close to the time clock as they could get them before punching out at the end of their shift. The next shift spent a good deal of unproductive time untangling the resulting forklift jam. This discovery was made through a root cause analysis of the labor data that tracked time between arrival and activity. Obviously people knew about this logjam, but they didn't understand its cost and impact on productivity. WMT technology added value to information; it replaced what people knew with what they didn't know about a situation.

Paying Unproductive (Nonworked) Time Accurately

Speaking of unproductive time, many union contracts guarantee employees a minimum number of hours even though they may be sent home after five minutes, which reminds me of the story about the hammer and the broken furnace. A repairman was called during the weekend. He arrived, assessed the problem, took out his hammer, hit the furnace, and it started working. He charged $51—a dollar for his time and $50 for knowing where to hit the furnace.

In real life, an off-duty repairman might be called in during the night shift and spend five minutes fixing something that was holding up production. The company may have a guaranteed minimum of two hours' pay if someone is called in to work this way. So the repairman must be paid two hours for five minutes' work, 1 hour and 55 minutes of which is nonworked time. According to government guidelines, this time does not count toward "hours worked" and doesn't have to be counted toward overtime. The company is also not obligated to count those hours toward the accumulation of paid time off (PTO) or other benefits. But in a manual system, if Mr. Fixit has already worked 40 hours and two more are put on his time sheet, he's likely to be paid at an overtime rate because the people keeping track aren't aware of, or may overlook, this detail.

Key Idea

According to government guidelines, nonproductive (nonworked) time does not count toward "hours worked" and doesn't have to be counted toward overtime. The company is also not obligated to count those hours toward the accumulation of paid time off (PTO) or other benefits.

Another problem with manual processing of this type of compensated, nonworked guarantee time is that it is often paid at a higher rate than required. If an employee is called back in to work late in the week and is already over his or her weekly overtime limit, that employee will be owed the overtime rate for the hours worked. But the nonworked portion of the shift guarantee—the hour and 55 minutes not worked but paid for—does not have to be paid at the overtime rate because it is not worked time. This is a very common mistake that overobligates the employer to pay for the guarantee time at a higher rate.

We also see instances of workers being underpaid during such premium shifts because those processing the pay associate the activity with the pay code or earnings type assigned to that program. Call-back pay is often paid at 1.5 x base rate, and a special earnings type is set up with this rate programmed into it. When hours are put into this bucket, they are paid at this rate regardless of whether the employee is eligible for overtime (also 1.5 x base rate). Hence, workers put down their time in the call back category, regardless of whether the hours are under or over 40 for the week, thinking this is correct. They both pay time-and-a half, right? Wrong. In fact, employees who have exceeded the weekly overtime limit of 40 hours may be owed more than 1.5 x base because overtime is to be paid at the *blended* or weighted average rate of their earnings for the week. Putting the hours in the call back flat 1.5 x base category could be *underpaying* an employee because it is less than the blended rate.

This is fairly technical. But it is important because it directly affects cost and compliance. Employees paid in the call back pay code rather than in an overtime pay code on Friday may be **underpaid**. While the difference could be minor for that instance for a given individual, these issues are significant when added up over time and across the organization. The liability issues incurred if an employer is found noncompliant as to wage and hour guidelines could be really significant.

Similar programs are known as "on call" and "call in." On call staff are routinely scheduled for "on call" duty. If the employee works only a short span of time and the rest of the "guarantee" is paid as a "bonus," the hours can be treated differently from true "worked time," and the cost of those bonus hours reduced. In a manual system, particularly in large organizations, this complexity in pay practices is difficult to administer consistently and accurately. It also requires a good deal of training and data manipulation. WMT takes care of all of that.

The potential savings that come from splitting the worked and non-worked portions of the call back shift can be very significant. Replacing the 1.5 x base rate with the flat base rate saves .5 x base rate for those nonworked hours. Again, for the single employee, it may not seem like a lot of money. But these programs are used frequently, and the overspend that employers suffer can be tremendous.

Call-in is a favorite device employees use for "working the clock." Many executives have no idea how employees set themselves up for repeated call-ins, racking up bonus hours like frequent-flyer miles. These employees work 30 minutes for a two-hour bonus, clock out, get called back again, and rake in another two hours for another 30 minutes. If you don't believe me, ask a nurse working in a hospital that has little or no technology behind its timekeeping processes. Even with a time clock, some systems are unable to curb this abuse completely.

I encourage rewriting these policies and setting up the system or audits to shut down these "frequent flyers" and to cap the well on call-in bonus time. Moreover, tracking call-in pay will reveal the real problem, which usually has to do with attendance and understaffing issues such as poorly executed labor deployment, manipulated workflow, or missed routine maintenance. Use the database available through WMT to reduce the dependency on call-in and on-call or whatever mechanism is in place to supply workers at a moment's notice.

Checking Training and Certificate Requirements

In certain industries, employees must maintain specialized certifications that require recurring training. Employees whose certification expires may no longer be eligible to work until they become "current." Learning management systems track these certification requirements and alert managers to upcoming due dates and violations. The ability to forecast training absences and sunsetting skills enables companies to plan around these staffing issues. Some systems tightly integrate training with scheduling and time and attendance, giving managers the full picture of availability and qualifications for a pool of workers.

The Forgotten Areas: Attendance and Leave Management

Before time and attendance, scheduling, and sophisticated analytics solutions arrived, companies had few tools to use to help manage absences. Attendance is an operational issue as well as a cost concern. Employers all too often leave it up to individual supervisors to manage attendance as a part of the daily performance routine. Even with a clear attendance policy, operating without an automated system ensuring that each supervisor administers the policy consistently is risky.

Leave management poses its own set of problems. The government has stepped in with burdensome regulations about the guidelines for allowing time off, reporting leaves, and replacing workers. Employees are becoming masterful at manipulating the system and taking advantage of loosely managed leave programs. The vendors have answered the industry's cry for help with systems that track the occurrences and automate the processing of leave.

If your organization is not managing attendance and leave with the latest software, significant dollars are being spent needlessly.

Absence Management: Out of Sight and Out of Pocket

Absenteeism as a business problem is a little like the common cold. We all expect to suffer from it, and we usually try to ignore the symptoms and continue to chug along despite how it drags us down. It's contagious and annoying. We spend a lot of money treating the symptoms because doctors have yet to find a cure. We know exactly how long we spent on crutches or in the hospital, but we have no idea how much time we spent blowing our noses last year. A cold can lead to much more serious ailments, but we generally believe we just have to live with it and eventually we'll be all right.

Business leaders suffer from a similar affliction called absenteeism. Every manager knows his employees will be absent some of the time but rarely complains about or takes time to evaluate how it impacts him. Absenteeism can spread, infecting employees with its sense of entitlement, racking up the costs as its symptoms must be dealt with. No single manager in the company owns the direct and indirect costs of absenteeism as a line item in the budget. Most companies have only limited ability to track the time and expense this situation creates. Leaving it unexamined and untreated, most companies simply don't understand the cumulative affect it has on the business—the costs, the reduced productivity, the risks, and the negative effects on morale and turnover. As some business leaders begin to recognize the price of absenteeism and start to manage attendance better to become more competitive employers of choice, executives who ignore absenteeism will pay dearly in lost profits, productivity, and employee morale. The pie chart in Exhibit 4.2 illustrates how absenteeism affects the total cost of labor.

Absenteeism comes in three "strains":

1. *Planned* (scheduled) absences: vacation, PTO, leaves (military, jury duty, personal, and so forth)
2. *Unplanned and unscheduled absences*: sickness, disability, Family Medical Leave Act (FMLA), worker's compensation, and leaves such as unpaid, bereavement, and so forth
3. *Partial shift absences*: Late arrival, early departure, long breaks, personal appointments, and so forth

Unplanned absences are perhaps the most costly of all. One in 10 hourly employees in the United States is absent on average, amounting to 10 percent of the workforce. This represents a chronic problem with an estimated

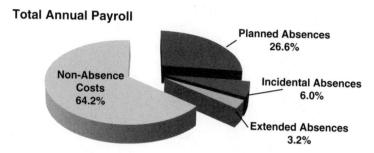

Total Annual Payroll

EXHIBIT 4.2   Total Cost of Absences Averages 36 Percent of Payroll

Source: Survey on *The Total Financial Impact of Employee Absences* by Mercer, 2008

price tag of $3,600 per hourly employee per year. The higher the rate of absenteeism, the greater the costs. According to Circadian Technologies, Inc., a leading international research firm, **overtime is 28 percent higher in companies where absenteeism is high. Idle time is 3.6 percent higher in these companies and turnover rates are greater in companies that suffer from poor attendance.**

Productivity suffers because of absenteeism. Unexpected call-offs, late arrivals, and illnesses all disrupt the planned activities and waste the time of managers and supervisors who have to process them and adjust staffing. The quality and speed of the work may also be diminished because less-qualified employees may have to take over. Employees who have to take up the slack can also become overworked and overburdened.

Absenteeism of any type increases costs and impedes productivity, and employees who work excessive overtime to cover for absent workers or who work in jobs for which they are not properly skilled, are more likely to have accidents and succumb to poor health. The indirect costs that result include those from additional worker's compensation claims and greater health care costs and represent very expensive side effects.

Financial managers need to be concerned about accurately tracking attendance, because without adequate estimates of the company's accrued benefit liabilities they may not be able to meet the minimum accounting requirements of regulations such as Sarbanes-Oxley. This can indeed be costly, and the implications for these managers should give them a scare on a personal level—think Enron executives. Out of sight, out of mind takes on a new meaning. The pie chart in Exhibit 4.3 shows the large percentage of indirect costs resulting from absenteeism. These are the most often overlooked and difficult to quantify without an intelligent system. Failing to make these connections may result in money coming out of

Total Annual Payroll

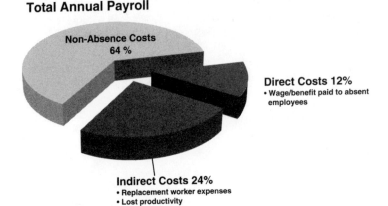

EXHIBIT 4.3 Indirect Costs of Absenteeism Are Twice the Direct Costs

The indirect costs of absenteeism—lost productivity, unexpected overtime, cost of replacement workers—make up two-thirds of the cost of absences.

Source: Survey on *The Total Financial Impact of Employee Absences* by Mercer, 2008

the personal pockets of these executives when they are forced to defend inadequate accounting processes and practices.

That's the diagnosis. The good news is that the prognosis can be good. WMT offers a remedy that's very easy to swallow.

The keys to effectively managing absenteeism include:

- **Communication:** visibility, meaningful information and timing
- **Alignment:** synchronization with overall goals and control
- **Standardization** of policies, terms, processes, and objectives
- **Tools**
- **Training**

Organizations need a way to track absenteeism and to identify the patterns and root causes. Such a system needs to enforce tracking consistently across the organization and total the findings to show the overall magnitude of the problem. Once this is understood, managers should share the information about patterns, offenders, and seasonal issues with supervisors. They ought then to set absenteeism goals in line with the company's strategic objectives. A standard plan of action needs to be created that includes common terms, policies, and practices that are clearly defined and easily followed. These standards should next be configured into the system, which will become the new workspace for absence management throughout the company. Training is the final key to success. This will be necessary not only because a new system is being introduced, but because roles, responsibilities, and expectations will be different than in the past and employees will need coaching and follow-up for these to take effect. Remember, we're talking about a serious "illness," and periodic checkups are needed to measure progress and eventually keep the "patient" well.

Some WMT systems offer management a dashboard designed with the interests of managers as far up as chief operating officers. There are a range of metrics that are important to this role: total headcount, labor cost, absenteeism cost, overtime, and productivity. Each metric has an indicator (a color-coded arrow) that shows whether the value is up or down compared to the last period. The color indicates whether a threshold has been exceeded so that major variances are highlighted for immediate attention. If the absenteeism cost indicator worries the manager he can investigate further using a linked document such as an Absenteeism Report.

These dashboards are configurable to the metrics that make sense for the customer. Behind the on-screen view of the dashboards are settings that allow the customer to design into the system the inputs from events that impede his operations and budget. The system continually collects and assesses the activity of workers, computes the cost, and measures it against predefined targets. The result is a better understanding of the true causes and cost of absenteeism.

Planning that engages everyone in the effort to manage attendance can be a benefit unto itself, because it will raise consciousness about the issue, as will the use of new technology and data that measure and forecast absenteeism. Software applications can empower employees to manage their own time off and influence the schedules to which they are assigned. Automating scheduling will enforce leave and compensation policies, resulting in more equitable treatment and improved employee satisfaction. Researchers have found that absenteeism is lowest where specialized software is used to manage schedules and attendance. Its effects are even more dramatic where employees are allowed to manage the balance between work and home life. The difference could mean savings of up to $3 million per year for a company with 5,000 employees.

The effects of FMLA represent a growing problem for companies, but applying technology to this category of time off can significantly reduce its financial and operational impact. Employees aren't simply using this program for long-term absences such as medical leave, the birth of a child, or caring for an ill family member. Increasingly, they are becoming aware of the leniency this program offers and use it as a "wild card" for intermittent, last-minute call-offs and partial shift absences. Automated systems enable companies to accurately track this manipulation of the system and to compile total time off. Lacking such a tool, companies are hard pressed to prevent overuse of the program. It's a generous benefit on the employee side; failing to track it adequately will obligate the company to excessive "generosity" and expense.

Best Practices for Absence Management

Best practices for absence management include tracking and identifying patterns and root causes of absenteeism. Using this information, smart organizations learn to manage, forecast, and plan for absenteeism. They use the system to enforce compliance and tracking, and this reduces their risks as well as the negative impact of excessive absenteeism on cost and productivity. The technology allows them to react in real time to staffing issues and to take corrective action to change behavior.

Each of the following types of absenteeism involves a different reaction time:

Planned absences. Advance notification of vacation requests and planned leaves allows for schedule adjustments and staffing solutions to be provided at a lower cost, less disruption to services, and better ability to staff with appropriate skill match (less impact on productivity). According to Circadian researchers: An average employee takes three days of unreported PTO per year.

Unplanned absences. Real-time response is essential. Data is required from operations to assess needs, resources, and costs. Unplanned absences can disrupt operations immediately, cause delays, increase costs, decrease morale, and leave an employer understaffed in the number of employees and the skills required. Circadian: Two-thirds of unplanned absences are non–illness related (e.g., for personal reasons, entitlement-related, family issues, etc.).

Partial shift absences. Absences are often unseen in real time. Immediate awareness and response are required. The partial absence must be identified. Needs must be assessed, along with resources and costs. Others on premises become burdened and productivity is hampered. Overpayment often occurs when workers are paid for nonworked time or because time off was not charged toward accrued benefit time. Circadian: 0.72 percent is average payroll inflation cost due to partial absences.

According to Circadian in the 2005 white paper entitled "Absenteeism—The Bottom Line Killer," the benefits of WMT applied to absence management include:

- Reduced costs (Circadian: A company of 5,000 hourly employees has the potential to reduce costs by $7.9 million or more per year, or 3.2 percent of payroll on average, using WMT/Absence Management.)
- Improved compliance, consistency and reduced risk

- Fuller awareness of unreported partial absences
- Faster reaction time
- Better scheduling decisions
- Improved productivity and resource utilization
- Improved quality and service
- Increased employee morale and retention

Attending to Attendance Policies

Some companies have policies that require points to be given for poor attendance. Attendance issues that create staffing and budget problems for companies include absences, late and even early arrivals, long shifts, short shifts, and unscheduled shifts. These are also known as "partial shift absences" or "shift variances." Leaves of absence of a longer duration—hours and even days for jury duty, military duty, personal or medical reasons, or sabbaticals—also interrupt the supply of labor. Managing each of these requires a special approach.

Companies that recognize those shift variance issues and want to do something about them create attendance programs to monitor the activity and manage the employees. At each occurrence, the employee racks up a point. In some programs, the various types of attendance problems carry different weights. These points accumulate, and after a specified number is reached, an individual may be "written up." This citation may need to be considered immediately; accumulated over a set period of time such as a month, three months, or six months; or taken into consideration at the annual employee evaluation time. Doing so takes time, attention to detail, and persistence. Such policies must be administered consistently throughout the organization. Allowing managers in different departments to administer an attendance policy with varying degrees of adherence to the letter of the law will open up the employer to poor morale at best and litigation in the worst case.

One employer related the story of three employees who had been dismissed for violating their attendance policy. The employees' supervisor had followed the company policy with escalating warnings and consequences to the point of termination. Unfortunately, these employees knew that similar offenses by employees in other departments had not been dealt with so stringently. Their supervisor was more lax in his adherence to the company attendance policy and had failed to take such severe action. The terminated employees filed suit. It cost the employer $40,000 just to investigate the claims; it involved digging through months of attendance records and supervisor paperwork. The end result was that they had indeed been treated according to the policy but they also discovered that other employees had not. Supervisors were not acting consistently to enforce the policy. These employees, who had poor attendance habits, had to be reinstated.

The good news is that there are attendance systems that will ensure that this situation is avoided. These systems are configured based on the company policy rules concerning types of absences and the consequences. The system evaluates employee attendance, determines whether the attendance behavior meets the criterion of a violation, accumulates all offenses over a defined period, and automates the process of enforcing the policy. When enough "points" for offenses have been accumulated and a supervisor action is warranted by the policy, the system automatically notifies the supervisor through an electronic notification, typically e-mail. Along with the notification are the completed forms that the supervisor must use—a script for a verbal warning, a letter for a written warning, a formal dismissal, and so on. These forms are delivered to the supervisor immediately; all she has to do is print the form, sign it, and contact the employee. To make certain she does her part, along the way the system has also notified human resources and the supervisor's boss. This makes the supervisor accountable for doing her part. If the supervisor doesn't take action and notify human resources that she has done so within a certain amount of time, the issue is automatically escalated by the same system. No gaps, no inconsistency in enforcement, and no lawsuits for unfair treatment.

Conversely, there are "perfect attendance" programs designed to motivate employees to come to work on a regular basis. Obviously, just getting one's basic hourly rate isn't enough of a motivator. Time and attendance systems come right off the shelf with mechanisms that track and count these activities as well. And the same type of automated workflow can be put in place to make certain that the incentives are deployed consistently as well.

No supervisor wants to spend time keeping track of absences. Tracking employee time manually takes away from more productive work. What is that time worth? It's difficult for supervisors to remember exactly when an absence reaches the point at which it becomes grounds for dismissal. When supervisors don't remember, it's extremely counterproductive to have disgruntled employees who know they are being treated unfairly. How much can your company afford to spend on investigations, grievances, audits, back pay, and lawsuits? It's so much more cost-effective to use technology to administer these issues.

Key Idea

The U.S. Department of Labor estimates that the average cost to defend a leave case is $78,000. Considering that on average 7 to 15 percent of a company's labor force is out at some point on leave during the course of a year, it may only take one employee to justify the cost.

Equally as troubling are the increasing challenges of managing employee leave. Things are changing in this arena as well. Congress has attempted to alleviate some of the pain that industry leaders have been suffering, but significant problems persist when it comes to successfully managing compliance with FMLA regulations.

It's no surprise to many that the Family Medical Leave Act (FMLA) is wreaking havoc on employers. In June 2005, the U.S. Senate held a roundtable discussion of FMLA as a competitive threat to U.S. manufacturing. Case study examples of the abuse of FMLA leave and the impact on businesses were cited with disturbing implications. Intermittent leave, including tardy, early departure, and Monday and Friday absences, has grown five times as fast as use of the program for continued leaves. For example, on Super Bowl Sunday one employer experienced a 50 percent spike in FMLA absences during game time. Occurrences of tardy and early dismissal at this employer averaged 110 per month, equal to six employees calling in late or leaving early every day of the month.

Industry representatives at the Senate hearing complained that FMLA regulations negate any contractual agreements between employers, employees, and unions, leaving the employer with little or no recourse to contest FMLA absences or to apply attendance policies to employees with habitual attendance problems. FMLA use has exploded in manufacturing and is circumventing employers' efforts to curtail poor attendance through policy. Unions have even held on-site classes to "train" employees in the use of FMLA. One employer estimated that FMLA absences cost $8.1 million annually. (*Source:* Lancaster Testimony 7.5.05 American Axle & Manufacturing, Family Medical Leave Act, U.S. Senate Roundtable Discussions Report.) All an employer can do in the present regulatory environment under FMLA is to react effectively to the disruption and work to mitigate the costs. If your company is caught in this situation and does not have a powerful tool to respond to employee absences, you may pay a very heavy price.

Compliance Is a Growing Concern

Many companies are learning the hard way that failing to enforce compliance to company policy, government regulations, labor agreements, and fair labor standards can be a very costly mistake.

Enforcing Policy Compliance

Automation can also insure that incentive plans, wage and hour guidelines, and overtime are administered properly. Let's say a policy is instituted that if an employee works an extra shift, he or she will get as an incentive two dollars more per hour. But a requirement is that the employee must work at least four hours beyond the regular shift. In a manual system, this might be tricky to administer, and there will be the ever-present temptation to bend the rules. An automated system will eliminate this temptation and administer the guidelines without missing a beat. More important, the most sophisticated systems can be programmed to prevent managers from scheduling employees into overtime situations by setting up overtime "violations" and warnings. This would be almost impossible to do in a manual system.

Including Exempt Employees

Exempt employees are another group for which time reporting and analysis of labor activity may be lacking. Here compliance concerns are reversed, and employers often worry that requiring exempt employees to participate in the WMT system will put them in noncompliance relative to their exempt status. Fortunately, this is not true. I surveyed the Department of Labor and all 50 states and could not find any statutes specifically prohibiting exempt punching.

Normally set up for a straight 40 hours per week or 80 hours of pay per biweekly pay period, exempt employees often are required to report only exceptions. If one takes a sick day, the onus is on the employee to report that he didn't work, and a day of sick time will be deducted from the employee's available balance. Salaried employees who fail to report this will still be paid the full biweekly amount. Often, because exempt employees don't submit time sheets for approval, the day off can easily be overlooked. The payroll coordinator has no idea whether the salaried employee worked or took time off, so the automatic 80 hours passes through the system as normal. The practice of exempt "autopay" has also put companies on "autopilot" when it comes to managing exempt labor.

An employee may have little incentive to report that he was sick. If no one notices, he'll be able to use that eight hours another day. Using an automated labor management system requiring exempt employees to report into the system at least once a day validates that they were at work that day. In addition, having some form of verification, such as biometrics, will validate that the employee was physically on site.

Another troubling consequence of underreported exempt time off is that the exempt employee can continue to "bank" that time off, increasing a potential liability for unused time off payouts when the employee retires or terminates employment. Companies that are forced to downsize may be surprised to discover the full price tag for these benefit hours that employees have, in essence, cashed in twice.

Key Idea

Companies that are forced to downsize may be surprised to discover the full price tag for these (exempt employee) benefit hours that employees have, in essence, cashed in twice.

There is a widespread misconception about, or perhaps an overly cautious approach in, handling the reporting of exempt worker time. Exempt status is a well-defined classification of worker types. All sorts of criteria are used to establish whether people's job responsibilities, not just their titles, qualify them as exempt from overtime. Wrapped up in this characterization or litmus test is tracking time worked. Employers are under the impression they cannot track an exempt worker's hours without being obligated to pay overtime. But this is not so; it is an exaggeration of the guidelines. Employers have every right to keep a history of a worker's time. I'm not a labor attorney, but I've spoken with some who assure me that when handled properly, exempt employees may be required to use an automated time and attendance reporting system without endangering their exempt status. And just to be certain, I contacted the Department of Labor and every state's department of wage and hour administration. Not one of them came back with a restriction against exempt employees punching in and out of a time-reporting system. It's not the existence of this information that counts; it's what employers do with it relative to compensation. So don't be afraid to include exempts in the process of implementing workforce management technology and thereby receive the full benefit of having this data in the system.

Adhering to Worker Age Regulations

Employing minors under a certain age involves restrictions, because in some states limitations exist on the number of hours they can work, as well as which shifts they can work, particularly during the school year. For this reason, minors can be flagged in the system so that their hours are limited, and other regulations are abided by, such as not being able to work past 10 P.M. on school nights. Eager teenagers may want to work the late shift, and weary supervisors may welcome a helping hand at closing time, but the system can prevent these violations of wage and hour regulations. Automated scheduling can make this sort of thing easy, enforce compliance, and put labor to work at the optimum place and time.

Achieving Equal and Fair Treatment of Workers: Reducing Risk

Having detailed time and attendance data at one's fingertips can help in other ways. Suppose an employee claims his employer didn't pay or treat him fairly. For example, most states require employers to give employees breaks after working a set number of hours. Some states allow an employee to waive his right to a break and work through the break period under certain conditions. A policy might be set up so that a supervisor is required to give his approval in such an instance, and the supervisor in turn might have the employee sign a release. This can be entered in the system, which will be important when troublemaker Charlie gets canned for habitually being late. He may realize his habitual tardiness has been documented but still want a pound of flesh.

"They wouldn't let me take lunch," he might say to his lawyer. "I should be paid for all those lunches they made me work."

When an employee makes such a claim, it's up to the employer to prove that either the employee was actually given the breaks or that he waived his right to them and was paid for the time he worked. Without documentation, the employer would be up the proverbial creek. With it, a disgruntled employee will simply have to move along and put the squeeze on someone else.

A labor attorney once told me a story about one of her clients. One supervisor in a company decided to institute a policy that if an employee under him didn't give two weeks' notice before quitting, that employee would not be paid for accumulated paid time off (PTO). According to the attorney, this practice is illegal in the state where this company is located, and one employee complained to the state about her client's company. This precipitated an investigation.

The lawyer went on to say that the state authorities didn't look at just that one employee record. Of course not. The company's entire system was audited. The authorities assumed that if one employee was mistreated, the company potentially mistreated them all. It happened that this company's problem was systemic, and its exposure to penalties and additional financial obligations turned out to be much more serious than what was indicated by just that single employee's complaint.

Let's think about the company where Charlie claimed he didn't get his required break. If management had employed the WMT system we've been discussing, this might not have happened, and if it did, after documentation upholding the company's position was presented, it's less likely that the authorities would have moved forward to take a look at all the records. In the first place, employees could have been required to clock in and out for all break periods. In the second, supervisors would have been entering in an employee's waiving of his break rights. The system would have forced each employee to be handled in the same way as every other employee in the company. The authorities would quickly see this and have less cause to investigate further. Automation would have prevented a wayward supervisor from making up his own rules for his department. At the very least, employers are in a much better position to defend themselves because the data is easily retrieved from their time and attendance databases. Running a few reports will be a lot less labor intensive than sending a crew of people down to the basement to sift through boxes and file cabinets full of paper records.

The reduction of risk—exposure to liabilities for noncompliance, employee grievances, external audits, fines, and so forth—is often understated and undervalued. The financial benefit of reducing expenses related to these issues should not be overlooked. Workforce management technology will elevate your organization to a higher plane, thereby mitigating risk and reducing costs.

Foiling Those Who Are Working the Clock

What's "working the clock"? It's a lot of things. Most companies don't pay minute to minute, so a cutoff usually exists for rounding the time of a punch. For example, if someone punches in at 8:08, this is rounded to 8:15, whereas a punch of 8:07 is rounded to 8:00. Employees know this and are savvy about its implications. Every organization needs to look at safeguarding itself against abuses. Are employees "cashing in"?

At what time will employees aim to arrive? Some might come at 8:07 every day and play this game at every punch. They punch in, punch out and in for lunch, and punch out at the end of the day right at eight minutes before or seven minutes after. This can add up to a half hour of non-worked time every day. That's two and a half hours a week. In a year that's 130 hours, more than three weeks of paid-for time that wasn't worked. In a company that employees hundreds or maybe thousands, this can add up to big money.

We evaluated a sampling of employee punches at one employer and found a significant spike in punches right at 00:23 minutes. For the minutes leading up to 23 punch activity had a noticeable decrease. At 23 minutes the employee's time rounded to the half-hour mark and they gained 7 minutes of paid time. When we looked at the individual employees and found many who consistently punched every day right at 23 minutes that proved that employees were gaming the rounding rule to gain the 7 minutes every time they punched out

Exhibit 4.4 illustrates how employees at one organization were abusing the punch rounding rule. It demonstrates how employees took advantage of the rounding rule, which rolls the time forward to the next quarter hour.

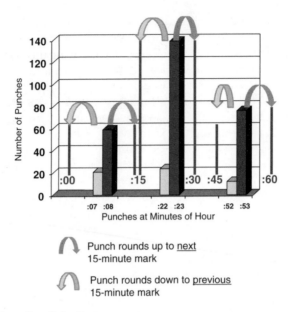

EXHIBIT 4.4 Rounding Rule Abuse

Source: Client-based research conducted by Athena Enterprises, 2009

Employees punching at these "change points" (8, 23, and 53 minutes) gain 7 minutes per punch. The dark bars represent employees who punch at the change point and gain 7 minutes of unworked time. The light bars represent employees who punch right before the rounding occurs. The difference shows how employees are waiting for the change point to gain the 7 minutes of paid time.

Of course, it can be argued that this rounding mechanism works to the company's advantage as well. Employees' time can be rounded back in a way that shaves minutes off what is paid. In theory this may be true, but only for the computer. People aren't computers, and they quickly learn how to "work the clock" and do so with abandon.

Key Idea

Industry estimates place intentional and error-driven time theft in the range of 1.5 percent to 10 percent of gross payroll, costing U.S. businesses hundreds of billions of dollars each year.

Source: "Biometrics: High-value Workforce Management—The Critical Role of Biometric Time and Attendance to Workforce Management Solutions," white paper by Acuity Market Intelligence, February 2008

Let's talk about the lunch break, because it's a slightly different animal. A lunch period is a span of time. It's an interval between two punches. At lunch time, an employee could leave at 11:53, knowing this will be counted as 12 o'clock. He could come back at 12:37, knowing this will show as 12:30. According to time records based on each rounded punch time, he took a half-hour lunch. In fact, he took 44 minutes—almost 50 percent more. Interval rounding enables employers to shut down this game and pay employees for their true time.

Interval Rounding Offers Savings

What's interval rounding? WMT systems can be set to round the interval or span of time rather than the punch time. Jane punched out for lunch at 11:53 and back in at 12:37. That's 44 minutes, which rounds to 45. The entire shift can be rounded as well. Please be aware, however, that if your company bills based on hours worked and you decide to try shift interval rounding, you need to make certain this method is consistent with your billing policies and contracts.

The system can also be set up to flag those workers who do not punch at all for lunch. If they couldn't take lunch because they had to work, they should be paid for it. But if they forgot to punch, or just didn't bother to punch and took lunch, they should not be paid for that time. WMT systems can easily be set up for automatic deductions and flags to report errant activity.

One of my customers requested an on-screen workspace that would display the employees who did not punch for lunch. Upon hearing this request, I was taken aback.

"You mean we've got to get the system to tell us something based on data that isn't in the system?" After all, the tool would be used to report employees who were *not* punching. Show me what doesn't exist was what I'd heard my customer say. Furthermore, for this tool to be actionable, we had to ignore missing punches (the nonexistent data) if the employee worked only a few hours and should not have taken lunch. This was incredible. Sometimes my client wanted to know whether a meal had not been punched, and sometimes he didn't.

The good news was the technology could do it. We devised a way to configure the pay rules and build logic into the system that told the computer to expect a set of lunch punches and what they would look like and under what conditions. If the system registered this activity, then nothing happened. But when the expected activity didn't appear, the system sent up a "missed meal" flag, giving the names of employees who may have forgotten to punch for lunch. An individual's supervisor could then look into what happened. Mind you, we did not customize the system, we configured it. WMT systems are designed as tool kits.

Early and late punches, relative to when the employee is scheduled to arrive and depart, can easily be dealt with in an automated system. Here's another scenario. Suppose Earl E. Bird likes to get to the factory at 7:30, punch in, and then go have a cup of coffee at the cafeteria until his shift starts at 8 o'clock. If Earl isn't supposed to clock in before 8 o'clock, the data collection device can be programmed so that it won't allow Earl to clock in before 8 o'clock. Or the system can allow the punch but round to the scheduled start time unless a supervisor overrides this restriction because Earl E. Bird really was supposed to come in early.

In addition, don't forget to document this new restriction for early birds in your compensation policies so employees clearly understand what they will be paid for.

Making Paper-Based "Fudging" Disappear

A parallel is the running of old and new systems simultaneously for testing and comparison. When going from paper to PC, the manual system is kept going while the automated system comes up to speed. Something I've frequently noticed during this time is that payroll costs go down during and immediately following the parallel period. People are aware of the additional scrutiny; they know that the two systems are being compared. So you might call this the "Big Brother syndrome." As the parallel process is used to validate the data, a dip will occur in the amount of payroll dollars paid out. Somehow, reported time becomes very credible. Paper system "fudging" disappears. As the paper system goes away, the payroll figure may creep back up. The good news is that it often will not reach its previous high level.

The previously high levels of fudging will disappear because controls are put in place, and what's going on is more visible. As time goes by, if it's possible to do so, some people will learn subtle ways to work the new system. That's why it's important to devise controls that discourage and limit the amount of manipulation that results in "working the clock."

Does this mean people are dishonest? Perhaps some are. But consider what you'd do in a typical situation. For example, think about what might happen when a person is late and it isn't really that individual's fault.

"There was a huge backup on the expressway. A tractor trailer turned over. I shouldn't be docked for that."

With the old manual system, it was easy enough for that person's supervisor to fix the problem. All he had to do to help the employee out was to add the time back in by adjusting the punch time. But in an automated system, doing this will not be so easy, and if everything is set up correctly, such an adjustment won't go undetected. One vendor shared a story about a juice producer that was implementing its software. The company had already been taking some measurements of overall labor costs to obtain some pre-implementation benchmarks. But when the company announced to the employees its intention to start to track overtime and productivity, a significant drop in labor costs occurred before the implementation actually started. It merely took the anticipation of greater scrutiny for this overspending to decrease.

WMT systems can identify the user, the device, and the location, date, and time of all entries and changes made in the system. Reports can show who is editing, deleting, or adding data in places where they shouldn't be. There is no eraser in an electronic system. In other words, the adage that "what gets tracked gets done" proves very true with WMT.

Eliminating Flex Time Abuse

Flex time is what comes about when employees are allowed to work a flexible schedule by adjusting their work hours to accommodate special, personal needs. Or it may be offered simply to provide greater flexibility to employees who want time off during normal business hours. Some examples of flex time are programs that allow employees to work longer shifts and take a day or a portion of a shift off without penalty. For example, employees work "eight nines," which means they work eight nine-hour shifts accumulating eight hours of flex time. They then use the flex time as a paid day off. Flex time might also be used to compensate employees who worked an especially long shift to handle an emergency or who were required to travel and experienced long work days because of the time required to get to a distant work location. Let's say a person works 10 hours one day. The person may work only six the next day to make up for this. In a paper system, the individual may simply write down eight hours for each day. But this misrepresentation of actual time worked cannot be accomplished in a system where data is time-stamped when entered and "actual" arrival and departure times are accurately represented.

In a manual system, it's easy for flex time to be ripe for abuse. One common misuse occurs when a supervisor hands it out as a discretionary bonus to a favored employee. It can also easily be overstated or overdrawn. Employers may unwittingly violate wage and hour regulations by allowing flex time to cross pay weeks or pay periods and not pay overtime appropriately. These are serious infractions in the eyes of regulators. In addition, flex time that is not recorded accurately can skew labor cost reporting by attributing productive time to time frames when no hours were actually worked.

But there is a solution. Use WMT systems to bank flex time and ensure that it is used in accordance with company policy. It can apportion productive time accurately and reflect compensated nonworked time appropriately. Incorporating flex time policy into an automated system ensures that the time is used and paid in alignment with labor regulations. And it can do all this while providing visibility into how the benefit flex program is being used.

Tracking flex time allows employers to evaluate the flex time program against operational and staffing needs. Since it represents a variance from the normal work schedule, it makes sense to monitor it to make sure it doesn't impede productivity. Tracking flex time allows the employer to measure the true cost of the program by relating flex time hours to any additional labor expenses that arise because an employee has to be replaced during the missed shift. Often, the flex benefit means others have to work overtime or, in extreme circumstances, that agency or contract labor must be brought in. The resulting additional expenses incurred need to be taken into account when evaluating such a program.

On the other hand, flex time might encourage employees to defer using other benefit time. Benefits such as paid vacations and holidays mean employees receive pay for nonproductive time off. The flex time program presumably pays employees for productive time and may create an illusion of paid time off similar to a vacation or holiday. This might actually work to an employer's benefit if employees get caught with excess vacation time in a "use it or lose it" program. In such a situation, the employer's obligation to pay for vacation time is eliminated when the employee fails to take the time off within the allotted time frame. The employee may have received several days off away from work during the period, but the employer may actually have paid only for productive time. The employer is making a payment for something it received—hours worked. With benefits, the employer's not paying for services rendered. So from the company's perspective, it could be that a flex time program may be a viable alternative to a vacation benefit program.

Whether or not such a program is appropriate for your industry and category of workers depends on how competitive the labor market is, along with regulatory factors. But it may be something your Compensation Manager should evaluate. Using workforce management technology to develop a critical analysis of the program can provide valuable data on which to base a decision.

Chapter Summary

- WMT systems work because they offer the tools that have been missing to ensure that the right person is at the right place at the right time. Operations benefit when they gain visibility into real-time activity and cost.
- The information gathered by WMT systems can be used to examine production variances caused by employees (e.g., absenteeism), payroll (e.g., work rules), and operations (e.g., material delays).
- WMT systems provide a new measurement—Overall Labor Effectiveness (OLE). OLE is a metric, based on the interdependency of labor utilization, labor performance, and quality. It measures the impact of the workforce on the business and helps to improve costing and labor utilization issues.
- WMT systems can provide on-premises reporting, support gatekeeper issues, and enforce compliance.
- The costs of absenteeism and poorly managed leaves of absence are often overlooked or considered an unavoidable cost of doing business. Because the direct and indirect costs are not understood, an average of 36 percent of total payroll is virtually unmanaged. Reducing and managing absenteeism can result in significant and immediate savings and operational improvements.
- Absence management tools enforce compliance, encourage good attendance, and mitigate the negative impacts of unavoidable absenteeism.
- Leave programs, especially FMLA cases, are extremely difficult to manage and put companies at significant financial risk if not administered properly. WMT systems relieve operational managers of much of the headache of managing leave cases.
- Regulations are an increasing distraction to operations as they struggle to focus on production while managing compliance. Time and labor systems are designed to handle all of the rules and help managers effectively manage their people within the constraints to which they are subject. Without the latest technology employers are at a disadvantage and employees may be working the clock, banking on the company's lack of oversight.

CHAPTER 5

How Automated Systems Make Life Easier

Who doesn't want the "easy button" turned on when they come into work? That's the most basic benefit an automated, intelligent system should deliver. WMT systems accomplish "easy" when they are designed to be flexible, easy to use, and intuitive. In this chapter we'll take a look at what makes life easy with time and labor management technology and why that's good for the organization. The benefits range from easy to administer, easy to track, and easy to report and solve problems with to easy to compute and forecast.

Configurable Software Supports Complex Rules

The beauty of a configurable system built on a tool kit of parameters, settings, queries, and workspaces is that it can be made more powerful. It becomes customized to your organization. Perhaps the vendor did not design every desired feature into the system, but its software engineers did design in the capacity to make the outcomes possible. The lesson is, if you don't see what you need in the canned product, look for a system robust and flexible enough to be configured to suit your needs.

What makes a system robust and flexible are the parameters, qualifiers, counter mechanisms, and zone features. The system needs to support the types of logic that your policies stipulate. Payroll practices are often built on Boolean logic, which says, "If so and so, then such and such." In a sense, employees qualify for their compensation and the complexities of the qualification process can seem endless. A setup's features must be able to account for eligibility criteria in multiple layers (i.e., if X then Y, but only if A + B = C on Saturdays). It must be possible to define settings and expand them. So, in selecting the right software, it's important to look for the ability to combine the parameters, review data in the future and in the past, measure and total the data, average it, and compute it before a result is given.

We've seen incredibly complex compensation programs configured to entirely automate the qualification and calculations of pay. The key is to know your practices. Know how and why you pay employees today and what you need to be able to do tomorrow. Then find a system that can best handle those requirements, sit back, and enjoy the evolution.

Historical Edit Features Maintain Accuracy in Any Time Frame

As is the case with politicians and modern movies, Payroll is frequently "rewriting history"—that is, trying to revise the record of what happened in the past. For Payroll, however, unlike political pundits and Hollywood producers, that history must be 100 percent accurate. Payroll history is checked and rechecked by government revenue agencies and internal auditors. Payroll records are subject to checks and balances, reconciling bank statements and general ledger accounts. They must square vertically with subtotals and grand totals and horizontally within every individual withholding account. This becomes increasingly challenging with each adjustment, correction, and manual check that must be written.

Manual processes for payroll corrections and hand checks are fraught with difficulty and prone to error. Payments cannot be made based simply on newly submitted information. The past must be reviewed and the new information applied to the historical data to determine whether the new information changes the old. A good record of the adjustment must be maintained so that when subsequent inquiries occur, the inquirer can locate and comprehend the history of those changes. Time sheets must be recalculated, notes made, and new records appended to the original time submissions. The new payment must be tracked both in terms of its historical impact and for its inclusion in current payroll data.

Fortunately, however, with the introduction of computer-based time and attendance systems, rewriting history is much easier than in the past.

Key Idea

Software products today include historical edit features that allow everyone in the process to keep track of records and payments for any time frame, past or present. Historical edits don't merely append additional information to records of employee activity and expenditure; they allow new information to update the past period and adjust anything that should have been impacted to accurately portray the total cost and work effort.

Date- and activity-specific records exist that can be updated with new information, recalculated, and merged with current payroll data for payment. Adjustment entries are electronically appended to historical records so that finding the corrections and preventing duplicate adjustments is avoided.

Payroll can update employee time cards with a record of an additional payment, whether it is paid with the next normal payroll cycle or done with a manual checkoff cycle. Reports can be run with labor management software that show labor costs for specific periods of time or activity as they were actually paid in real time or as the information accumulated over time with additional adjustments and corrections.

Group Edits Make Life Easy

Let's say a supervisor has a group of people attend an offsite meeting. Since they weren't at the plant, they couldn't punch a time clock. In a manual setup, this would have meant locating the time card for each of those individuals and manually adding the time. Or a report would have been sent to Payroll, and Payroll would have had to manually add the time to each individual employee's payroll record before processing.

Today, we have the ability to grab all of those employees at once, whether they are all in the same department, all work the same shift across the plant, or even if they all are working on a common project but represent a diverse group of employees and different functional areas. After the "group" has been selected, we can now input the activity and apply it to all the selected employees in a single stroke. This works well for bonus payments as well, and systems often provide a confirmation that each record was updated successfully. No more is it necessary to find each employee's paper time card or electronic record individually and input the same thing over and over. This is a tremendous time-saver.

Reason and Comment Tracking

Is it important to your organization to know the reasons why? What value does attaching a reason or description to labor activity and payments add? From an audit perspective knowing "why" can be crucial in determining whether a user has made a change in the system for an appropriate reason.

There are two types of comments—fixed and free-form text. A fixed comment setup in a WMT system provides the ability to create predefined reasons that can be used in the system. Typical comments include "family emergency, bereavement, weather related, missed punch, low census, late materials, and supervisor approved." These comments are attached to time card events and schedules to show reasons behind employee activity and attendance. These comments allow for standardization across the organization so that everyone uses the same set of reason codes. What isn't standard, however, are the underlying definitions (e.g., what constitutes a valid family emergency?) and how these are applied unless workers are well trained and there is thorough documentation on how these comments are to be used and defined. It may not matter to the organization as a whole, but if it does, it should be deployed accordingly.

The second type of comment and newer to the industry consists of free-form text comments. This feature allows users to type in whatever commentary they want to add to the employee's activity. "Bob was late because he picked up Bill after his truck broke down" or "Extra duty paid because two other nurses were out sick." Free-form text comments are very popular, but they do have their drawbacks. First, space is limited and access should be limited. Second, clear guidelines about how much to write and what to include are also needed. Third, what can be used can also be abused. Make certain users know what is acceptable language and commentary. Remember the audit trail!

In many organizations attendance is a big problem. Comments can help manage this issue. For example, each time a person is late or absent, the record may be appended with a reason why. Maybe she overslept or got stuck in traffic or the baby-sitter didn't show. When tracking trends in employee attendance, a spike in late arrivals due to road construction may be revealed. You might ask, "So what? What can an employer do who knows traffic is a problem on the second shift?" Having the second-shift employees consistently arrive late is going to disrupt the first shift, the customers being served, and production schedules underway during the transition. The employer may decide a temporary change in the schedule would alleviate this problem by allowing employees to travel during non-peak traffic periods, thereby making it more likely they will arrive at work on time. Or the employer could simply remind employees that they will need to leave for work earlier to ensure on-time arrival.

Comments can also be integrated with the attendance management module discussed in previous sections. A comment after the third late arrival could show in the time card that the employee was given his verbal warning.

Attendance can immediately impact a business's bottom line. If no one performs an authorized, reimbursable, billable service, the revenue that would have been gained is lost. The retail industry is particularly sensitive to the attendance problem. A retail store may not be able to open until a manager is on duty or enough cashiers are in place. I once went to the movie theater and stood at the back of a very long line. As the crowd grew, we noticed workers behind the concession stand inside but soon realized no one was manning the ticket windows. The line grew longer and longer as show time approached. Finally, the manager came out and let us all in for free. Ouch! Would it have been useful later, when looking at weekly revenues and expenses, to have recorded that occurrence and planned better for it next time?

In manufacturing, someone missing from a line can throw production off-kilter. This is particularly true in lean environments that operate according to predetermined takt times. (Takt rate is how many of each product configuration needs to be produced during a given time.) The line may have to "flex down" to a significantly lower output level if not enough people are available to staff each workstation, because those who are present will have to be redistributed in a way that keeps the line in balance.

Comments can also help justify production problems that were not the fault of the employee. Delayed delivery of parts, power outages, a local outbreak of the flu, or other unforeseen events can be legitimate reasons that explain why employees were sent home early (they worked short shifts) or failed to meet their quota. Reason tracking helps put production realities into context and gives greater insight into how to better manage the business.

Error Reporting Is the Sonar of WMT

Another important thing automation can do is identify errors in transmission. For example, it can automatically answer such questions as "Who is not going to be paid?" and "Who is going to be paid who shouldn't?"

In a manual system, when time cards are being keyed in and one slips under the desk, unless someone happens to spot it, no one may suspect something's wrong until the employee goes to her supervisor when she doesn't get a check. If a terminated person happens to receive a direct deposit into her account, how quickly do you suppose she will report the error? But filters can be established in an automated system that will raise a flag if an employee is missing from the register that shouldn't be, or if an employee who has been terminated is going to be paid. All that's necessary is for an automatic audit to be in place, ensuring that inactive employees are not being paid and that all active, working employees are. We routinely set these up as part of the basic workspace so that supervisors are made aware each week of potential problems. The automated part is the system finding the problems and making them visible. The important part is the person who takes action to correct the situation. What is often missing is the information, and WMT systems remedy that.

Variances in payment amounts can be monitored as well. Managers can review significant increases or decreases in payroll by having the system compare today's figures to a base line or to prior periods. Remember the

Key Idea

Filters can be set up in an automated system that will raise a flag if an employee is missing from the register that shouldn't be, or if an employee who has been terminated is going to be paid. An automatic audit is created to ensure that inactive employees are not being paid and that all active, working employees are.

$50,000 check mentioned in Chapter 1? If anyone had been reviewing just the totals for that group of employees, the increase from any prior period would have jumped right out. It's even easier for an automated system to catch this type of problem and alert management.

Calendars Reveal Chronic Tardiness and Absences Easily

Let's say a company has a few employees who have attendance problems. They might be habitually late or absent. Management would like to replace these people, but firing can be difficult. On top of this, a person with an attendance problem might also be someone with an attitude problem, a person looking for a reason to make things difficult for the company. So what the boss needs is good, solid documentation that enables him to let that person go without fear of repercussions. The right automated system can deliver this. For example, it will allow the employer to review the past six months or the past year and identify every time that person was late or absent and the reason given.

One of the best examples of this as it appears in a WMT system is an **onscreen calendar view of employee activity.** More than just a simple note, the screen can display several months in one view with color coding identifying various types of activity or absence. It's very easy to see patterns and the gravity of the situation. If a wage and hour specialist, an Equal Employment Opportunity Commission (EEOC) representative, or a labor attorney become involved and say it looks as though an employee was dismissed unfairly, the calendar is readily available to demonstrate the opposite. Pull up the data for the delinquent employee and then pull up data for any other employee as well. The disparity will be easily visible. And those comment codes and free-form reasons will also be there at the click of a button behind any date that is flagged. With a manual system, it could take many hours of tedious work to go through filing cabinets and pull out time cards to support a case.

The ways employees will attempt to slip past controls are practically unlimited. People can be quite skilled at avoidance techniques. "Slippery" folks will try it all. Late arrival? "I forgot to punch." Late arrival again? "I lost my badge and couldn't punch." Late arrival again? "The clock wasn't working." Like children, aren't they? Why do people try this sort of thing? Because it works! In a manual system supervisors can be like parents. They're busy, distracted, and forgetful. They don't have time to keep track of the excuses, and they are usually relieved that the employee has finally arrived so the work can begin. And like children who quickly catch on to the latest fad, such avoidance techniques can be "contagious." Suddenly, other employees have forgotten their badges. But this poor attendance behavior can be cut short in a hurry with an automated system and the proper management response. Marking occurrences with reasons and comments will bring to light problems and the frequency with which they occur, and it won't be long before word of this gets around.

And don't forget, we've already talked about full-blown attendance management modules that automate the disciplinary process that accompanies this type of behavior pattern. When it comes time to build a case, the system will qualify and count the occurrences from a strict calculation, and the manager will have the notes to back it up.

Make Tracking Operational Issues Routine

While we're on the subject of tracking, here's another story. During a WMT implementation at a large hospital, I overheard a nurse commenting about a new regulation requiring employers to track staff illnesses. I asked how she was planning to comply with this new rule. She looked at me with a twinge of incredulity and replied something to the effect she'd have to create some sort of new paper report.

Absences were already being set up automatically to be a part of the new system, so I suggested to the project team that they flag employee absences with a comment describing the illness causing an absence. This seemed the most logical place to store this data. What was needed to help fulfill the new reporting requirement was to include the type of illness associated with each employee in the comment list of the system the hospital had already purchased. With this feature in place, the supervisor could easily add the comment when adjusting the schedule to reflect the absence or when entering time off so the employee would receive benefit pay. This solution proved to be quite handy. Management could record illnesses by individual, and any spread of the contagion across the organization could be mapped and a record compiled of when and where it started, how many employees were affected, and when it tapered off. If an epidemic occurred, the cost could be tracked. It would be possible to see if some areas were immune or contained the spread more effectively. Because tracking was a requirement, an outside entity looking at this data would have an easy time applying standards and ratings to this organization's figures. What better way to ensure that the hospital would score well than to be actively collecting data and managing any problems?

Manage Holiday Complexity

Holidays are so pervasive and widespread there are Web sites devoted entirely to all the holidays ever imagined and set aside as special days. One, www.earthcalendar.net, will tell you what today is. You see, somewhere in the world, today is bound to be a holiday. I happened to type this sentence on August 8. Did you know August 8 boasts two international holidays in addition to holidays in six countries?

    Queen's Name Day—Sweden
    Father's Day—Taiwan
    Independence Day—Bhutan
    Day of the World's Indigenous People—International
    Peace Day (end of the Iran/Iraq war)—Iraq
    Peasants' Day—Tanzania
    Universal and International Infinity Day—International
    Saint Mary MacKillop Day—Australia

Let's face it. We like our holidays, our heroes, our celebrations, or any excuse to have fun or just to take time off. In addition to holidays most of us have never heard of, in the United States there are six "standard" ones: New Years Day, Memorial Day, Independence Day, Labor Day, Thanksgiving Day, and Christmas Day. Additional government and bankers' holidays include Martin Luther King Day, Columbus Day, and Veterans Day, and of course, there are regional holidays such as Patriot's day in the Northeast, and local holidays such as Mardi Gras in New Orleans and Oaks Day in Louisville (the day before the Kentucky Derby). And there are religious holidays, such as Easter, Good Friday, and Yom Kippur. For businesses operating overseas there are unique national holidays to be observed as well.

Holidays can be observed on different schedules. Some observe the day as midnight to midnight. Others observe the holiday from the start of first shift on the holiday to the end of the third shift on the day after the holiday. Some holidays begin on the "eve" of the holiday. This is often true of New Year's and Christmas. For example, the Christmas holiday might start at 3 P.M. on December 24 and run to 3 P.M. on Christmas Day. Some companies will tack on extra holiday hours to Christmas Eve, making the Christmas holiday longer than 24 hours. There are floating holiday programs whereby an employee can take off her birthday or bank an unused holiday for future use. Some industries that operate 24 hours a day, 7 days a week may designate when the holidays will be observed, particularly those that fall on weekends. Within an organization, holidays may differ based on the functional area. Administration may observe standard Monday–Friday holidays only, and operational employees may see their holidays fall on weekends as needed.

Are you beginning to feel overwhelmed or left out? Imagine how difficult it is to administer this monstrosity in a company with a manual system that administers systems with employees in multiple states or countries and numerous unions and religious groups, while employees enjoy any variety of holiday benefits.

Some employers have holiday programs that are administered as a benefit in the same way as vacation and sick days. As with other nonworked paid time off, every employee may not qualify because he or she may not meet the eligibility requirement. For example, such a holiday program might stipulate that the employee "must be employed at least 90 days prior to the holiday" or "must work the scheduled shift before and after the holiday" so that no one can make a four-day weekend out of it.

Holiday pay can be granted in a set number of hours or based on an employee's regularly scheduled shift time. More equitable programs base holiday pay on the average number of hours worked per shift for a certain number of days prior to the holiday. There are endless ways to specify who gets how much.

Holidays are also opportunities to pay employees an additional incentive for working on a day most would like to take off. Holiday worked time usually must meet qualifying criteria. The payable time must fall within certain zones of time or may not be paid in combination with other premiums such as overtime or shift. And finally, benefit holidays as mentioned previously—those nonworked paid days—may not be the same dates as holidays that are payable for working the designated holiday.

This discussion may open your eyes to new holiday possibilities. Or it may make you shudder. What is great about the technology now available is that no matter how your organization administers holidays, enough flexibility exists to handle a variety of policies, even within a single institution—even across international boundaries. And generally the systems handle these programs in an entirely automated manner. When you assess your holiday programs or take the opportunity to tweak what you have in place prior to automation, the important thing to keep in mind is that the more consistent your guidelines are the better. Avoid too many "if/then" criteria and determine what happens when other pay programs are also payable on the holiday.

Key Idea

Integrating holidays into schedules and timekeeping and planning for holiday shortages and premium payments are essential when trying to optimize human capital.

Automate Administering Long-Range Programs

There are benefit programs that take an entire year to administer and qualify for. If managed manually, these types of programs are difficult to manage and nearly impossible to forecast from a cost perspective. However, for an automated system these programs can be easily tracked and the pending financial liability quickly computed at any point in time.

An example is one where the policy states that if someone works five of seven holidays a year, he or she would earn a $500 bonus. Manual tracking of a program such as this presents several difficulties. As the year draws to a close, employees invariably will want to know whether they have worked enough holidays to be eligible for the program because they want to decide whether to work the remaining holidays. Where do they get this information? They either have to keep their own records or ask their supervisors. How will supervisors know? They either have to keep a manual tracking system up to date or go through a year's worth of time cards for each employee who asks. In addition, when a supervisor puts a holiday schedule together, she will often have no idea whether scheduling specific employees will obligate the company to more bonus payments or fewer.

During one implementation, I uncovered such a program being administered jointly by HR and Payroll. I started to ask some probing questions and found management had issues with this policy as well. How was such an incentive program being budgeted for? Technically, there were no program limits to the gross amount that might have to be paid out. Every employee was eligible who worked the required days. In a large organization with thousands of employees a lot of money might be involved. Before automation, estimating the funding of the payroll bank account, including the holiday bonus, was practically impossible.

It's not uncommon for such practices to elude the radar of the discovery team that's preparing for time and attendance automation. A program may have been handled in a certain way for a long time. It may have existed outside the time and attendance system entirely or partially, with the result that no one thought to include it in the requirements for the new system. Fortunately, in the example given, our thorough examination of the company's pay programs during initial project discovery identified this as a great opportunity to replace an unwieldy manual process.

Using the tools in their WMT system the solution we designed enabled the customer to instantly identify any and all eligible employees at any point during the year. Employees could quickly determine their eligibility, supervisors could quickly find out how many holidays each employee had worked year-to-date, and management could extrapolate the financial obligation from the list of employees and their rates of pay. **The customer gained ease of management, accessibility, and a financial forecasting tool.**

Calculate Paid Days Off

Many employers manage paid time off in their Human Resource or Payroll systems. These systems vary in the tools they offer to calculate accrued time off (e.g., vacation, sick, paid time off (PTO), etc.) and the means they have to disseminate that information to supervisors, employees, and the payroll system. The most significant shortcoming of handling accruals in systems outside of workforce management applications is the lag in communication. HR and Payroll systems typically work on a biweekly basis and generate updates only every payroll cycle. They can also fail to keep up with corrections on manual checks that are needed to update the system about an employee's available balance.

The problem with this lag in communication is that employees and supervisors need to know up to the hour how much available paid time off an employee has earned and taken. The use of paid time off happens in the real world in real time, not according to the biweekly or monthly payroll cycle. The result is that employees can take time off they haven't earned and be paid for benefits they have not yet accrued. Today's time and labor systems offer full feature accrual engines to handle complex accrual rules and integrate the calculations with real time information from the timekeeping, scheduling and attendance systems. The best place to manage accruals is within the WMT system.

Managing benefit time within the WMT system also allows planned time off in the future to be considered when the need for an unplanned day off arises. Inside WMT the employee's vacation plans for the summer can be scheduled and input far in advance. While the employee has not yet taken that time off, taking those hours into consideration when using their benefit time today gives everyone a better picture of their available benefit balance for the year.

Some employers compensate their employees for time off based on the average shift length they have worked during the past, say, six months. In other words, employees don't automatically get eight hours pay for Labor Day if their average shift worked has been six hours. This is very difficult to keep track of in a manual system, but easy to do in one that's automated. The computer is able to easily go back over the past six months for each employee and calculate the average length of shifts worked. If someone is working only six-hour shifts, it would be unfair to those working eight-hour shifts to give that person eight hours of pay for a holiday.

This type of program rewards employees based on hours worked. It also provides a way to reduce the cost of the benefit if the current policy is to pay all employees the full benefit amount regardless of their contribution of time, thus keeping the benefit in line with the business.

Chapter Summary

- The message of this chapter is that rules and regulations can become quite complicated, and managing attendance and compensation over time may be difficult using outdated processes.
- What can be defined can be configured into an automated WMT system. This can make life easier for those in Payroll, HR, Finance, and supervisory positions. More important, these improvements also save significant sums of money and improve processes.
- Use a system that allows the organization to make changes with ease and is flexible enough to handle change in a complex environment.
- Some WMT systems can handle changes to historical data and provide an audit trail to track changes.
- WMT systems should offer the ability to make mass changes easily.
- Effectively managing the workforce relies on analysis and WMT systems provide rich root-cause discovery when reasons and comments can be attached to labor activity. Electronic systems shouldn't be so rigid that the everyday nuances of the workplace are lost. Reason tracking can be a valuable and time-saving tool.
- Filter mechanisms allow managers to focus on what is urgent and important. These tools highlight exceptions and variances and reduce the amount of time managers must spend on managing issues that are not mission critical.

- On-screen views of labor activity, such as calendars, can display large amounts of information in a single, intuitive workspace. These and other graphical views in WMT systems allow managers to identify trends in employee behavior.
- Holiday pay has become an incredibly complex management issue, particularly in large organizations in multiple locations. Optimizing human capital can't be done without effectively managing holiday scheduling and compensation.
- Administering and computing earned paid time off (accruals) in WMT systems (instead of in HR/Payroll applications) makes sense because it offers real-time integration with worked time and schedules.

CHAPTER 6

The Human Side of Technical Implementations

Perhaps the most underappreciated (or neglected) aspect of time and labor system deployments is the people factor. Too much is expected of workers when technology is introduced in ways that dramatically change their roles and responsibilities. In this chapter we'll explore resistance to and fear of change and how to mitigate these natural reactions. Human capital has become a remarkably larger component of the company's asset mix; therefore, managing talent, like managing any major, valuable asset, is critical to a company's success. Several employee-related problems such as employee turnover, fairness, management styles, and generational differences to time and labor management systems are mapped to show how the technology can be used to address these challenges.

You Must Understand Your People

A successful implementation of any new technology is largely dependent on how well the people part of the equation is understood. Planning for the human side of an implementation is vitally important and should not be underestimated. People aren't robots or equipment on the shelf. You can't reprogram them with the flip of a switch or expect computer software to upgrade their mental and behavioral processes automatically. Humans react to change differently, learn differently, behave differently, and have a variety of needs. The environment influences them; the person next to them influences them; and their thoughts about the past, present, and future have an impact on their performance.

Time and labor systems will change the way people do their jobs. They will change their perceptions of their importance to the organization and the way they are being treated. The systems may even change the hours they work and the money they are paid. In addition, these systems change the way they interact with other people. Like it or not, the culture at work changes.

There are situations when companies and people are more or less inclined to want to change. Organizations with little incentive to care about cost, lack a sense of urgency, or are detached from their customers are not likely to be motivated to change. Companies that are about to die or are facing extreme competitive pressures are apt to be highly motivated to change. Change is relative. If people see a relation to their survival or mission, changes take on a positive flavor.

Knowing what this technology is going to change related to work patterns or culture is crucial. Is the new system perceived as emanating from a lack of trust? Is Big Brother monitoring us? People need to understand the reason for the technology. Honestly, it's rarely purchased solely because employers don't trust any of their workers. It's simply a matter of automating processes that are terribly inefficient or inaccurate when left in human hands. Perhaps during or after implementation people can be retrained to perform tasks that are more valuable to the organization or more directly affect its customers.

Will the system still meet everyone's unique needs? Technology can threaten an employee's sense of being special or unique in the eyes of his employer. He may have worked hard to curry favor with management and fear that the system will wipe away the perks he has enjoyed. If favors equate to unfair treatment or expensive choices, then the change may be unpopular but necessary.

Sometimes there is resistance to change because the cost is just built in or through force of habit. In other cases, people resist change because it isn't a glamorous and exciting thing to champion. There is also a resistance to change things that are intangible—the soft targets. A company that wants to get an immediate "hit" can easily grasp the value of downsizing x number of workers. Such hard targets are things they know and can easily quantify. They can flip the switch today and see the result.

But if an even larger target, such as giving front-line managers decision-making tools to better manage their workforce, improve output, and lower costs, is put in front of managers it may be too nebulous and foreign for them to comprehend. Obviously, decisions are being made today, and the work is getting done. And implying they could make *better* decisions means that managers have to accept that perhaps they aren't making the best decisions *now*. Does that mean they haven't been managing and doing their jobs well? Can a system really be smarter than they are? This kind of change will also mean that along with the new system they will have to do some training and work with their own managers to help them become more effective. The return may seem very far down the road.

It's frustrating when managers have only a superficial approach to the human side of the technology. Asking how many people you can eliminate with the technology is an example of not thinking deeply enough about what the technology has to offer. Understanding how the technology can change the organization and make people work smarter is the better approach. The habit is that people are often on autopilot and fail to stop and think carefully about fundamental change.

Key Idea

Resistance to change and fear are the most common obstacles to successful organizational improvement. Anticipating how employees will perceive a new system is leadership's responsibility.

There may be a fear factor about technology and change that is cultural. Installing anything new is a risk. If the organization is risk averse and doesn't encourage innovation or reacts strongly to failure, people may be very concerned about their job security when the new system comes along. This may be what limits a lot of organizations from engaging the system to do little more than replace current processes. The fear may also stem from worry that employees won't be able to quantify their success to the satisfaction of management. Understanding these fears and planning strategies to alleviate these problems will help.

One of the more common fears is fear of the unknown. The answer here is to let people know what is happening, why, and what it will mean for them. Sharing success stories from other customers or internal business units and promoting role models will alleviate these worries and demystify the changes. Providing adequate internal communication, keeping a lid on negative advertising within the organization from disgruntled workers, and ensuring that everyone is thoroughly trained will demonstrate that the organization is planning for everyone's success.

Plan for changes to take time—a lot of time—when it involves changing people. Installing a new computer system is the easy part. Managing the human changes required for successful use of the system is much more difficult. Be prepared to see change happen gradually and be committed to the effort it will take to transform the organization over time.

Overcoming the Perception of Insignificance

If you want to get really creative and help people be more open to change, put their current processes or problems in historical context. If they are doing things the same way they did back in the 1970s, pull up some photos of things that were going on back then. Who was President back when most companies did that? What kind of cars were people driving? Are they positioned competitively when they are operating several decades behind today's technology?

The perception of insignificance can be a huge barrier to change. People tend to focus on what is urgent rather than what is important. That's how organizations can be stuck with systems and habits that are so outdated. There is always something else more urgent or more enticing. Time and labor management competes for the attention of workers and organizations. The proper perception may be that a new system is *both* urgent and important.

Human Capital Is a Bigger, Costlier Asset

A serious problem confronts many companies today—the difficulty they have attracting workers and retaining them. Some must replace up to 70 percent of their workforce each and every year. There are industries in which the average turnover rate is 30 percent. Why is this a serious problem? Not too long ago when a study was made of the manufacturing companies in the S&P 500, for example, 80 percent of their assets were in capital equipment and tangible goods. The remaining 20 percent of assets were intangibles, related somewhat to labor. Today, that allocation has been turned upside down. Now 80 percent of an average company's assets are intangible, and most of that is wrapped up in the quality of the workers. This change is represented in Exhibit 6.1.

Today's paradigm is knowledge and information, and this requires businesses to look at the "machines of knowledge" (i.e., labor) differently. The entire process of acquiring, managing, and maintaining this new "machine" is changing. Like an asset, it must be selected, purchased (recruited and hired), installed (brought on board and oriented), scheduled into the process (assigned a job and task), and maintained (trained, provided benefits, and supervised). Labor has a life cycle that involves team-building, gaining tribal knowledge, promotions, and mentoring. Eventually it will be retired and replaced with younger assets. The problem is, there's a limited supply of this resource and quality can be hard to come by. The investments companies make in labor are significant, and not enough is done to protect that investment and make certain it remains in place through maturity.

The price to recruit and train new people is substantial, and lost productivity while new hires are in the learning mode is costly. A generally accepted measurement of the cost to a company to replace an employee is 30 percent of the employee's annual salary.

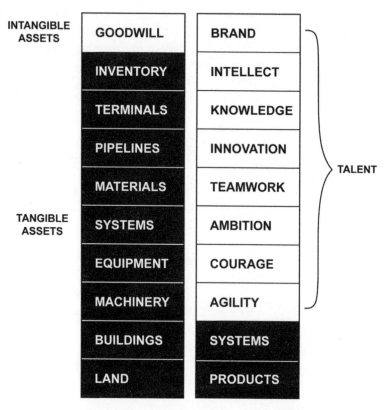

INTANGIBLE ASSETS	GOODWILL	BRAND	
	INVENTORY	INTELLECT	
	TERMINALS	KNOWLEDGE	
	PIPELINES	INNOVATION	
	MATERIALS	TEAMWORK	TALENT
TANGIBLE ASSETS	SYSTEMS	AMBITION	
	EQUIPMENT	COURAGE	
	MACHINERY	AGILITY	
	BUILDINGS	SYSTEMS	
	LAND	PRODUCTS	

80% of S&P Assets Today Are Intangible

EXHIBIT 6.1 It's a New Economic World

The importance of the workforce to the organization is shown in a comparison of assets. In the past, labor-related capital, an intangible asset, was largely discounted. Today, nearly 80 percent of the organization's capital consists of intangible talent.

Source: 2006 Human Capital Institute

Let's examine one case. The company has to replace about 300 employees a year. If each one earns $20,000 per year on average, the cost would amount to $1.8 million ($20,000 × 30 percent = $6,000 × 300 employees = $1.8M). That's a lot of money, for which the employer gets absolutely nothing but headaches. But lost productivity and a big bill for headache relief aren't the only downsides. Consider the tremendous drag this creates on the organization's quality of service. It takes time for newcomers to get up to speed. The more that people do a job, the more experience they have under their belts, and the more their performance improves. The truth is, new people are likely to make mistakes because they don't yet know the ropes. High turnover creates a limited pool of talent for promotion and makes business continuity a real challenge.

In most cases, money isn't the primary reason people leave. According to one expert, Michael N. Abrams, Vice President and Managing Partner of Numerof & Associates, Inc., what departing employees would term a "difficult" boss coupled with a lack of empowerment are the top reasons employees leave their job in the United States. People simply don't like serving at a boss's whim. And they don't like to lack information or a sense of control. People spend a lot of time at their places of employment, so perhaps it's no wonder an agreeable and pleasant work environment can be a major factor in keeping employees happy. Without one, they are likely to jump at the chance to hurry off to greener pastures.

Treat Employees Well

Take the opportunity to use the technology to improve how your workforce is treated. Examine every problem and map it to features that can enhance the employee's experience working for the organization.

Boosting Employee Retention

When the issue of employee retention is considered, management often focuses solely on why employees leave. Exit interviews, for example, are widely used. While there's nothing wrong with finding out why someone has decided to go elsewhere, this can mean the statistics used to measure employee retention show only the negative side of the equation—the number of people who leave and why. Laurie Friedman, a talent management consultant, suggests that it also makes sense to ask, "Why do employees stay?" When it comes to boosting employee retention figures, understanding what employees like about working for a company can be a good place to start. If the company is doing things right for some, can these things be done even better? Can other attractive workplace offerings be added to what already exists? Friedman says making an organization "an employer of choice" is a lot like positioning products so they will sell well. In addition, understanding the positive things about an organization from an employee's perspective helps management understand the types of employees they should be working to attract.

How can an automated time and attendance system help in keeping employees on board? One way may be to involve them directly in scheduling the shifts they work. This will give them a measure of control over their lives and a sense of involvement. Empowerment is an appealing aspect of work life. How does this work?

Some software applications allow employees to go online and enter their names on the shift they wish to work. If tenured employees have first dibs, the system can be configured to grant those with seniority exclusive access to the process during a specified period of time. Workers can also register their preferences for working certain schedules. This communication allows the employer to be a better "fit" for the employee's work life schedule. As everyone knows, in many families both parents work, and there are more and more single-parent households. It's no wonder a work schedule that conflicts with family needs can be much more than inconvenient, which is why a scheduling system that takes into account an individual's availability gives that employee a sense of control and respect. Earlier I mentioned that a difficult boss is the biggest reason people give for leaving a job. Not liking a boss may have a lot to do with the boss's expecting you to work at times that may cause difficulties.

Several strong products have been introduced into the market in recent years that provide robust, flexible staffing solutions that are integrated with time and attendance software. All the major vendors offer a scheduling module with self-scheduling capabilities and templates for building schedules based on business needs. Each has various "bells and whistles" to answer the market's demand for intelligent scheduling. Some of the underlying functionality differs, however, so purchasers need to be sure to understand their company's operational needs before watching a vendor's demo. These programs are not all alike; each offers a unique package of features. Knowing what to look for allows a prospective purchaser to stay in the driver's seat and understand the differences.

The management of a large hospital network in the Fort Lauderdale area decided to go with one staffing solution. In spite of being in an industry plagued with high turnover, this particular employer had a very low turnover rate. Part of the reason could be its use of automated self-scheduling. Schedules at this hospital network are electronically posted, and employees have 45 days to sign up for shifts. When management elected to go with an automated scheduling solution, one hospital was using a standalone nurse scheduling system and two facilities were still using paper systems. None of these could be integrated with other workforce systems. All required double entry, were difficult to compile, and were not user-friendly. No wonder schedulers were happy to have the benefits of a new system that eliminated those issues. The new system also was able to project when an employee would begin earning overtime, so that managers could now avoid overworking individual employees and level the workload. Nobody likes bearing the burden of working more than everyone else, so it's easy to see how this solution brought more satisfaction to workers.

Numerous industry studies have found that when nurses were given the ability to self-schedule, total absenteeism and turnover are reduced by as much as 20 percent. This shows the power of such a system and the advantage of investing in one. Attendance and retention are significantly boosted just by giving employees a greater measure of empowerment.

In addition, putting the scheduling process into an automated system removes some of the bias and politics that can be a part of a manual setup. Fairness and opportunity are benefits of using workforce technology to assist in the scheduling process.

Sophisticated scheduling modules are designed to make managers aware of scheduling issues. The scheduling system can be set up to call attention to excessive hours, under- and overstaffing situations, and employees who fail to show up for work. The scheduling systems with the most functionality will show open shifts in the schedule—slots where workers are needed but no one is assigned. These systems display the schedule on screen (or in printed reports) allowing the manager to view or post his staffing by skill, job, area, or time of day. With employee demographic information, the manager can also find contact information and job qualifications making locating the best employee fast and easy.

Letting People Set Their Own Hours

One company in the business of transcribing medical records lets employees set their own hours. Workers can do this job from home, interacting with the company via the Internet. I discussed this with the company owner. He said his employees don't brag about how much they make an hour, but they do like to tell people they can work whenever they want. They are completely free to schedule their time.

A major reason employees take this work is that they can do it when they want. This benefit costs the company nothing but nonetheless pays a dividend in the form of a fairly stable staff at an affordable price. Workers like the arrangement because they can stay up until midnight working if they want, then take the next day off.

Of course, this is not going to work for most businesses. The point is that more and more people want to arrange work around their lives rather than the other way around, which is not surprising. It's often difficult to take a job because it conflicts with the children's school schedule, a husband's job, or a class a person would like to take. Maybe someone's not a morning person. People want flexible scheduling. In health care industries in particular that operate 24/7, more and more companies are finding ways to implement flex scheduling because it can be a win-win solution.

With an interactive system, a manager can monitor these self-scheduled shifts, even remotely, and ensure that the work will be completed or the work site adequately staffed. If the load isn't going to be right, he can make reassignments or pull in extra resources. He doesn't have to keep his fingers crossed to find out at the end of the week what got accomplished or missed. He is assured that the supply of workers meets his needs and his crew gets to work at their preferred times.

Overcoming High Employee Turnover

In what other ways can automated time and attendance help in the area of retention? Labor activity can be tracked against turnover to find out what's causing employees to leave. For example, is there a higher incidence of turnover in certain jobs? Do certain shifts seem to turn workers away? Does being forced to work more than 40 hours lead to high turnover? Does retention improve at certain wage levels? What's the effect of having to work weekends often? Is there a higher incidence of turnover in certain job, skill, or demographic categories? If so, is the company hiring the right people? Maybe those who do the hiring aren't selling the job correctly, and when people come on board they find it's not what they expected.

What incentives work to reduce turnover? Exhibit 6.2 illustrates some of the contributing factors to improving employee retention.

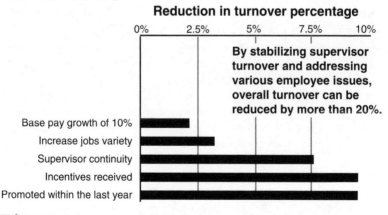

EXHIBIT 6.2 Know What Retains Employees

By stabilizing supervisor turnover and giving people adequate incentives and a sense of career opportunity, turnover can be reduced by as much as 20 percent.

Source: Working the Clock: How to Win the Race for Productivity and Profits with Workforce Management Technology, Lisa Disselkamp; The Oaklea Press, 2007.

Treating Employees Consistently

We seem to be born with an innate need to be treated fairly. If you have children, you know that the "fairness meter" turns on very early. Everybody is measuring how they are treated versus anyone and everyone else. An automated system delivers consistency in how people are handled. This can lead to fewer disgruntled employees and in turn to a higher rate of retention. Why? The technology makes it difficult for managers or supervisors to play favorites by giving breaks to people they like, and it's hard for them to make things difficult on those they don't care for.

Human interpretation, or bias, almost always comes into play in a manual system. People's intentions may be good and honorable, but it's human nature to treat our buddies one way and those we either don't know or don't like another. Not only can this cause morale problems, but the company is at risk of overcompensating some workers, or of suffering through grievance actions for inconsistencies in how different employees are handled.

In the left-hand side of the chart in Exhibit 6.2, the number-three reason employees stayed with the job was "supervisor continuity." Obviously, the supervisor is liked and probably doing a pretty good job of treating everyone equally. WMT makes every manager "the good supervisor" by standardizing practices and making good management the norm.

Key Idea

A WMT system isn't something that will walk out the door with supervisors when they quit or retire. It can be a stable and favorable aspect of the employee's work environment and promote job satisfaction.

Let's look at an example. An incentive program named after and attributed to Baylor University Medical Center comes to mind. As the story goes, management instituted a bonus program for clinical practitioners to encourage people to work on weekends. Nowadays, "Baylor Pay" commonly refers to a pay program designed to give employees an incentive to work difficult-to-staff shifts, typically on the weekends. In its current form it may differ from what was actually used at Baylor, but today such programs work by rewarding employees who work a combination of specific shifts with a set amount of hours during a pay period. The programs are designed to meet business needs and minimize staffing issues. They stipulate the number of shifts, the shift durations, and the number of bonus hours payable and sometimes include qualifiers that penalize employees who are absent during a period of time before or after the Baylor shifts. They may also require a set number of worked shifts over an extended period of time for a worker to be eligible to participate in the program. The idea is to encourage good attendance and a commitment to working less-desirable schedules.

Here's how one such program worked. Provided an individual worked two 12-hour shifts on the weekend, that person was credited with eight hours of additional time. But, as everyone knows, life happens and sometimes employees fail to meet the letter of the law. When a manual system is in place, it's easy for the system to break down because there are often people around (i.e., supervisors) who will try to "fix" the problem.

Suppose a person works one 12-hour shift, and then only 11 and a half hours because her child gets sick. This person would not be eligible to receive those bonus hours, would she? No. But what do you suppose is likely to happen in a manual system? The supervisor might look at the situation and say, "Gee whiz, look at this. Greta is a half hour short. Old Greta's a great gal and a loyal worker. It wasn't her fault her son got sick at school and had to be picked up early. I'll just ignore that half hour."

But maybe a supervisor doesn't like Greta or is displeased with her performance in some other area. Then the response is, "Sorry, Greta, but here's the policy in black and white. I simply can't add an extra half hour. Uh-huh, no way. I don't care if you will work three extra hours on Monday. I can't go against company policy, Greta. You know that."

Unfortunately for the supervisor and the company, Greta and her coworkers talk. They talk a lot and they talk about what they get paid. Greta knows full well the same thing happened last month to Suzy and she did receive the bonus hours despite her shorter shift. They also know the supervisor will come up with a good explanation for this and that complaining will do little or no good.

After this happens, where do you suppose Greta is going to fall on that continuum we discussed earlier where employees are positioned somewhere on a line that runs from "engaged" to "disengaged"? (See page 31.)

The message is that an automated system ensures consistency. It removes the discretionary nature of manual pay programs. Consistent programs establish stability in the workforce. Stability results in fewer turnovers.

Compensating for Management Styles

Automated scheduling has all kinds of flexibility, which makes the institution of best practices fairly easy. But what if it turns out that scheduling methodology is not the reason for the difference in a department's performance? Another question to be answered might be, "Do these managers have different management styles?" You may recall what we discussed earlier: "People don't leave companies, they leave bosses." Autocratic managers, for example, often have trouble holding onto employees. Customer service may suffer and other problems may persist because the employees under an autocratic manager are reluctant to make decisions that may incur the boss's wrath. In other words, they are not about to stick their necks out and are quite likely to take a hike when the opportunity arises. A computerized scheduling system may help mitigate the negative effects of such a manager. It may even lead to fewer no-shows, fewer late arrivals, and a lower level of schedule disruption overall. How so?

Not only can a scheduling system be set up to allow people some flexibility in scheduling themselves, as previously mentioned, but it can empower employees to find their own replacements when they need time off, giving them a measure of control and empowerment. A system can, for example, be set up to allow schedule swapping. Automated "shift swapping" is gaining popularity. The system allows employees to identify their own replacement, submit the request for time off along with the suggested replacement (who also registers his approval or request for schedule change), and receive an automated notification of the supervisor's or the system's acceptance of the change. The supervisor's approval action will then automatically update both workers' schedules and notify them of the approved schedule change.

These systems update the supervisor periodically about any open shifts. If no one signs up, the manager can go through the normal selection process. If everyone is online, then no paper or phone calls are required. If not, at least the only call the supervisor or scheduler needs to make is to the employee he already knows is willing and capable of working that shift.

There are a number of benefits to this arrangement. There's less likelihood of an interruption in labor supply, the employee did not have to complete any forms or contact the unpleasant manager directly, the manager was prompted to adjust to the schedule change as needed, and the entire staff had the opportunity to bid on additional work opportunities. And most important, employees in this situation enjoy a heightened sense of autonomy and control over their work life. In an area with an autocratic manager it's one less situation in which these employees feel powerless.

Addressing the Challenges of Generation Y

I spent some time talking with Libby Sartain, an HR thought leader with interest in the effect of generational issues on the workforce. Libby was CHRO at two great brands, Southwest Airlines and Yahoo!, as well as many others. Both Southwest and Yahoo! had a young workforce, so she had firsthand experience with Gen X and Gen Y. And, as part of her research for her recent book, Libby investigated what other organizations were experiencing in their efforts to employ Generation Y workers. What Libby has found, and a lot of you may already realize, is that the younger workers don't place the boundaries between work and home that older workers do. These workers don't compartmentalize their business and personal lives. They work at all different times, they take iPhones, BlackBerry's, and cell phones with them everywhere to stay connected to their peers, bosses, and family. They want more flexibility in their work schedule, often demand more attention, and probably expect to change jobs a lot during their careers. They may even expect to completely change careers more than once. What's really interesting is that these expectations are giving everyone else permission to demand the same things.

These workers have some pretty high expectations about their role in the organization. They've been given a sticker or trophy throughout their lives just for participating. Accommodations have been made for their "special needs" in school, where curriculums and testing processes have been changed so that everyone succeeds—at least to some degree. They've been asked to journal their thoughts from a very young age, and so they believe their opinions should matter to those in authority. According to Libby, the most important difference is that this generation will seek mentorship and daily feedback. They'll want stroking and probably won't like anything that implies they are simply "average."

Workers in this new generation also spend a lot of time online, texting, and blogging. Their communication style is brief and cryptic and interspersed with humor and commentary. For them, the line is also blurred between entertainment and everything else (work, news, shopping, communication, etc.). They've been raised with an infinite amount of information at their fingertips and instant access to anyone on the globe.

What does all of this forebode for workforce management technology? According to Shira Harrington, a senior recruiting consultant, quite a lot. First, these workers won't have trouble gaining competency quickly on new systems. However, they may also be better at finding any gaps in the system or opportunities to game the process. They can also share and compare information rapidly with anyone. Security, audit trails, and ironclad configuration of rules will be essential, and so will competitive salaries, benefits, and employer attitudes.

Second, the ability to instantly communicate information will appeal to them. However, they will use that to communicate their needs at the last minute, particularly when it comes to schedules, deadlines, and time off. This generation believes that personal life should take priority over work. That will make scheduling a more difficult task. Third, dashboards that show their progress won't appeal to their tender sensibilities about their performance. Remember that they've been praised and rewarded for mediocrity and for merely showing up. The Millenials (the generation born between 1980 and 2000, also known as Generation Y) want constant mentoring from their boss. If the system indicates they've done something wrong, they will want to know how to make it better. Managers may have to find ways to make certain these workers feel appreciated and understood despite what the raw numbers in the WMT system might show.

Finally, features like self-service and anything that empowers these workers to make choices will be welcomed. As Harrington puts it, "Parents and teachers said they could do anything. Now they feel entitled to show what they can do." (Shira Harrington, "Myths vs. Realities: The Mulitgenerational Workforce Revealed," Sept. 18, 2008 WMAC APA, Washington, DC; a presentation.) But these systems may not be enough to completely satisfy their desire to have input and control. WMT champions will need to communicate these benefits and connect them to this generation's attitudes.

WMT systems may offer an unexpected middle ground between the demands of Gen X and those of Gen Y. According to Harrington, Millenials are so accustomed to technology and the ability to Google everything, that they tend to approach problem solving with "menu-driven" thinking skills (coined by Robert Wendover; www.gentrends.com). This lack of independent problem-solving skills is countered by Gen Xers, who tend to have the opposite problem of not consulting enough people when attacking a problem. WMT systems will channel them both into a collaborative, menu-driven workspace helping mitigate the negative aspects of these behaviors.

Ultimately, some experts are concerned that the impact of Generation Y on the workforce as a whole will create a less competitive pool of labor. Companies may go elsewhere to look for the best workers, no matter where they are. It will be interesting to see how far these newcomers to the workforce push the envelope and what technology can and can't do to make the workplace productive and hospitable for business and workers. Sartain believes employees will be in the driver's seat, offering their talent to the best employers regardless of location. Brand, career advancement, technologies that empower employees and meet their demands, as well as a talent-centric culture will be important success factors for employers.

Managing Talent Successfully

The WFM industry has recognized that there is a close relationship between the traditional time and labor management systems and hiring processes. Who isn't familiar with the old adage "consider the source"? It means "Where did it come from?" It can matter a lot where labor and activity come from. Who is doing the work? Who is keeping track of things? Hiring the best workers is one of the first steps to ensure that all of the other processes that are put into place perform well. In several industries, finding and keeping qualified, skilled workers is very difficult. Increasingly companies are looking for intelligent ways to seek and select workers with the right talents and temperaments. The vendors have software solutions that help in this area.

Time and attendance and scheduling solutions deal with employees already on staff, but a new field known as "talent management" works to ensure that the right types of workers are brought on board in the first place. The process of attracting, developing, and retaining labor resources is a growing area of workforce management, and software vendors offer a number of products in this area. Clay Ritchey, Senior Product Manager for a major industry vendor, for example, boasts that their applications actually get smarter over time as data about an organization and its staff builds and the record grows concerning how well employees perform, how long they stay, and so forth. In addition, hosted solutions offer the advantage of leveraging this accumulation of data across an industry or a region. The data can then be shared by each customer.

Key Idea

Applications actually get smarter over time as data about an organization and its staff builds and the record grows concerning how well employees perform and how long they stay. Worker profiles are further enhanced by accumulating data across an industry within hosted/shared solutions.

Using this data, companies bring on board employees who are a good fit and keep them longer. Money is saved because less training is required, productivity will be higher, and turnover will be lower. Better employees, those who fit the organization, are absent less and more productive, lowering the amount of overtime that might otherwise be required and generating greater outputs in volume and quality. This being the case, why wouldn't an organization work to improve its talent management? Unfortunately, traditional habits and processes persist when it comes to acquiring good workers. Most companies are not very far along in the maturity curve for this technology.

Know How to Change Behavior

I had the pleasure of talking with Aaron Faustz, a leader in the industry in terms of change management. With a background in industrial organizational psychology, he has a keen take on planning for change within the organization. One of the biggest challenges he sees is front-line managers who are so slammed with the day-to-day business responsibilities that they are not managing their workforce. In many instances, managers have abdicated their responsibility for overseeing their own employees and have delegated that function to timekeepers or even Payroll. Faustz tries to help customers see that WMT is a tool for front-line managers and that there is a wealth of information for managers to use in planning for effective operations. His customers struggle to get managers to spend time with the system because of the perception that workforce management is not important work. Not only do managers think it's not important, they don't see the rules and regulations they focus on as their own. Rather they view the wage and hour rules as penalties used for managing workers, not guidelines for productivity or cost control.

How do you get front-line managers to pull away from what they are doing today to make time to effectively react to WMT information?

Step 1. Prioritize from the executive level. Create a framework that shows managers how what they are doing is helping their team and supporting the overall success of the organization. Organizations should strive to use mission-based communication in conjunction with WMT and create a line of sight from the individual to the department to the company up to the highest levels. As managers being asked to do many different things they will understand which three or four things are most important to focus on. Make a direct connection between the aspects of managing their workers and how that relates to strategic goals. This helps prevent equating busyness with accomplishment.

Step 2. Adequately train managers how to manage. Know what a good manager does and invest the time in showing managers how to manage their people.

Step 3. Train people how to understand data. Do they know how the organization makes money or what is important to their customers? Do they have enough education about how the business runs and how they fit into that the overall scheme? Without training, managers are likely to react to data by instinct, gut, habit, or experience. Mapping a reaction to data to the right actions and the success of the organization are critical to using data. Managers need to understand the appropriate actions to take with the data they are given. Although we are in the information age, many organizations operate very primitively with data.

The data is valuable because it shows trends or urgent situations. But things are not static, and the numbers are always changing. The data can seem like chaos unless it's put into context and unless the user knows how to interpret and react to the information. WMT systems with sophisticated dashboards and configurable indicators are designed to help managers understand the information and respond appropriately. They are easy to read and can be powerful enablers but it does require some training.

Step 4. Know what you want people to do with the data. This step could easily be Step 1, the place to start. It should be an ongoing step, a routine review to make certain the actions taken are having the desired result. It's a matter of commitment. If managers are reacting as they should but outcomes aren't improving, it's time to reevaluate the processes and the incoming data. Your company will grow and change, and so will the employees. Take a holistic look at the processes and behaviors end-to-end to ensure that they are still lining up properly.

Step 5. Recognize competency on the system. Create a form of incentives and rewards for gaining new skills. Make it worth learning and behaving accordingly. As is done with Six Sigma training, certify users according to their level of ability: green belts, yellow belts, and black belts. Measure calls to the help desk, system edits and errors, manual checks, productivity, and anything else that shows how well people are using the system. The black belts could be used as field trainers. Managers would know whether their supervisors and employees were progressing.

These steps might seem common sense. They are. The final step might seem too radical or too involved. But if you're struggling to get commitment from your workers and managers to follow strategic plans, it might be that they sense a lack of commitment from senior management. This kind of approach is more likely to trickle down to those front-line workers resulting in a much more effective workforce. Planning for that human piece of a technology implementation could be the secret to your new success.

Chapter Summary

- Labor and talent have become a significantly larger part of the asset mix as opposed to not long ago when capital and tangible goods were the major components of a company's valuable assets.
- Employee turnover is so costly that increasing employee retention can have a considerably positive financial impact. WMT systems offer a variety of employee-centric features that make working at the company more amenable.

- Fairness in the workplace can be institutionalized across the board by using WMT systems that enforce consistency and objectivity.
- Younger workers are changing the demands that are placed on the employer and the means of compelling employees to produce good work. In addition, technology has changed how people communicate and where they work. WMT systems answer these demands accordingly when the right features are installed.
- The first step in creating a strong workforce is hiring the right people. Applicant processing systems are accumulating data across industries and building a knowledge base about what defines a good candidate that employers can tap into.
- The success of any WMT implementation largely depends on the manager's performance inside these systems. There are five steps for training managers to effectively react to time and labor information.

CHAPTER 7

The Many Benefits of Workforce Scheduling Technology

E mployee scheduling is a skill that is rarely taught but one that directly impacts the operational efficiency and bottom line of any organization. Regardless of the process or system used to schedule employees to work, it's important to understand the fundamentals of good workforce scheduling. In this chapter we explain the different types of schedules and what must go into a scheduling decision, as well as some fundamental principles to apply to labor scheduling. We'll discuss how to create an optimal schedule, the various models for meeting the unique scheduling demands of various industries, and pitfalls to avoid in creating a scheduling system. Finally, we'll offer some talking points concerning resistance to automated scheduling and how to use schedules to increase profitability.

The Science of Workforce Scheduling

To understand the benefits of an automated scheduling system it's important to appreciate the intricacies of workforce scheduling. What makes up a schedule? A schedule is a calendar of days worked, unpaid days off, and paid days off. It is a work plan made up of shifts, duty assignments, and benefit allowances. The assignments are shifts with defined start and stop times or projects or assignments by job, department, and location. Shifts may include meal and rest breaks, transfers to other areas, and extra compensation.

Schedules are dictated by policies, regulations, safety, demand, and availability. At the same time they are constrained by the nature of the demand (e.g., volume, quality, and deadlines) and supply (e.g., availability of resources, equipment, and people). Resources that put a limit on schedules include budgets, inventory, energy, and infrastructure. On the people side of the equation, numerous factors limit what can be done in a schedule, including skills, preferences, seniority, cost, total hours worked, availability, and proximity to the work. It doesn't take long to recognize there is a long list of inputs into scheduling decisions. As with an iceberg, there is often more below the water line than what you see floating by. In Chapters 2 and 4, we talked about the interdependence of men, machines, and materials when managing production. Schedules are complicated and diverse.

There are a number of types of schedules:

- **Continuous**—businesses that operate 24/7, 365 days a year, with equal levels of workload around the clock or unbalanced loads varying by shift
- **Variable demand**—based purely on demand, unpredictable
- **Rotations**—patterns that attempt to establish some stability in the schedule while equalizing the burden of working undesirable shift times
- **Seasonal**—businesses that experience significant peaks and valleys in demand

Out of all of this complexity and variety comes the simple truth that no matter what method or system is used to create schedules, there is a decision process that presents ample opportunity to make good and bad decisions. I sat down recently with scheduling guru Tom Benson to talk about some of the fundamental truths and best practices in scheduling. We agreed on the following indisputable aspects of labor scheduling:

- **Schedules are impossible to dictate from a single, central authority.** The end users should be in command because they are closest to the operational activity. It is virtually impossible to enforce rigid schedules from on high; people will simply avoid such a schedule because it will not meet their business needs.
- **Scheduling is 100 percent political and 200 percent personal.** Scheduling is a personal art form, a relationship-centric business process. It is a domain people are resistant to relinquish to outsiders and machines.
- **"Global" and "scheduling" are two words you cannot use together in most organizations.** Schedules vary widely by department, team, and time.
- **The impact on cost and people is unusually large.** Scheduling matters to the bottom line and to the people involved.
- **Scheduling is a form of compensation.** It is a very tangible benefit to employees, but the costs are hidden and don't appear as a line item on any budget.

Key Idea

Out of all of this complexity and variety comes the simple truth that no matter what method or system is used to create schedules, there is a decision process that presents ample opportunity to make good or bad decisions.

The last two items in this list are probably the most profound and the most ignored. Scheduling in any business is occurring, whether it is formal or informal, automated or entirely manual. And it is having a huge effect on the bottom line. The more primitive the methods, the greater the likelihood that the impact on the bottom line will not be positive. The output of a schedule is what hits payroll. As Michael Gondek, another expert in the scheduling space, puts it, "By the time the employee gets to the clock, it's too late. You have to pay them."

How to Create the Optimal Schedule

Designing the optimal schedule requires considering many factors from three primary areas: the business needs, employees, and the rules. When the requirements are satisfied without neglecting to answer to the needs of each area, an optimal schedule is achieved. The diagram in Exhibit 7.1 illustrates this harmony.

So how do you do it right? Creating a schedule is a five-step process, according to Benson. He has been helping companies understand and improve their scheduling process and systems for most of his career.

Step 1. Create the forecast.
Step 2. Create the workload.
Step 3. Create the master schedule.
Step 4. Populate the schedule.
Step 5. Adjust the schedule.

Benson's recipe for good scheduling includes investing more in implementation and less in technology. By that he means that a schedule is only as good as the logic on which it is based. All of those variables and inputs and options in the preceding list are important factors in generating an efficient schedule. If you shortchange your ability to provide good information at the right time and place in the process, you will sabotage the

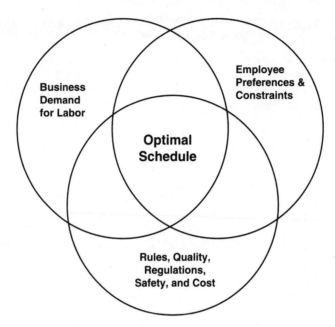

EXHIBIT 7.1 Designing the Perfect Schedule

Companies that use WMT to create schedules that take into account business, regulatory, and employee needs effectively manage a major driver of overall success.

eventual outcome. You have to find that area where things satisfy the business, the employees, and the rules. That's the way to develop the optimal schedule.

Scheduling Technology Models Vary

Incorporating the use of electronic scheduling into the time and labor management system is essential to extracting the most meaningful data from time cards and to effectively managing labor resources vis-à-vis business needs. There are important factors to keep in mind when deciding just how to deploy this piece of the technology.

There are different types of automated schedule systems based on the business logic inherent to the operational needs. In the retail and hospitality industries, mathematical optimization is used based on algorithms that use history and trend analysis. In health care, manufacturing, and many service sectors, optimization of supervision is employed, engaging the organization's own rules and allowing for human inputs. A more recent evolution is graphical optimization for sectors like the gaming industry where physical layouts of work space and tasks are simulated graphically, almost like a video game, providing the owner with a virtual, intuitive, but intentional planning tool.

Three types of automated schedule logic can be recognized:

- Mathematical optimization
- Supervisory optimization
- Graphical optimization

First, there is a difference between "scheduling" and "staffing." The terms mean different things within different industries. For our discussion, scheduling is defined as documenting the assignments of people in the time and labor system. The scheduling component allows the employer to house information about who is assigned, where, and when and perhaps how much they will be paid for working that shift. Simple scheduling applications are a record of planning and decisions that take place outside of the time and labor system. Scheduling systems offer efficiencies in terms of entering and reporting the data. But they have no built-in logic about whether the schedule is being built properly relative to business rules or demand.

A staffing application is more sophisticated. It is an intelligent system that depends on parameters and must be fed data about certain variables such as demand (i.e., volume). Staffing systems also take into account specific characteristics about each person: their skills, availability, and cost, for example. Where scheduling is rather passive, staffing modules are much more energized and are used to build schedules and assign staff based on the logic according to which they are configured.

Note: Many sophisticated systems use the label "scheduling." This passage is not meant to define or characterize products using the term scheduling or staffing. The use of each term here is to help distinguish the difference between what various systems can do as they are discussed.

Scheduling systems require rather dry, flat inputs, either from a person or from another database—who, when, where. They can be set up once to be ongoing into the future (unchanged), or they can be adjusted periodically to reflect changes in the schedule or even refreshed nightly from an outside source. It's akin to an electronic stock trading system. If you are a buy-and-hold investor, you're in good hands with a scheduling system. You'll be able to handle the exceptions and minimal changes you need to make. Basically, you operate off of fairly stable trends in scheduling. If, on the other hand, you are at the other extreme and you're a "day trader" when it comes to your schedule, making changes every hour with multiple variables taken into account, a staffing system is going to be more in line with what you need.

Staffing systems require dynamic inputs on a regular basis so that the staffing levels are kept in line with both demand and business constraints.

Staffing systems must be routinely supplied with key volume data. The business must know what kinds of work must be done relative to the amount and type of demand. Businesses that are currently run "by the seat of the pants" of management aren't good candidates for deploying a staffing system, because they are not in touch with the requisite business drivers. Because staffing systems are automated, the frequent changes to the schedule are not as labor intensive. They can handle multiple parameters and hierarchical logic in the decision process much more efficiently than the average human supervisor. And they can make those decisions and transactions quickly. Staffing systems are high-performance processors that take demand-driven labor deployment to the next level.

The second factor to keep in mind about scheduling and staffing systems is that neither one is there to completely replace the human dynamic that is essential to successful labor staffing. Do not make the mistake of thinking that the system, however sophisticated and high-tech, is better 100 percent of the time at creating a schedule that results in success for your organization. Computerized optimization may work for machine production schedules and investment trading, but the employer who forgets that ultimately he is working with human capital—not capital goods or trading capital—is bound to hurt his business.

Third, deciding on scheduling and staffing systems is not an all-or-nothing proposition. Very little in workforce management systems is. If you deploy time cards to hourly full-time workers and not to seasonal part-timers, that will work fine. Likewise, if you decide to use basic scheduling for some departments, sophisticated staffing modules for others, and perhaps nothing for salaried employees—all in the same application—that will work. Over the years, we've seen these systems deployed in numerous combinations. It's a matter of form, fit, and function; decide which best meets your needs and where.

Key Idea

Computerized optimization may work for machine production schedules and investment trading, but the employer who forgets that ultimately he is working with human capital—not capital goods or trading capital—is bound to hurt his business.

SCHEDULES THAT ARE BIASED TOWARD BUSINESS NEEDS WON'T WORK   Scheduling practices have become a topic of interest at the academic level. Susan Lambert is an Associate Professor in the School of Social Service

Administration at the University of Chicago. She is a "work and family scholar" and studies how firms structure opportunities in hourly jobs. Recently she studied more than 20 work sites in retail, hospitality, transportation, and financial services and 88 hourly jobs. Lambert's study looked at whether the opportunities provided to workers by these corporations are equally accessible to hourly employees. What her findings reveal that is relevant to workforce scheduling systems is that there can be a significant price to pay for placing too much emphasis on optimizing the schedule based on business rules and not enough on balancing the equation from the human perspective.

If the scheduling technology focuses solely on eliminating all variance, risk, and rigidity in the schedule in order to supersynchronize with demand, then labor bears the brunt of such overoptimization. Her study found that highly optimized business-centric scheduling practices affect a worker's ability to stay in that job, access benefits, and even make good use of non-work time. These practices are characterized by fluctuations in shift timing (A.M. shifts some days, P.M. shifts other days), posting schedules only a few days in advance of the workweek, and schedules that don't sustain an employee's benefit eligibility because of too few hours. As systems take a purely mathematical approach to schedule assignments, employees find their hours significantly reduced, their schedules erratic, and their work/life balance entirely unpredictable and difficult to manage. The evidence shows that when hours fluctuate, it can create higher absenteeism. When employees have to miss a shift because of a conflict (because they've picked up a second job to supplement their income or can't find transportation or child care) they are not likely to get those hours back. In addition, employee turnover rises because these scenarios are a huge barrier to accessing benefits and career paths.

The remedy is for employers to balance the actual cost of a schedule against the opportunity cost and the value of their human capital. Lambert also suggested that employees need to figure out how to manage risk instead of simply passing it on to workers. For example, she suggests that employers post the majority of the schedule farther in advance, establish core hours around certain operations and store opening and closing, and guarantee at least a minimum number of hours to all employees. Things like self-scheduling, shift swapping, and shift bidding can also help, given that employees are pretty good at *not* scheduling themselves for times they *can't* work.

Michael Gondek urges customers to think about creating schedules that have a reasonable minimum shift length, rest between shifts, and sleep time. He also agrees that giving a minimum notification (more time between when schedules are announced and worked) of shift assignments is a part of supporting a work/life balance that meets workers' needs. Essentially, employers need to understand the benefit of having tenured, satisfied employees at the front lines of the firm, who often have the most customer contact. Stable and predictable hours equate to opportunity, training, career advancement, and feeling valued. Remember, the schedule is a form of compensation and you may get what you pay for.

Key Idea

Scheduling is a form of compensation.

For these reasons, it's not likely that automated scheduling systems will ever fully replace the human scheduler role. Let your managers take a leadership role in looking at scheduling not just as a cost or production issue. The technology can institutionalize good business decisions and make schedulers more accountable for the direct and indirect costs.

Accountability is important because it's about alignment with your goals and best practices. Scheduling systems can have whatever degree of restriction may be needed in a particular situation. If scheduling parameters aimed at managing costs, skills match, preferences, or any number of variables are violated, the system can flag, warn, require a manager override, or completely prevent the assignment. The system is doing its job by providing visibility into what is about to happen with labor utilization and cost. And to make sure the best course of action is being followed, the process can require the involvement of multiple layers of management so that staffing decisions are validated and approved.

How a Scheduling System Accomplishes Its Goals

When a work schedule is put together, it is typically done for a set period of time such as a week, a month, six weeks, or whatever is the company's defined "schedule period." In a manual system, who is to work on a given day at a specific time is written down. This process is repeated for each "period." The manager sits down, looks at the calendar, and starts putting together a schedule, just as he did six weeks before. He has to think about who is on his team, who might be taking vacation time, who likes to work on which days, perhaps who works well together and who best gets the work done. He may look at last period's schedule and start from there. Or he may start with a blank page. He may be able to fill in 75 percent of the schedule without checking with anyone, but then the phone calls come in and cajoling, wrangling, and negotiations must begin; this is time the manager could use to review patient status if he is in health care, oversee production outputs in manufacturing, help customers in retail, or engage in other more productive activities no matter what type of organization he is in.

In an automated setup, a number of tools exist to make this process faster and easier. Scheduling systems can fully automate the process, assigning staff to shifts as the anticipated workload requires. Alternatively, such systems can provide a toolkit of templates and repeating mechanisms that simplify the building of a schedule but still allow the manager to use her own judgment.

Full automation allows a manager to enter business data that reflects the volume of work, such as the number of parts to be produced in manufacturing or the anticipated volume of customers in retail. The system will be preconfigured with a set of special criteria that use the volume data in combination with parameters for selecting staff in order to build the schedule. Selection criteria can include settings that tell the system to select the employee with the lowest base pay rate, the fewest hours worked, the best job skill match, or those who prefer to work a particular shift. A company can establish criteria that are unique to the organization. Parameters are limited only by what data is stored in the system and the ability to qualify an employee based on the characteristics. For example, if management wanted to select employees based on their hair color, this could be done, it simply needs to be identified in the system. (See Exhibit 7.2.)

What Degree of Automation to Use

The system evaluates needs. It's demand-driven workforce management. A retail outlet that expects a high volume of customers at a work location— whether it's a car wash, a department store, or even an amusement park— will have to have a number of car washers, stockers, salespeople, or entertainers and cashiers to handle these customers and to generate the maximum sales.

Suppose a printing company receives a huge rush order for tri-color brochures; machines have to be set up, materials collected, packaging lined up, and workers assigned for each workstation. Every print job is unique; every project schedule requires a different plan for labor.

Every industry has its demand drivers, production peaks and valleys, new orders that change the production landscape, and bread-and-butter products that must get pumped out day after day, rain or shine. Employers have to adapt when orders or conditions change. In some companies, things change all of the time. In others, labor demand stays relatively the same. Managers have to adjust plans for their people. People adjust instinctively if and when the situation dictates. But what about systems?

EXHIBIT 7.2   Mapping Scheduling Processes to System Features

Process	Description	Scheduling System Features
Forecast	Determine the demand.	Forecast engines, interfaces to other business systems (ERP, HR, Payroll, etc.) to pull key drivers
Workload	Evaluate the supply, consider the restraints.	Workload templates, supply side rules, hierarchical decision logic, timekeeping, accrual (time off) information
Master Schedule	Create schedules by task, location, time, etc.	Workload planning, schedule templates, calendar views, etc.
Populate Schedule	Assign the right employees.	Selection tools, communication tools (automated workflow), self-service and shift bidding, communication with devices such as time clocks and phones, Web access
Adjustments	Modify the schedule in real time for variances in demand and supply.	Real-time visibility and alerts related to production side issues, automated schedule updates, quick and easy user interface to make manual changes, automated workflow to notify employees and supervisors, analytics to assess cost and production impact

WMT systems are designed to handle the primary processes in scheduling the workforce. This table describes each of those processes and identifies the mechanisms within WMT systems built to perform those operations.

There are varied levels of basic electronic schedule deployment: full, partial, and assisted scheduling automation.

In **full automation mode**, the automated schedule can populate employees into the work schedule for a specific period of time, or it can do so indefinitely into the future. For some categories of workers, such as nine-to-five office types, this works very well. Their schedule is populated once, and the pattern is automatically repeated into the future. Temporary changes, such as for vacation or special project work, are handled by editing the specific dates from the master schedule. This also works well for schedules that rotate staff in patterns such as seven days on, seven days off. Such programs are sometimes put in place for workers who commit to work in a particular program for an extended period of time, say six months. In these cases, the automated schedule works nicely for the pool of 7 on, 7 off workers and is populated on the master schedule well into the future.

In **partial automation mode**, the scheduling technology can be used in tandem with management input. A system can be designed to provide the manager with templates of common shifts, such as 7a–3p, 3p–11p, 8a–4:30p, as well as patterns such as Monday through Friday, Saturday and Sunday, Week 1: Mon, Wed, Fri and Week 2: Tues, Thurs. A manager can use such a system to select the best-matched employee according to job requirements. The system can then display a list of top candidates, ranked in order or according to preconfigured selection criteria. The manager can then choose workers from a list that gives her excellent business intelligence concerning the most qualified and willing workers. The manager can add the "human factor" (her personal preferences or team sensitive changes) in making the final selection.

The **assisted mode of scheduling** technology can be deployed in an even more basic manner as a computer-based spreadsheet on which the manager makes all schedule assignments "manually." This solution doesn't take full advantage of the available technology, but it does preserve older processes. More important, it moves the company forward in scheduling integration by supplying the time and attendance system with schedule data and providing greater access and visibility into what individual managers have scheduled for their areas. The manager may experience fewer time savings, but he will gain significant benefits in meaningful labor activity data and reporting. The schedule can also be distributed and shared more easily, because it is no longer on a single sheet of paper or within a standalone computer system.

Staffing works somewhat the same. A **fully automated staffing system** works well for creating a schedule that is quite complex due to the many variables that determine how many workers are needed and which workers are the best match. The staffing modules can generate the architecture of a staffing plan that identifies how many workers are needed, where and what they are tasked with. It will then go to the resource side of the system and look at the pool of employees. Using the built-in business rules for selecting the appropriate person for each job, the automated staffing system populates the staffing plan with employees from the list. Manually constructing such a schedule can be hard work. It also requires getting it right. If the workers who show up have the wrong skills, that's a big problem. Allowing an automated system to use built-in workloads and staffing guidelines frees the manager from what can be a time-consuming and possibly unrewarding task.

However, remembering what was said earlier about the human component of this process, the employer may decide to allow the system to generate the staffing plan and populate the schedule *but* require the manager to approve the assignments and ensure that the dynamics of the team and delicate personnel issues are accounted for. A good analogy may be found in cooking. A great meal isn't in the details and mechanics of the recipe but in the minor adjustments, taste-tested by the chef.

Making Schedule Adjustments Efficiently and Quickly

In today's work environment, the employee work schedule almost certainly will change. As employers look at labor as a variable to be actively managed and workers struggle to balance the demands of work and family, schedules will change. Whether the schedule is generated from a fully automatic process or is handwritten by a front-line supervisor on a paper napkin, demand for labor and employees' ability and willingness to provide it will vary from the original master schedule.

Companies must operate efficiently. In the recent decades, a dramatic surge has occurred in cost-conscious business processes such as lean manufacturing and just-in-time supply chain operations. Labor supply is part of this. Companies must acknowledge that the demand for labor does not remain constant. Highly competitive organizations are waking up to the realization that to keep labor costs low while meeting operational demands that fluctuate, they have to be agile in the scheduling of employees. Using scheduling technology within the time-and-attendance suite of applications provides the responsiveness needed. Changes in the schedule come from either a shift in supply (workers) or demand (work volume). On the demand side, if production plant A has a shut down and plant B has to pick up the slack immediately, management needs a tool to help determine what should be done. If a hospital has an unexpected influx of critically ill patients, the right staff in the right number needs to be called in immediately.

On the demand side, if half the student population at a college comes down with an epidemic of flu or food poisoning, campus student workers will be in short supply. Or if schools close due to a snow storm and parents must stay home to watch their young children, workers will be calling in to take the day off in droves. Scheduling to meet this type of change in a manual system efficiently is extremely difficult.

Workers experience unexpected events that prevent them from working their assigned shifts. With more parents working these days, when a sick child has to be taken care of by one of the parent-workers, one will have to call in and take the day off. Personal business such as closing on a new home may result in lost work time and an interruption to the set schedule. Management needs a tool to use to work these changes into the schedule.

There's nothing new about changes. Someone once said that change is the only constant. What's new is that instead of relying on managers to handle these business needs in an ad hoc fashion and with little oversight, smart business people are using scheduling technology. So, instead of allowing Johnny Laidback, supervisor of the shop floor, to scramble around and fill an opening with his favorite buddy, once he finally gets word from someone on the production line that Amal Tired didn't show up for work today, the scheduling system will generate an immediate alert that there's an absence because Amal Tired didn't punch in. It will simultaneously identify the most suitable replacement, using best practices and cost-conscious factors, and will notify the supervisor and replacement employee by e-mail or pager, thus fixing the problem in short order.

This scheduling repair process is possible because a schedule will have been entered into the system. Having a populated schedule in the computer makes attendance notification a no-brainer. Not only are these urgent situations more effectively managed, integrating schedules with time and attendance allows for attendance tracking over time, and tracking data can be used to better manage the business. For example, the number of arrival and departure exceptions can be tracked. The tracking can be done by specific employee—counting the number of times the employee is late and indicating how late the employee arrived each time. Attendance can also be tracked by group, showing attendance trends by work area, supervisor, job category, tenure, shift, or whatever makes sense for the business. The ultimate goal is to manage attendance better. To do this, a manager must know what, where, and when attendance issues are occurring. Schedules allow labor activity to be evaluated, measured, and characterized.

A time clock will record when employees arrive and depart and how long they work, but it alone will not paint a picture showing how the activity should be interpreted. Trends can be developed from this data. From trends come predictions that allow the scheduler to anticipate and forecast the variances in supply and time. Of course, not everything can be forecast 100 percent. Scheduling systems tell the manager about problems as they occur. Unlike managers, scheduling systems don't take vacations, call in sick, or go to meetings. So schedule repair can be done consistently, immediately, and wisely at any time.

These systems also work well under pressure. What if the demand for labor spikes and many employees need to be called in at once? The scheduling system can handle an increase in the volume of work more easily than a front-line manager trying to meet the operational needs of those employees who are on site while also figuring out how to adjust the schedule and call in relief. Increased efficiency, more meaningful data, automated processes, and good business practices will ultimately impact operations in a positive way.

Earlier, I mentioned some common objections to automated scheduling systems people typically raise. Some people will object to the implementation of a new system because they are used to doing things the way they have been doing them for years. There are ways to implement the technology even when the workforce isn't entirely ready to make the change.

Key Idea

The beauty of these systems is that they are flexible enough to allow the customer to implement "in degrees" and to have the technology turned on "low, medium, or high" in different locations throughout the organization.

Take a hospital, for example. Automated scheduling software has been used for years in clinical areas. A recognized need for the technology existed in these areas long ago, and vendors provided standalone scheduling packages designed to meet it. It's not surprising, then, when hospitals upgrade their time and attendance systems and include a scheduling solution in the implementation, that clinical areas in an organization can be very enthusiastic about getting a new scheduling system. At the other end of the spectrum, usually areas in administration, managers can be quite resistant to going to an automated scheduling system. Often, they simply don't see the need.

To accommodate this difference in buy-in, scheduling systems can be rolled out to some areas in a phased approach. The new system can be turned on full blast in a clinical area that welcomes an integrated scheduling system. After all, it will eliminate the need for double entry of data as well as the disconnect between timekeeping and the standalone schedule system. Immediately upon implementation, managers in these areas can have full access to all the system's capabilities. Typically, they can be expected to begin creating complex, unique, repeating schedules and to keep these schedules up to date on a daily basis.

For areas such as dietary and housekeeping, which may be lukewarm to the new system, scheduling can be implemented on "medium." Managers in these areas, who have not been operating on a computer-based scheduling system but have somewhat complex schedules and fairly volatile change activity, will be expected to create a master schedule in the system for all employees and make changes on a less-frequent basis. This might be done weekly or every pay period. In this way, more time is given managers in these areas to get used to the new processes and to learn the benefits without the expectation of intense usage hanging over them. Over time, these areas will be expected to begin using the system fully.

For administrative areas that refuse to be convinced of the need for automated scheduling, the system can be turned on "low." The expectation for these areas is that the master schedule will be created for all employees once. Managers are not expected to update the schedule. Exceptions that occur when work assignments change are dealt with in the time card, and the schedule is a loose image of the work schedule. Only when an employee's job or permanent schedule changes, such as when she switches to the night shift, is the schedule updated for an employee. These areas may never go to full scheduling usage unless a business need is identified that necessitates a more accurate schedule picture.

I've also seen the reverse. Standalone scheduling systems can be very entrenched within a group of employees. The idea of replacing the legacy system causes a good amount of consternation and resistance. Supervisors are worried that the system they are familiar with and that "ain't broke" is about to be fixed, but they aren't sure it's going to be a good change. Thorough analysis of the business requirements for these areas is the answer. Decision makers must assess what these areas need in terms of staffing and how the legacy system meets those needs. How dependent is the success of their operations within that business unit to the legacy system? Next, perform a gap analysis comparing the legacy system to the new technology. Are any of the business requirements left unmet? Will the business unit be able to continue to operate effectively? Are the concerns warranted, or is education about the features and benefits of the new system the answer?

Don't make the mistake of dismissing these internal voices. They are, after all, experts at what they do today. Bulldozing over them with a new system and hoping for the best is a recipe for mutiny and disaster. Make it your mission to win these stakeholders over by taking the time to listen, analyze, and communicate and be open to various options and timetables.

The benefit of having flexible deployment options and allowing each area to use scheduling at a different level of involvement is that all areas are working toward being on the system, and management throughout the organization has the opportunity to work with the technology and evaluate its benefits and costs. This reinforces the importance of the objectives that were identified when the system mission was established. Requiring all areas to use schedules lets everyone in the organization know that scheduling is an important part of the organization's human capital strategy and that using this piece of the technology is key to its successful implementation.

Common Reasons People Resist Automated Scheduling

1. **It takes too much time.** It is true, the processes are new and may seem like additional work. However, *the time spent is "smarter time"* used to set up continuous schedules or to provide more visibility into schedule activities. The time spent creating and managing schedules may eliminate time spent reviewing and correcting time cards, requesting manual checks, revising schedules due to poor scheduling, identifying and locating personnel, and dealing with employee dissatisfaction or payroll errors. Changed processes frequently seem more difficult than the old way. It is often the case that

only the transitional period is difficult, and in fact the new processes are more efficient.

2. **Our schedules change too often to maintain in a computer system.** Supervisors often manage a volatile schedule due to employee absences and varying consumer needs. *The systems are flexible enough to allow managers to decide how much they will be involved in keeping the schedule up to date.* Some managers may be able to keep their scheduling systems up to date on a daily basis. It may only be reasonable to expect others to update them periodically throughout the pay period. In extreme cases, a system can be built around fixed schedules. Managers may be eased into the process by choosing the lowest level of maintenance until they are comfortable with the system, recognize the benefits of the automated scheduling system, and can handle more maintenance. It should be noted, however, that each level of maintenance provides a different degree of credibility based on how up to date the schedules are.

3. **Scheduling is a personal art form, or "my system is not broken."** Often managers are committed to "their way of scheduling," including their tools and personal time frames. They may be concerned that an automated system will be less effective than their accustomed method and restrict them because of technical limitations. But the system features do *allow managers to duplicate their manual practices* and create templates for recurring shift patterns. An automated system also *institutionalizes their expertise* and allows for training and proxy sharing of their scheduling know-how. Although scheduling is an art form, it is also a logical, repeatable task that can free up manager time.

4. **Scheduling forms relationships.** Without standard methods or processes, managers devise their own systems and identify their key resources for staffing. They cultivate individuals who are willing to fill scheduling needs. Employees and supervisors may enjoy, or resent, the way schedules are currently prepared, and introducing an automated system threatens to upset established relationships for better or for worse. A relationship-based scheduling methodology often has little to do with business objectives, such as holding down costs or ensuring operational quality, and a great deal to do with employee or personal preferences. On the other hand, automated scheduling systems provide consistent cost- and quality-based management of schedules. They draw on all employees' access to staff shifts based on employee skills and business needs. The system also tends to level out the hours worked among employees while at the same time reducing overtime and preventing premium stacking.

Using Ghost Schedules for Efficiency

Just about everyone is happy when someone takes care of something for them, especially when they don't have to ask. One day, for example, my son and I had lunch at my parents' house. After my mother and I went into the other room, my then 13-year-old got up, cleared the table, and began to wash the dishes. My mother and I came back into the kitchen and surprise! Everything was cleaned up. Who did that? Boy, would we like it if someone did that every day.

Automated schedules can be like this, doing unexpected things for employees. When schedules are integrated with time and attendance, data from the schedule carries over to time cards automatically without the employee having to do anything. These are called "ghost punches." For example, a schedule can include a chain of work activity events that are expected to occur throughout an employee's shift. The employee may begin work at one location and be scheduled to move to a different location three hours into the shift. When the employee arrives at work and logs into the system, whether by time clock, Web, or telephone, the data goes into the time card. The schedule in the background recognizes that data as the in-punch and tells the time card "I know what this employee is going to do." The employee goes about his day and completes his shift. He goes to the system and logs out, which is his second and final entry that day. The time card registers the out punch, and the schedule fills out what the employee did during that shift. The transfer to the second location appears in the time card as a "ghost" punch, allocating the employee's time to the two different work locations. No effort whatsoever is required on the employee's part. The less time spent going to the time clock, the less chance there is of entering the wrong data or forgetting to enter the transfer.

More can be done with schedule data ghosted into time cards— changing jobs, changing rates of pay for specific scheduled labor activity, scheduling time off such as vacations and leaves of absence—far in advance. All this can be entered when the schedule is put together, and at the proper time, the data will go into the timekeeping module for payment automatically.

Budget and Schedule in a Dynamic Environment

Budgets ought to be considered the approved plan for labor expenditures. They should be a yardstick for measuring performance, but not a straitjacket. Scheduling is, as some managers argue, an art form, even in a mechanized environment. Give managers the right information and the best tools, and value will be the result.

As production increases or decreases and demand for labor hours changes, the schedule needs to reflect this, and the budget may have to be reworked. This is why it's a strategic imperative to use a scheduling mechanism that can quickly and easily adjust to fluctuations in the amount of labor required to produce a projected volume of work. It would not make sense to prevent, due to budget restrictions, a manager from scheduling more workers if demand was up and the imposed limit would result in a production shortfall and, therefore, less revenue and profit. It's important to keep in mind that the cost of not putting more labor to work or not using the most expensive workers may be greater than the amount that would be saved by holding back. It may help to have processes surrounding mechanized scheduling that include a "sanity check" or override feature that gives the manager pertinent information about risks and factors that would cause a negative impact.

Such factors might include winning a new contract, a competitor going out of business, or an important customer with a rush order request that necessitates labor efforts above and beyond the norm. The result of not meeting the customer's demand for the product might be that the entire account will be lost, making the investment in additional labor expenditures for the extra labor worth the additional cost. This is where complete data integration becomes indispensable. Enabling a front-line manager to assess how critical a situation is and to make important decisions about deploying his staff can be invaluable. For automated staffing systems a different, urgent model could be deployed so that the system adjusts for the importance of the project, not just the short-term costs.

Staffing at Levels to Maximize Profits

A schedule for a company that builds complex machines to customer specifications might project that a particular machine assembly will be ready to work its way through the production process next week because that's when the subassemblies are due to arrive. So the machine is scheduled for production on a certain day. It's simple enough to determine the manpower and specific skills that will be required to complete this assembly, and thus workers are scheduled.

What happens if there is a delay? Suppose it turns out a critical component will not be available? This sort of thing is bound to happen from time to time.

The scheduling system needs to be flexible and able to reschedule the number and location of workers on a real-time basis. In such a plant, a newly refreshed schedule could be generated and posted periodically, telling skilled workers where they are assigned and what they are slated to be doing as the day unfolds. The same sort of thing can and does happen in all kinds of business environments. In business, people have to be able to react quickly and intelligently.

No one wants to pay employees to sit around and twiddle their thumbs. But what's the right level at which to staff when history shows there are certain to be peaks and valleys due to seasonal fluctuations in demand? Lean manufacturers typically deal with highly seasonal markets by establishing production capacity in the middle, between anticipated peak demand and the minimum demand expected. For one thing, it's almost always easier to expand capacity than to cut it back. As a result, many lean producers plan on hiring temporary labor or on adding shifts during peak periods. But there is also another way to deal with seasonality.

Exhibit 7.3 represents the varying demand for labor and how it can be misaligned relative to labor supply. The demand curve represents the driving forces behind the volume and type of work needed. It's natural for there to be fluctuations in the demand. The workforce curve illustrates the labor that was supplied. There is an attempt to respond to demand, but it is not in sync.

When there are not enough workers, quality or timeliness will suffer. When there are too many workers, waiting just in case, payroll becomes excessive and labor standards are not met. The key is to align the supply and demand curves so that they closely match keeping costs low, quality high, and timeliness on track. This is the goal of demand-driven workforce management.

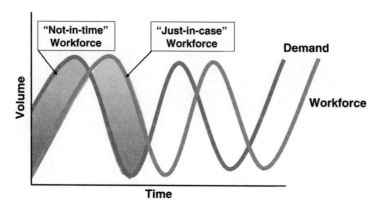

EXHIBIT 7.3 Challenge—Align the Workforce with Demand

Managers must align labor with demand constantly. With too many workers, there is an oversupply (more cost); with not enough workers, production and service suffer (poor quality, lost revenue).

Source: Used with permission.

As most business people know, inventory is a dirty word to lean manufacturers, and they try to eliminate it to the extent possible. Even so, it may make sense for a company that has a good idea of what's coming in terms of demand to build some inventory in advance of seasonal peaks. This is done during slow periods when daily demand is down. The products built are usually standard, off-the-shelf items, or in the case of build-to-order operations, units completed only to the point that customization can begin to occur. Then, during peak-demand times, standard products will for the most part be delivered out of inventory, and production capacity will be devoted largely to keeping pace with custom or specialty product demand. In this way, a lean manufacturer is able to even out the peaks and valleys and get maximum value from the workforce he has employed.

Identifying best practices, measuring, fine tuning, and measuring again are made possible with WMT. The ability to constantly ratchet up performance in this way makes software-assisted scheduling and labor analytics indispensable tools in the push for continuous improvement that's become so necessary and important for companies to remain competitive in today's global economy.

Chapter Summary

- There are four general types of schedules: continuous, variable demand, rotations, and seasonal.
- The principles of good scheduling include the following:
  - End users are allowed to be in command of flexible scheduling options.
  - Scheduling is 100 percent political and 200 percent personal.
  - Schedules vary widely by group, even within the same organization.
  - The impact of schedule decisions impacts costs and people.
  - Scheduling is a form of compensation.
- Schedule creation follows a standard process of five steps.
- Three models of automated scheduling optimization are mathematical, supervisory, and graphical. The workforce management technology vendors offer different products based on these models.
- Schedules that are overly optimized in ways that focus only on business needs will not work.
- Employers must avoid passing all of the risks of labor scheduling on to employees. Employees must have a minimum level of schedule predictability. Schedules translate into benefits and

compensation in very real ways. Sophisticated scheduling modules can help balance business and employee needs while abiding by the workplace rules.

- Organizations can deploy automated scheduling within their organization to varying degrees based on each business unit's needs and over time as the organization matures.
- It is possible to overcome resistance to electronic schedules.
- When staffing is aligned with demand, profits rise. WMT systems offer the ability to respond to the forces behind labor demand and budget constraints reducing conditions of over- and under-staffing. Highly configurable solutions allow any company to input its unique drivers of needed labor volume.

PART II

Workforce Management Technology Systems and Installation Considerations

CHAPTER 8

Adding Value to Data through Collection, Storage, and Distribution Techniques

I cannot emphasize too much the importance of the data inside a WMT system. The ability to use the tools and benefit from the information produced out of these systems depends on having the right data. Data must be collected at the right time, from the right people, and for the right reasons. There are a number of devices for collecting data that meet just about any need. It is time to begin collecting data from people and places that might not have been considered before, because the information is so important and the tools allow you to handle it appropriately. Not only can data satisfy the obvious need for information, it empowers the system to control activity, ensure security, spotlight problems, and even maximize revenue. Using time and labor management systems the right way makes information about the business "glow in the dark"—showing management things they could never see before.

Because data is so important, it's essential to evaluate a number of aspects related to data in the products you evaluate. Going through the list of considerations will tell you whether you really understand your data needs and ensure that you acquire the right system. From many years of watching companies struggle with data issues, I've gained insight into some things to watch out for.

Data Is for Everyone, Everything, and Everywhere

"No boundaries" aptly applies to our discussion of data. For the time and labor management system to be fully utilized it must collect and analyze all of the important data. This is where keeping WMT in the payroll box limits the potential benefit. Payroll data can be "plain vanilla" and still produce accurate paychecks. But workforce management data must be specific, timely, informative, and complete. For data to do its job, it must be collected at the right time and place, include all of the important information, and be shared with the proper decision makers.

Location, Location, Location—Now "Where" Is Important Too

What are the three biggest things to consider when buying a house? Location, location, location, of course, and it's the same when it comes to collecting and distributing workforce data. Where the data is collected, where the employee performed the activity, and where the data goes after it is reported by the employee are crucial to the value and integrity of the information and the ability to control the labor activity being reported. Payroll data has historically been simply a matter of capturing who and when; processes collected the names of people who worked and when they worked. In some cases, it might have included what the employee did. That was all that was needed for payroll.

But operational activities don't exist in the two-dimensional world of only what and when. Operations take place in a location. People work in teams, on wings or floors, or in units. They are assigned to equipment and production lines, buildings, and geographic zones. If the work is more conceptual than physical, they are assigned to projects, cases, or clients. The point is their work relates to a third dimension of data that historically hasn't been a requirement in the payroll department. That third component is what relates their work to the organization's products and services. It is the connection between an employee's work contribution and whatever is being sold. When an employee is in the correct location, doing his job, his work should be adding value.

Management should want to collect time, location, and task-related data because it will help them better manage human capital. Having an employee go to a particular spot to report on and start an activity is a crucial element in collecting value-added data. A phone might be located there, a PC, or a bar-code reader or some other device.

An employee might be required to clock in when he begins an activity and to clock out when he finishes. This isn't limited to any one type of company. The work that goes on in many industries can easily be viewed as something the employer is interested in tracking. Manufacturing, health care, retail, transportation, gaming, government, and education all need to understand their labor activity. This sort of information can also be extremely helpful to companies that bill clients for the time people spend working on their behalf; lawyers and management consultants are two examples. In the service industries it is imperative to have time records to justify client billing. Yet, workers, across all industries, might not fill in manual time sheets until the end of the day. More often, it is at the end of the week, in the last half hour before time sheets are due. As a result, many are based primarily on memory.

How accurate do you suppose they are? How much legitimate, billable time do you suppose is lost? I'm willing to bet that over time the accumulated effect is substantial.

For the most accurate picture, then, of an employee's labor cost and the value it adds, data collection ought to be done at the moment closest to when work actually begins. This is why improving the ability to collect data at the precise moment productive work begins should be a goal when time and labor data collection is being automated. The ideal setup is for the employee to report his beginning time at the exact minute and location an activity starts. That setup may not be a time clock by the entrance door or next to the break room on the other side of the plant. Fortunately, technology now provides the opportunity to locate collection devices in proximity to work locations.

Locating the collection devices in actual work areas ensures that compensated time is productive time, supervised time, engaged time. It lessens the gaps between the time employees report to work and the time they actually begin to work productively. It may not seem like much of an improvement, but small savings repeated day after day add up.

What's really exciting is that the technology is rapidly evolving in a way that will make "location" of the device a non-issue. Collection and reporting devices will go with the worker and will be everywhere, unencumbered by cables or power cords and not needing a wall to hang on or a desk to sit on. By the time the next generation enters the workforce, it's likely that relatively inexpensive devices such as these will be available. These devices are already in the works. Think cell phones, and you'll begin to see where data collection devices are headed.

Enabling workers to report their activity as it occurs also reduces errors and omissions. Filling out a time sheet at the end of the week, relying on memory, can lead to mistakes and honest omissions. It is also presents opportunities for unscrupulous workers who may choose to fill in the blanks with data that is not representative of their true work activity. The more this type of waste, fraud, and abuse occurs, the more entitled workers feel to continue it, and the more money employers lose.

"Fred never gets here in the morning till 8:30, and I'll bet he doesn't mark that on his time sheet. So I'm not going to put down that I left 20 minutes early yesterday. It's only fair."

A Legal Perspective on Data in WMT

The value of data collected through time and attendance systems becomes important in the context of employer records and, in some cases, audits and lawsuits. The technology is relevant to lawsuits because in a wage and hour case you're dealing with off-the-clock work, total hours, breaks, and the like. According to Rod Fliegel, an employment law attorney and shareholder with Littler Mendelson, the nation's largest labor and employment law firm, investigators will look at scheduling, records of hours, and all of the things the technology is geared toward capturing.

The first thing that happens when an employer is pulled into something like a class action suit is to consider whether and how to implement an appropriate litigation hold. In huge, multistate systems with thousands of employees, trying to locate all of the records and lock them down can create all kinds of practical issues. People who could destroy evidence have to be prevented from doing so, and storage has to be provided for all of the information and supporting documents. Typically, these cases can go back as far as three to four years. The WMT system is the repository for capturing and safekeeping the evidence for long periods of time.

Fliegel shared that he would be hard-pressed to find many general counsels who don't worry about getting involved, or who haven't already been involved in costly law suits in California. Even though a case may be resolved up to a certain point in time, the door is open to what are known as "copycat class action" cases for successive violations from that time forward. These open-ended cases can easily make a WMT system a valuable component of defending a lawsuit and even preventing further losses. Managers have to be aware, however, of the intersection between law and technology. The technology is in many ways fantastic; it centralizes things and eases the administrative burden on companies, but it can be expensive in terms of storage and e-discovery. Plaintiff's-side attorneys try to use this impending expense to leverage settlements. Although technology can be a great tool for querying data, the systems are not static. Upgrades and conversions move technologies to new platforms, and going back into legacy systems that are no longer being used today can be a challenge. Fliegel routinely meets not just with his client's legal representatives. But in this day and age he must also involve IT, because data retrieval can be an issue.

The lesson here is that archiving records involves more than simply storing the data on a server. Someone has to be able to go into that system, retrieve the needed information, and produce some sort of report. It's important to document the processes, keep track of security and login information, and simultaneously maintain compatible legacy reporting systems (or be familiar enough with legacy systems to explain to a court why retrieval would be cost prohibitive). The benefits include the ability to access huge amounts of information and data with full integrity.

Fliegel recommends that any time you set up a WMT system, you should keep in mind how the data might need to be queried. Keep the data flexible. Wage and hour class action suits typically involve negotiation over classes of employees. One suggestion is to use discrete job codes so that when payouts are computed based on a specific group of employees, that group is narrowly defined, keeping the cost to a minimum. You may have a position such as engineer that is involved. If the case covers only a specific subset of this job class, having well-defined job classifications is important because having this kind of quality control and precision inside the technology can be a way to minimize the losses.

Data Is Collected from a Variety of Devices

As shown in Exhibit 8.1, data is collected from a variety of devices.

Many workers use computers in their jobs, and a growing percentage in many businesses have them on their desks. When an employee arrives, all she has to do is sign in, and the system knows she's there. The employee can also use the computer to access information about herself, such as how many days off she has earned, year to date, or hours she's already worked this pay period.

It might be more practical for telephones to be used in some locations. This is particularly true in large locations, such as a medical center, a business with numerous small (by employee count) locations, or for mobile workers. Time clocks can cost $2,000 to $5,000 apiece or more, and not everyone who works is assigned his own computer. Using telephones is an excellent solution, because they are ubiquitous in most workplaces, and today, most people carry a cell phone.

Telephones can also save time. In a large building or an office complex, the nearest clock might be 10 minutes away from the employee's workstation. A phone is usually right at or nearby the workstation, the work site, or the client site.

Using a phone the employee might call in and punch a code (Note: It is not advisable to use Social Security numbers for privacy reasons), an employee ID, or a personal identification number (PIN). Voice validation is also a possibility. Whatever the case, the computer on the other end knows which device was used (based on the device's electronic "address" or the phone number), the time of the call, and who is on the line once the code is entered. The computer might prompt the employee to punch in another code that will enter a specific activity. When the employee is finished signing in by phone, she doesn't have to hang up if someone else

EXHIBIT 8.1   Types of Collection Devices

Device Type	Ideal for	Requires	Device cost/ Overall cost	Benefits	Limits
Time clock	Fixed work sites; locate near entrances or break areas	Hardware, network, power	$$$$/$$$$	Ideal for sites with more employees, interactive inputs, supports security; biometric capability, add-on bar code readers	Not portable, may need multiple clocks for high-volume usage, some limits on total number of employees stored in single clock
Telephony	Numerous remote sites, mobile workers, locating device close to work-station	Phone lines, phone management software, hardware	$$/$$$$$	Inexpensive, readily available, easy to use, supports security, ideal for sites with few employees, easily located at work station, few limits on number of employees	No display, less interactive communication, cannot read bar code
Computer PCs	Users who have access to PC, kiosk setup	Hardware, network, power, user network IDs	$$$/$$$$	No additional hardware needed, located at work station	Users need computer access
Mobile devices (e.g., PDA)	Remote or mobile workers who cannot get to a fixed device	No installation, wiring or configuration; connection required	$$/$$$	Ability to track regardless of location; high performance, relative low cost	Although able to work off-line does require some connectivity

Data collection devices have expanded to include tools that offer solutions for a variety of situations and requirements.

is waiting to check in on the same phone. She can simply punch the pound sign and then hand the phone receiver to the next person.

The collection device can also be set up to give employees information if they want it, such as how many hours they've worked this week, the next shift they are scheduled to work, or how much paid time off (PTO) they have coming to them. The device can also allow the employee to request time off, change a scheduled shift, even read an e-mail. But we'll get into all of that a little bit later.

These paperless capabilities are increasingly in demand. Going paperless can save considerable expense. However, to keep a system from being overloaded at peak punch times, it may make sense to limit the hours in a day in which this type of device interaction can be accessed at equipment that is used for arrival and departure reporting. Clocks and telephones aren't the only channel through which employees can interact with the system. Computer kiosks can be set up. Otherwise, to support the added traffic at the clock or phone it might be necessary to add servers and other IT infrastructure in order to accommodate the volume—lots of calls or entries—at peak times.

The amount and type of information a particular person can access can also be limited based on an individual's position in the company and what he needs to know for his job. Collection devices readily administer "security" profiles that tell the device what each employee is allowed to do at that machine.

In addition to telephones, personal digital assistants (PDAs) can be used to enter and access data. So can the types of devices UPS and other delivery companies use to track packages. Given that there are 262 million mobile subscribers in the United States—which is equivalent to 83 percent of the population (*Source:* CTIA Wireless Association October 2008)—and some 78 million (and growing) remote workers, this technology will increasingly be used to manage these employees, who cannot use a fixed device. With these devices, employees can enter information from their workstations to track idle time, materials consumed, and scrap at each work area, as well as to monitor production costs along with their time and attendance information.

As noted previously, device vendors are working closely with WMT vendors to develop new technology that will be available soon, perhaps not too long after this book is published, designed and manufactured specifically for the purpose of WMT data entry. One device in the works resembles a memory stick and is about that size (2 in. x 1 in. x $\frac{1}{4}$ in.), making it easy to wear around the neck on a lanyard, clipped to a belt or lapel, or attached to a key chain. The cost is expected to be relatively low, less than that of a cell phone. To check in, an employee will simply press a button and state her name, along with other pertinent information—"This is Jane Smith, reporting to work in sporting goods."

In addition, the employee will be able to use this device to give and receive information such as an upcoming work schedule or how much paid time off she has accumulated, initiate a message to another manager or employee, or instruct the system to take an action, such as run a report.

Either with global positioning technology or by noting the point of entry into an Ethernet or cell phone grid, the device might also keep the system informed about the approximate physical location of the employee. This will come in handy when trying to track someone down—a doctor in a hospital, for example—although this level of sophistication may not be available quite as soon as more basic capabilities. There is lot of technology in development or on the cusp of being more readily available and easy to own. Radio frequency identification (RFID) and active-badge technologies will be more prevalent in the years to come. In addition, advances are coming via mobile devices that will allow workers to simply punch one button or send a text message and thereby send alerts to their managers or to a call list to create and fill an open shift, among other things. Workflow to personal electronic devices with cell and wifi capabilities will be common place in the not too distant future.

Finally, there is the time-honored time clock. But these aren't your father's time clocks; they can do much more than punch a card. As with those that have been around for decades, time clocks are usually positioned near an entrance or a high-traffic area. But today's clocks are connected to a computer network or system. Once the clock is punched, data enters the system and is instantly available. This allows management to see who is working and where at any given time.

Exhibit 8.2 shows a time clock with a biometric device and LCD screen for entering and reviewing information. The clocks can be preprogrammed to automate sign-in to special categories of work and compensation such as call-in, extra shift, special premiums, temporary supervisor or line leader rates, work orders and so forth. "Time clock" has really become a misnomer; these data-collection devices are now tools for two-way exchanges of much more than time-related information.

Is Any Data Exempt from the Clock?

In Chapter 4, it was explained that no one is prohibited from punching at a time clock or entering actual time-worked data into a time and labor system. An exempt employee is an employee who, because of his or her duties, responsibilities, and decision making authority, is exempt from the overtime provisions of the Fair Labor Standards Act. Although exempt employees are expected by most organizations to work whatever hours are necessary to accomplish the particular goals and deliverables of the position they hold,

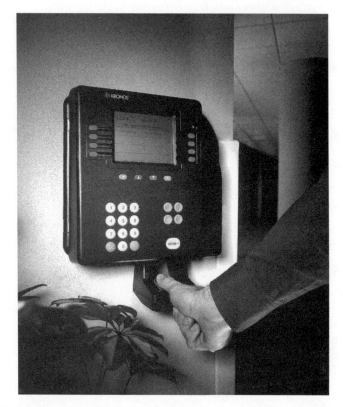

EXHIBIT 8.2 Photo Image of Time Clock with Biometric Device

Photo: Kronos 4500 Touch ID Terminal

Biometric devices (e.g., finger scanners) validate the identity of the user and deliver security and savings. Payroll inflation from buddy punching accounts for 2 to 5 percent of total payroll. Seventy-four percent of organizations experience payroll losses directly related to buddy punching when no validation measures are in place.

Source: Nucleus Research 2006, APA 2004, KY CPA Journal Fall 07

they usually have some flexibility in their schedules and can come and go as necessary to accomplish their work.

Let's say a number of workers on staff meet the exempt requirements. Management may want to track their activities for reporting or cost accounting purposes, or to provide information that will be used to bill clients for services rendered. Certain service sectors have strict guidelines as to the number of staff required relative to the number of "customers"—that is, patients, residents, tasks, or clients. For these organizations, capturing exempt time data is a critical operational need. They must report and prove that they staffed adequately for a particular case load. In many situations, exempt employees should also be included in time and attendance data so that the figures management uses to make decisions, provide services, and bill clients will be representative of the whole.

But this can be problematic. Exempt employees aren't being paid by the hour and are often considered "professional workers," so they typically don't punch in and out at a time clock or report their actual arrival and departure times in time reports. Often they record a duration to represent their day such as "8 hours." They are, of course, expected to work a full week, but technically their pay cannot be reduced if they leave early every now and then or don't work a full 40-hour week. If it takes more than 40 hours to get the job done, they are expected to put in the hours necessary, but their pay does not change. Therefore, because exempt employees' actual time worked and pay are not related, many companies have historically not closely tracked the time they put in. Businesses feared being scrutinized by regulators for their classification of these workers and even potentially fined for wrongdoing. The result is that many companies are reluctant to track exempt employee activity. They don't require them to punch, and they don't have them call in to a phone system to report time worked.

Other reasons why exempts typically do not punch their time are cultural. Professional employees expect a greater degree of autonomy and liberty. Today, there are fewer visible distinctions between production workers and professionals in the workplace. Requiring exempts to punch in at today's workplace further blurs the line between the two and diminishes the status and perks that go along with being in the higher ranks.

But times have changed. Technology has introduced data integration into management's toolbox. Workforce management technology systems now deposit labor data into the corporate data warehouse and parse it into reports that are used to make business decisions. Omitting exempt labor data would lead to an incomplete labor activity picture. Suffice to say, the old principle that recording exempt employee time equates to tracking time for hourly employees isn't true in today's info-centric business environment. So long as the data isn't used to compute salaries or earnings on an hour-for-hour basis, companies are safe to collect the information.

There are numerous ways to record exempt employee activity. Some companies are satisfied with manual processes that allow exempt employees to report their time on a weekly basis. Some require salaried personnel to allocate their time to cost centers, projects, or customers. These processes do provide some sense of exempt labor activity and cost but fail to provide real-time data and are not as accurate and verifiable as those for hourly employees, who use a data collection device such as a time clock or a computer.

SOLUTIONS FOR THE SALARIED WORKER There are some things to consider in planning to track exempt employee time in a new workforce management system. For consistency and reporting purposes, it may be preferable to have exempt employee hours come from the same system as hourly employees. A problem may arise, however, because an exempt employee may work fewer than 40 hours, or he may work more, but his pay should not change accordingly. In other words, actual hours worked may vary each week, but the employee's earnings do not. I have encountered systems that are easily configurable to limit the number of hours passed to Payroll for an exempt employee, thus eliminating the potential problem that excess pay might be automatically generated. A problem I've run into is that the same systems sometimes are not equipped to guarantee the weekly minimum hours to support the salary payment, which might result in an underpayment. Turning on an "auto-pay" isn't a great solution, because it doesn't take into account benefit time and actual instances when the employee should be paid for less than a full week, such as with a termination or leave. I strongly recommend including exempt-hour tracking requirements in the technical specifications when selecting a system and verifying that it can support the payroll system side of the process.

One solution is to set up the labor management system to recognize "one punch" as a valid entry per day for an exempt worker. If an employee calls, punches, or checks in at any time during the day, or his supervisor validates that he worked, the system will log in a day's work (e.g., eight hours) for that employee. At a minimum, this can help keep track of days worked so that paid time off is taken appropriately. If the system registers no punch at all, then a manager has a right to question whether an absence occurred or paid time off should be applied. The one-punch system also allows the exempt employees to be included in "on premises" reporting so that management knows who is physically onsite in real time. It can also verify coverage in work environments that require specific staffing levels, because the employee's "punch" can be used to validate her identity and location. As the section on scheduling explained, a schedule in the background could be referenced to provide more detail about when the employee worked that day.

Auto-populating punches from a schedule can also work to enter exempt employees into the system without the need to track their work days in real time. This way the time card shows the employee's planned work schedule while generating the hours that must pass to Payroll for payment. Systems that employ auto-populated punches from schedule don't require the exempt employees to clock in. This also accomplishes more accurate cost accounting than would otherwise be the case by attributing the exempt employee's wages and costs to the business activity in the same way the time of hourly employees is recorded.

ON-PREMISES NOTIFICATION IS INCREASINGLY IMPORTANT   Various ways can be used for the system to know who has punched, who is on premises, and who has failed to arrive as expected. A person might have a badge with a magnetic strip that's swiped. Some systems require a PIN in addition to this. More and more, however, employers are using biometrics. All an employee has to do is touch a pad on the clock with a finger, and the system will identify her. In these ways you can know to varying degrees of certainty who is at each location.

Key Idea

Market estimates indicate that nearly 400,000 biometric devices have been deployed worldwide.

Source: "Biometrics: High-value Workforce Management," white paper, *Acuity Market Intelligence*, Feb, 2008

What happens when someone forgets to punch? The system can be programmed to generate a list of those employees with missed punches or who fail to show up and provide this to the appropriate supervisor. Call this the "workflow" component. In selecting a system that's best for your organization, you must know how the information needs to get to the manager. Some systems will generate an electronic page to cell phones or PDAs. Others provide the notification only within the application, requiring computer access. On-premises notification can be a powerful tool. The key is to purchase a system that adequately delivers this information to the right individuals, at the right time, and via the available technology.

You Cannot Manage What You Cannot See

Collecting data from an employee at the time and the place an action occurs provides real-time data. What makes it even more valuable is that this data is visible and accessible. Where can the data go? Wherever it needs to.

Data should travel on a need-to-know basis. Does Payroll need to know minute to minute who has reported to work or ended a shift? No. Pursuing real-time data is for operational purposes. The immediate dispersal of the information collected is to provide a tool—a window into today's activity.

As the saying goes, "You cannot manage what you cannot see." So who should the data be for? It's for the Subway shop scheduler responsible for ensuring that each of the five stores he or she manages in a 10-square-mile area is staffed at all times. Obviously, this person cannot physically be in five locations at once. But the WMT system can tell her who is at each location and who has not yet arrived. It's also for the foreman on the shop floor who gets the production line ready. It's for any scheduler who needs to make certain the entire crew has reported to work so that the work can begin on time. It's for the retail store manager who expects a rush of holiday shoppers and needs to direct staff to high-traffic areas. And it's for the business owner who must control costs and wants to be alerted to workers who are about to go into overtime.

Collecting data at specific locations provides immediate visibility into what is going on and where it is happening. Data can also go beyond schedulers and front-line supervisors. That's the beauty of a technology that collects data on everyone. It is of interest and value to other levels and can be made available to them via workflow notifications, on-line workspaces within the application, traditional reports mailed electronically, or printed hard copy, or it can be sent to the data warehouse repository. You decide where the data goes and when.

But you also need to understand what the data is for. Perhaps the new system can replace the need for some rudimentary data or arcane reports, because it is actually resolving the issues these reports are designed to address. A good example of an outdated need for data is a reconciliation report distributed out of the legacy system. The new system is probably going to eliminate problems with missing or out-of-sync data. Spending adequate time before a system is installed to evaluate who is asking for information and why is consistently one of the top "best practices" recommended to ensure that your new processes deliver real improvements.

Capturing Activity-Specific Time

Let's say a factory produces complex machinery that needs to be customized to each customer's specifications—for example, a heating and air-conditioning system for a large building or a shopping mall. The system is made up of valves and controls, air handlers, and ducts and vents of varying lengths that curve this way and that. Each person who performs a task in the building that system is installed in might clock in at the beginning of an operation and clock out at the end, perhaps by swiping a bar code with a wand. In this way, the actual cost of the labor it took to build a particular custom HVAC system can be determined, rather than simply estimated by the seat of the pants.

Accurate information about how long it takes to perform different tasks can be extremely valuable to manufacturers who want to run a lean operation. It's information they need so they can schedule items through production in the right sequence with the right number of workers deployed to maintain a predetermined rhythm of production and eliminate as much worker downtime as possible.

Collecting Product- and Job-Specific Data

How is the information collected about how much labor went into a particular task? We've mentioned time clocks and telephones. Another way is to use bar codes. Visualize a laminated sheet attached to a clipboard with rows of bar codes on it representing various activities, jobs, parts, and so forth. A bar-code-reading wand can be positioned nearby. As a product moves into a workstation for a subassembly to be installed, the employee simply scans the appropriate bar code. When it's done, he scans another. The product moves to the next workstation, and this is repeated.

This may already exist in an enterprise resource planning (ERP) system in some fashion. What's new is relating the data of a specific worker to the cost of that worker's labor, along with other trackable data about who is doing what. The latest generation of sophisticated WMT systems break away from a strictly employee-centric view and offer views of data based on work order, machine, and material. These views are aligned with the ways companies do business.

The information this produces can be used in several ways. It can be used for cost accounting as described previously. It can measure a particular individual's performance against others who perform the same task. A shop floor supervisor might want to pull up all shop orders that are late along with the employee data behind those items. It can help establish the interval of time required for a particular operation. Or it might be used to calculate the pay for individuals who are compensated on a piecework basis. It can be used to track quality and output—who is the most productive and proficient. The data can reveal the skill gaps that are hidden in a fog of general information.

Relating Data to Billing and Maximizing Revenue

An automated time and attendance system can be used to integrate time and activity with billing. Many health care providers, including nursing and rest homes, are remunerated by Medicare, Medicaid, and state agencies, based on the actual services provided to each patient. Let's say there's a house with five residents in it. There might be two workers on staff. Employee A might be in the activities room with Clients 1, 2, and 3, while Employee B is giving physical therapy to Clients 4 and 5. Client 4 may finish physical therapy and go to the activities room, at which time Client 1 may go to physical therapy. Does this sound complicated?

Agencies footing the bill require that invoices reflect all of this. In other words, the billing must identify the patient served and the activity. Obviously, recordkeeping in such a situation can be problematic. An older time and attendance system may collect only information about who worked and how long, so a separate system would be needed to record activities by individual patient. Sometimes it's hard to reconcile the two because the time card may say a person worked eight hours whereas the activity sheet adds up to 12 hours or more. How can this be? Two or more patients may have been served simultaneously.

An updated time and attendance system can bring these two record-keeping activities together, simplify the process for those keeping the records, make it possible to reconcile patients served and time spent on the job, and at the same time automate the billing of services rendered.

Respite service is another area in which this way of working can pay dividends. This service is rendered when a professional health care provider comes into someone's home to provide "respites" for family members who are caring for someone who is physically unable to care for himself. For example, think of a handicapped adult who still lives with his parents. Medicare allocates a certain number of respite care hours it will reimburse per month per individual. The idea is to give the primary caregivers a break for a weekend, or to go shopping, or to just get out of the house for a couple of hours.

Let's say Medicare or the state will pay for 25 hours a month of respite care for a particular individual. A health care provider should consider this as a purchase order. But how do most companies know whether they have delivered all the care they are entitled to deliver? In a manual system, the cumulative number of service hours is probably not known until the last time card and activity reports are submitted for the month. That's way too late. But with an automated system, it would be relatively easy to make sure none of this potential revenue falls through the cracks. Approved-care hours provide a "budget" for that patient. The hours could be scheduled over the course of the month, and direct-care staff could be assigned to the schedule. The system could be scheduled to give periodic reports and to highlight those who are in danger of being underserved. As the nursing aides work their assigned shifts, they report their time to the system, including the patient information. If an employee misses a shift or the patient is unable to be served on a scheduled day, the balance of hours would indicate that additional hours should be assigned to replace the missed shift. Periodic reports of budgeted versus actual hours would alert management to situations where revenue is being lost.

How does this work? Telephony-based solutions, some designed specifically for home care, allow employees to use a telephone to report their work activity. They call a number, the computer answers, the worker identifies himself with a PIN, and the computer leads the employee through a series of prompts, such as which patients were served and what the activities were. Unlike earlier telephony systems, this new home care telephony system is configurable and allows providers to program the system to collect the required business data that is unique to their services and clients along with time and attendance information. Providers can set up a system to prompt the employee to provide the patient-related information they require. Workers can listen to recordings that are based on their job or work location. The system then exports the data to the time-and-attendance database and to the company's billing system.

This is one way a vendor has answered its customers' demands for a system that allows an employee to report activity in multiple formats and to include critical business information as well. Time must be reported for payroll reporting, but equally important, client-based activity, including customer numbers, service types, activity durations, and concurrent events also needs to be collected. This program allows it to be done in a simple and cost-effective manner. Previously, employers had to continually reconcile two separate reporting systems, which was no easy matter. They realized that there could be significant gaps between what they were paying their employees (reported work hours) and what they were billing their customers (reported billable activity). That gap constituted their profit margin and involved considerable risk.

Key Idea

The telephony solution made a direct impact on the employers' bottom line in terms of process improvement, expense, and revenue.

Telephones are about as basic as hardware gets these days. They are inexpensive, easy to use, and readily available. Even cell phones can be used. Phone lines are also inexpensive and reliable. 800 numbers can be used for multistate operations, and T1 lines can provide enhanced bandwidth and speed. A reporting pathway must have very little down time, and telephony systems are very reliable.

Evaluate the System's Components

Technology today provides a number of functional options, devices, and channels in response to the needs of various business processes and data sharing requirements. There are considerations for selecting the type of devices to be used, the infrastructure, and the processes that carry the data from employee to paycheck to business manager. They include

- Cost
- Security
- Ease of use
- Functionality
- Standardization

Cost

Cost will certainly drive what your organization can afford in terms of sophisticated technology. Knowing what you can spend before you shop will allow you to focus on what you can afford. Workforce management technology when used as suggested by this book will deliver cost savings and a return on the investment. The only question is, how much? That's why the process of selecting the appropriate data collection devices should include a cost-benefit analysis.

Cost-Benefit Analysis

- Cost of the devices (hardware and supporting software)
- Cost of device infrastructure (networks)
- Installation costs
- Replacement costs and device life cycle (based on use; how long will the system last?)
- Cost of system support (personnel to manage and maintain or repair the devices and systems)
- *Determine the total cost of ownership*

You'll notice the list of costs includes more than just new equipment. The vendor should be able to provide guidelines as to how many FTEs (an FTE is a term used to refer to a Full Time Equivalent employee) will be required to manage a system of the size and complexity you are purchasing, or how many hours of administrative oversight the system demands each week. Have the vendor verify the ratio of FTEs or administrative hours to your system with actual examples from customers. It's a good idea to talk with current users about exactly how they are using the system in order to make certain the comparison is appropriate. It's not just a numbers game; 50 clocks installed at one plant all doing the same thing are not the same as 50 clocks installed at 50 different locations in three time zones configured 10 different ways. Understand your level of standardization, because system complexity will determine the economies of scale.

In addition, all FTEs are not alike. Your implementation may entail a significant staffing component. Employees will have to administer each piece of the system. Their duties and skill sets may vary widely, and their labor cost must be considered. The request for proposal (RFP) process should include obtaining detailed job descriptions and salary estimates for the new system's support staff. The people in the Information Systems (IS) Department who run the HR system today may not know anything about overseeing a sophisticated telephony system or patching PDAs into the network. And the Payroll coordinators who will no longer have to use their adding machines to tabulate paper time cards may not have the knowledge required to learn how to configure a new computer application.

Security

There are several components of security to consider when evaluating your system. The first is the ability of the system to validate the identity of the users and prevent unwanted access to the system. The system can also be engaged to provide facility security by tying it into gatekeeper systems that prevent entry to buildings or secure areas.

Second, the system should offer different security profiles for users based on their roles and responsibilities. Obviously an employee and a system administrator should not have the same access within the application. Make certain that the ability to define these profiles and a user's access meet your expectations. And last, but certainly not least important, is ensuring the security of the data collected.

Security

- User/employee validation
- System administrator security
- Tamperproof
- Protection of confidential data

Ensuring the data is legitimate and protecting the data once it is collected is crucial to providing credible data. For this to happen, you need to know in which locations you need the system to be a security guard and where opportunities exist for employees to use "the buddy system." Also consider the other security programs in use at your work sites. If there are already safeguards to ensure that employee must have their ID with them to gain access to the premises, enter the parking garage, or use the computer systems such as a photo ID, badge, or the like, it may be that these are sufficient to prevent buddy punching. If employees violate a strict policy requiring them to display their photo ID badges at all times and if they must use their badges to gain entry, they are less likely to share that badge with another worker. If employees would have to share their computer login ID and password with another worker in order for the coworker to clock them in and security is fairly tight around that, it may be that there is no need to worry.

Key Idea

"Buddy-punching accounts for up to 5% of the gross payroll."

Source: American Payroll Association 2004

For an example of the buddy system, suppose Bob says to his coworker, Charley, "Hey buddy, punch me out when you leave today. I'm going home early." If Bob can't exit the parking garage without the ID badge he uses to clock out, having Charley punch for him with that badge probably won't happen.

If these safeguards aren't in place and it's important to know it was actually Bob who punched out at 5:00 P.M., then make certain the technology has some sort of user identification validation. Phone systems can enforce voice identification or caller ID. Automated number identification (ANI) is provided today on most telephone lines. Telephony systems can compare the incoming phone number against a list of authorized phone numbers, preventing callers from attempting to call from an unidentified or unauthorized phone number.

Key Idea

"Biometrics have a projected 34.2% compound annual growth rate over the next five years."

Source: Acuity Market Intelligence Projections, 2008

Biometric technology allows customers to verify an employee's identity via fingerprint scanners, palm print readers, or optical retina identification. Once the system has approved the user, the data must be protected from manipulation or disclosure except by authorized personnel. If edits are allowed, the original data should be archived as well for backup and not deleted or overwritten. A number of systems that collect call information will overwrite that data when a supervisor makes an edit. Is that important to your organization? System security includes maintaining an audit trail of all data inputs, showing who entered what, when, and offering the user an opportunity to attach a comment or flag notation concerning why a change was made. Employees who are gaming the old system will constantly seek ways to outwit the new system and avoid detection. That's why when security is evaluated, it's important to think like someone who wants to circumvent the controls in the system.

There are some basic security issues to think about as well. If employees must enter an ID number on a keypad in a common, unsecured area and the keypad is visible to passersby, the question needs to be addressed: Should that ID number be kept confidential? It's not uncommon for employers to assign employees' Social Security numbers as their login ID numbers. Punching that number into a keypad for anyone to see could be risky. Asking the vendor if the display can show only an asterisk (*) instead of the actual numbers may provide all the security that is needed. For phones, the same numbering convention might allow the next caller to hit the "repeat" button on the phone and view the last employee's ID number, which would breach that employee's privacy.

PINs are also a concern. Such a number is only as secure as the employee wants it to be. Relying on the employee to keep his PIN private and using it to verify his identity is potentially fraught with trouble. Again, the "buddy system" can come into play when Bob shares his PIN with a coworker to punch in for him. Also, PINs are often forgotten and require continual reassignment. That assignment process opens up yet another opportunity for abuse when system administrators change an employee's security settings and must use some other means of verifying the employee's identity. Any number that identifies an employee in the system must be guarded. Screen views, reports, displays, and playbacks present windows of opportunity for unauthorized users to gain access to employee records.

In your evaluation of systems, ask vendors to explain how they view the security issue. Make certain the importance of guarding data is clearly understood.

Resetting passwords can be a major headache. Not every WMT vendor allows employees to reset their own passwords or request help with a forgotten password. Allowing employees to manage their forgotten passwords, as do online banks and services, is a tremendous time saver for the employer's help desk or security administrators. I've seen this become a part-time job for administrators of very large employee populations. This one feature alone is very valuable.

Ease of Use

It goes almost without saying that the system you want should be easy to use.

Ease of Use
- Employee/end user usability
- Ease and speed of acceptance by users
- System administrator—complexity of setup and management of multiple devices and the underlying infrastructure
- Scalability—ability to add devices, change configuration, and adapt to growth
- Impact on existing resources

The process should not be overly complicated or time consuming for employees to identify themselves to the system and enter their data. Obviously, it shouldn't impede their ability to get to work, and it should allow the next person in line to do the same. For many systems, administrators are able to customize prompts so that employees are given specific step-by-step instructions as data is entered in the system. These prompts may also be designed to "retire" after the employee gains proficiency and no longer needs the extended version of prompts or explanations he depended on when he first began using the system. The system should also have the ability to cancel or back up (the old "do-over" key) when a user makes a mistake or "fat-fingers" an entry. Accurate data is crucial, so people need to be able to correct their mistakes or abort before the system collects erroneous data. Systems that confirm (repeat back) the information entered are even better, assuming the process is not overly time consuming or involves a playback that could be seen or heard by other employees.

I often suggest that during orientation employees be given a "cheat sheet" the size of a business card with instructions covering basic steps for reporting activity or even for more difficult tasks. Posting instructions by the collection device is also a good idea. Including the phone number of the Help Desk can be a positive step.

More than end users should be considered in your evaluation. System administrators will benefit from technology that's easy to work with and maintain as business needs evolve and the system undergoes minor modifications. A configurable system, one that requires an administrator to be proficient in a common computer language or proprietary tool kit generally displayed in a graphical user interface (GUI) on-screen workspace, is preferable to a programmable system, because it will be easier to learn how to use, more stable, and require less skilled and less costly personnel. In addition, rewriting system programming may require extensive system testing and validation before changes can be put into effect. Configurable systems limit what the system administrator can change in the underlying software and should be fairly goof-proof as far as overall system stability is concerned. The desired outcome might not occur when an error in configuration is made, but the system is less likely to crash due to a configuration mistake than it would from a programming change.

Configuration skills are also important in planning for personnel. How widely used the application is in your area or industry may determine how easy it is to find qualified resources to support your system. If everyone in your market is using the same product and it meets your needs, such familiarity gives you a larger pool of workers to choose from and more competitive salary expectations. In addition, a popular system may call for less training of employees who are already familiar with the technology from their previous places of employment. It may be easy to use because they've already used it. You might even find local user groups for ongoing support.

Ease of use also translates into ease of growth. Over time, it is likely your business will grow or change or both, and the system will need to expand. As a result, vendors ought to be queried as to how many more devices a system can accommodate before more hardware or network infrastructure is needed or an upgrade is required. The architecture you are sold will be based on your current size. It's good to understand where you will max out that landscape as your employee base or device inventory grows.

Two areas of growth and size that often are overlooked are inactive employees and turnover. Employee populations are often counted based on active employee count for a given year. What this neglects to include is the total number of employees remaining in the system during that year because of turnover and leaves. Many industries have very high turnover rates; anywhere from 30 to 75 percent of their workers quit and must be replaced each year. Payroll departments can attest to this phenomenon when they issue W2 statements in February and the number of W2s far exceeds the constant for active employees. For the system, the scalability question hinges on the number that is more in line with the W2 count, because those terminated employees will load the database with more records. Similarly, employees who are on extended leaves of absence remain in the database as well, taking up valuable space and impacting those sizing decisions.

Functionality

The best way to define functional specifications is to diligently investigate every way data is handled today by current systems in your organization. These functions will differ by industry, location, by employee population and the general logistics of handling data in the employer's workplace. There are tactical and strategic operations the system must be able to perform. Remember that to become a business tool, the system must handle not only payroll data but also business rules and operational information.

One of the most common gaps in defining functionality is in the business rules. If functionality is not fully defined, the ability of the system to automate complex processes may fall short. Organizations with multifaceted calculations—tiered qualifiers that determine whether an employee is eligible or the amount of pay—often do not dig deeply enough into these rules early in the process. The result will be that the chosen system may not be able to satisfy these business needs and the customer will be left with manual processes or complex workarounds.

To select a system that will satisfy your functional needs, consider the following:

Functionality

- Options for data collection—type of data that can be collected and frequency of collection
- Data transfer—interfacing with other systems
- System performance—sizing the system for the appropriate volume of data inputs and outputs

- Specific rules for calculations and qualifiers—including tiered qualifiers, the source for important parameters or key performance indicators, and the range of time to be handled

Standardization

It's best to first determine whether procedures and processes are standard throughout your organization. There are several ways to do this through a sampling of data or perhaps an all-inclusive survey of each business unit and employee category. Onsite observations and interviews conducted by a business analyst are even better. If your operations are managed centrally and policies and processes are strictly adhered to, you may be in a position to interview a small group of employees and managers. This would probably be the case if everyone uses the same forms and systems, the same numbering systems and naming conventions, the same reporting cycles, and a similar organizational hierarchy.

Another indicator of standardization is locality. If all operations are in one city or state, it's more likely that processes and procedures are standardized than if an organization is spread out across multiple states and localities. A single line of business or homogeneous customer demographics also reduce the chances that a system will have to handle a lot of complexity.

Companies that grow by acquisition and allow new business units to continue existing practices instead of converting to corporate standards are likely to require system features different from those that have been standardized. Organizations that have been in business for many years and have expanded over time may be fairly conservative in their current practices but may be on the verge of benefiting from more advanced data collection features. Having a wide variety of worker types, from commission-based staff to exempt and project-oriented employees and hourly, per diem, and piece-rate workers, indicates a need to thoroughly explore the functional requirements.

Indicators of standardization:

- Uniformity of forms, naming conventions, policy, and language
- Age of policies and systems
- Number of manual checks issued and reasons
- Number of sites and proximity to one another
- Method of company growth
- Management—centralized or decentralized
- Turnover of management and administrators
- Types of pay codes (wage types, earnings codes, etc.)
- Lines of business—operational diversity
- How many different states and localities
- How many unions or employee contracts/agreements
- Date of last survey and findings

Once the type of discovery process (sampling, survey, site visits, etc.) has been identified, and whether it relies on a sample or is inclusive, the investigation should include what the system does today, what works, what doesn't work, what it should be doing, and what it should not do. The resulting functional specifications may even include levels of required functionality:

- Level I: basic/required
- Level II: enhancements
- Level III: optimum features (the gold-plated faucets you'd love to have but probably can't afford unless they come standard)

The important point to keep in mind is that it's imperative to know what your system must be able to do. You must uncover the full set of detailed functional requirements. If one group of employees cannot use the system because it doesn't do X, then X is critical and cannot be overlooked. If you know your processes are complex, nonstandard, or inadequately documented, the best approach is the most extensive discovery you can afford.

It's also important not to forget that paper time sheets are still a legitimate device and represent a process that may be the best workable solution for some organizations or subgroups, given the issues raised here. The most prudent exercise is to begin with an assessment of how current collection systems measure up against these considerations.

Scalability—Can the System Adjust?

If your organization plans to expand and you are looking at an automated time and attendance system, scalability is something that needs to be evaluated. No matter what your numbers are—whether you have 250 employees, 2,500, or 25,000—scalability is critical.

Key Idea

The different aspects of scalability include hardware, network, and software.

First, the software component should be evaluated. Some platforms are not designed to handle large databases or a high volume of inputs. Some vendor systems are designed on operating systems or database applications that are capable of handling only a limited amount of data.

I once discovered the hard way what lack of scalability can mean when working on a large-scale implementation several years ago. This time and attendance project included the purchase of a telephony system for data collection, which happened long before I came on board. Employees would use a telephone to call into the system, and the system would record a "time stamp" of their arrival and departure times, change of location, job, or activity. The company had more than 25,000 employees across the country. Employees typically called into the system several times a day to report a change in work activity. The system was rolled out gradually, adding a few thousand employees every few weeks. The telephony system worked well for the first few months. But a point was reached during the implementation when the system became unstable.

Little had changed from the initial rollout except call volume. More and more employees were added to the database, and an increasingly heavy volume of calls was coming into the telephony system. Suddenly, phone lines were down and the telephony database would freeze. Employees could not call in, and the telephony module could not transfer the call data to the time and attendance database. What had worked just fine for the first 8,000 or 9,000 employees now routinely crashed. Field personnel were increasingly frustrated by what had become an unreliable system. Employees returned to their manual time sheets. Management was dismayed at the direction of the project roll-out and upset with the vendor. The roll-out was temporarily halted, and some regions were taken off the new system to allow stability to be regained for the divisions that had been on the system for some time. Rumor had it that out in the field, the project was no longer called time and attendance; it was now referred to as "time and chaos."

I wrote a memo to the vendor detailing the state of affairs from a technical standpoint: how often the database had to be compacted and repaired, the occurrences of line outages, the volume of calls. I did not go into the soft-side impacts: the high level of internal frustration, the sense of being in crisis mode, and so forth; even so, the vendor contact called it a "toe-curling message." The problem rapidly ascended on the vendor side until it reached senior management.

To its credit, the vendor did an outstanding job of pulling together what I would call a "tiger team" of its key developers and product specialists. The vendor team held daily calls with the customer team and created a test environment on their premises that replicated the customer's setup. The frailties of the telephony system were identified, the hardware was beefed up, and the workload on the database was parsed out among a shared server network. The scuttlebutt internally, however, was most interesting, and provided a valuable lesson.

I had joined the team on this project long after the vendor had been selected. Apparently, the group that went through the request for proposal

(RFP) process consisted of personnel from several areas, including Finance, Human Resources Information Systems (HRIS), Payroll, Operations, and Information Technology (IT). IT had apparently raised concerns about the platform on which the telephony system operated, but the system was eventually purchased anyway. The primary time and attendance application selected was quite capable of handling a 30,000-employee database. But the telephony piece was in a Microsoft Access database. From experience and accumulated technical expertise, IT believed Access would not be a suitable environment for handling the expected volume of data inputs. Of course, the vendor assured the customer that the system would perform as required, and management dismissed the concerns within IT. But we later learned that no customers that had more than 10,000 employees were on the Access-based telephony module. This installation would be by far the largest database this telephony product had ever attempted to handle. Scalability—going from 10,000 to 30,000 employees—was a significant factor that even the vendor failed to appreciate.

Like people, systems are capable of handling only so much. Systems have to fit. Just like people, if they can't handle the workload, they will fail and the work will not get done. On a very technical aspect of product suitability, the technical experts in IT apparently lacked sufficient influence in the company to ensure that the appropriate product was purchased.

It's important to learn from this. If you are selecting a product based on technical requirements, listen to your technical experts, or require the vendor to certify or validate that their product will perform based on your sizing requirements. It would be best to go onsite for a demonstration to see the product up and running under the same conditions your company will impose on it. Stress-test the product, take it for a test drive, and see it actually do what *you* will need to have it do.

Beware of Potential Maintenance Nightmares

The preceding narrative shows one aspect of scalability. There are others that can be more subtle, but just as deadly, or sometimes just a dead end. Marketing departments are great at identifying customer demands. Programmers can be terrific at designing solutions that answer these demands. And salespeople can be geniuses at making every wish seem to come true, if only the product they are selling is selected. But the old saying "What you do for one, you must do for all" is very important in systems that are replacing manual processes for a large base of users. Managers of enterprise-size organizations need to be careful that the products they purchase were designed for an enterprise-size user community. Developers who are not designing for an environment that is constantly changing and growing, one where system setup and user features must be applied to large numbers of individual users, can create maintenance nightmares. Worse yet, the demands of an enterprise-size user base can mean that certain features in the system simply cannot be turned on. The heavy burden cannot be supported at the individual user level if the system is not designed appropriately.

An individual's or a manager's universe of employees and data in a manual system is quite limited. He or she has access only to what comes in on paper. But when these individuals become computer system users they are thrust into a much larger universe of data and functionality. In enterprise-size organizations, the data can be huge. The variety of functions needed can be vast, spanning the entire organization. Therefore, a system must have mechanisms for limiting what each individual user can see and do.

If the vendor says a particular user will see only that individual's small group of employees, be able to do only what you want him to do, and have access only to certain data or reports, you must ask how this will be accomplished. If the system can analyze data and give users crucial alerts in real-time situations, ask how that information will be distributed. In the military it's called logistics—acquiring and distributing supplies to the troops on the battlefield. The system must be capable of doing the same thing with the data. It must be able to identify who needs what, when, and how much, and it must provide an efficient means for delivery. In addition, it must be able to adapt to changes and work well for every business unit. Efficiencies in setup for large implementations are a must.

Key Idea

Data logistics—acquiring and distributing data among users at crucial times—can be a feature that works well only with a small number of users. Efficiencies for managing large user groups so that all features can be turned on should be a key assessment question for enterprise-size employers.

Let me give you an example. If you want a small group of individual users to have access to a query that shows them only the employees in a specific line of business, there should be a way to create the query once and assign it to that small user group all at once. In addition, if the line of business changes and the system data changes, the users should get the new information automatically. If a user owns access to a certain type of data—for example, employees in the southern region—he should receive the changes to that data. If the southern region acquires a new location with a new set of employees, then the definition of the "southern region" changes and southern region users should automatically get the newly defined southern region data. You don't want to have to repeat the process all over again; the system logically should know that those users need the new information. This may have been incorporated into the system design. If not, and data set definitions change frequently, this could be a huge maintenance issue. The logistics or maintenance features built into the system—how changes are inherited or delivered—are key components of scalability.

Consider Workload and Hardware Requirements

The last aspect of scalability we'll talk about has to do with workload and hardware. Vendors design products around assumptions about the product's utilization. Systems are built with functions and outputs, reports being a significant example of what is wanted from time and attendance systems. Vendors offer products that are designed to operate under certain levels of demand for these functions and outputs. The customer must be able to quantify what demands for these functions and outputs will be and to measure whether the product can handle the demand. No two companies are alike. What is sufficient output for one may not be sufficient for another. For labor management systems, the ability to access and use the data is crucial to enabling the technology to become more than a payroll reporting system. Some systems are remnants of applications designed basically to provide weekly or biweekly outputs. If their platform or programming has not been upgraded adequately to handle a greater demand for outputs, significant performance problems may be experienced when tasking the system to become a daily business tool. For the airline I worked for, the C.A.N. Reports worked well on the existing hardware, because for payroll purposes they were needed only periodically, and for marketing, the demand was not exhaustive. If operations had decided to use the reports on a daily or hourly basis, problems most likely would have occurred.

The introduction of automated workflow, including preprogrammed running of reports, is another workload requirement that can quickly get out of hand. In the early versions of today's time and labor systems, automated reports were intended for system administrators to assist in critical system operations. This was a small audience with few reporting needs. If the sales person mentions this feature, make certain automated reporting is intended for the entire user population and dig deeply into what it takes to set it up and the workload it puts on the system. I've witnessed a large gap between the "sales talk" and the reality of the product's offering.

If you conduct a thorough analysis of the way your operations and support areas use workforce data before purchasing a new system, you are more likely to avoid unpleasant surprises about the software.

Key Idea

Look at how needs may change and how having access to more information may actually increase the demand.

The technology has two important jobs to perform: processing information as it is received and manipulated by the users, and compiling that information to generate tools, reports, and actionable data for operational needs.

Each application relies on hardware—servers and the physical infrastructure of a networked system—to run the system. The software applications are just part of the package required. The servers are designed to handle the database, but their capacity to do so is limited. One server will support the application only to a certain size. If a potential buyer has 2,500 employees, a vendor may sell the software and indicate that a single server will support the system. But if the buyer expects growth, he needs to know how many more employees that single server can support. Scalability in the hardware area means buying more servers or beefing up existing machines. If a user doesn't have the financial ability to purchase more servers, the system won't perform well. Scalability can be limited in terms of what is affordable and deliverable.

Chapter Summary

- Data collection devices include time clocks, telephony, personal computers, PDAs, and even bar-code technology.
- WMT systems provide valuable data for mitigating losses resulting from class action suits by minimizing the affected employee population (through discreet classifications) and making discovery a less burdensome process. Electronic data records are not without issues. Over the long term, storage and retrieval must be carefully managed.
- Data is easily related to business information such as product, job, equipment, task, customer, and revenue.
- When evaluating a time and labor management system, consider cost, security, ease of use, functionality, and internal indicators of existing standardization.
- Appropriate scalability and ability to handle the expected workload will determine the long-term fit for a system.

CHAPTER 9

System Mission and Communications

The number of companies that neglect to create and maintain a clearly defined mission for their time and labor management system never ceases to amaze me. Whether it is an overly simplistic view of what the system is expected to do or a failure to sustain the vision for what the system is here to accomplish, the absence of a well understood mission severely inhibits anyone's ability to make things better.

In this chapter, we'll discuss what a mission means for a time and labor management system and how a mission-based system differs from a basic replace-and-move-on implementation. Achieving the mission for the system is no small task and takes a well-thought-out game plan and the right resources. Testing and system validation will be explained, including guidelines for parallel testing.

The chapter will wrap up with suggestions for communicating the changes and benefits that are expected from the new system as well as using project champions to ensure success throughout the organization.

What Is the System Here to Do?

If the management of a company for which we are working wants its new system to help reduce labor costs, we consider this a mandate to configure the system to enable managers to do just that.

Key Idea

"Mission-based configuration" is our terminology for a system that is set up to do more than simply pay people.

It means approaching each pay rule, each user workspace, and each system feature as a tool to be used to help accomplish specific business goals. These tools need to be action oriented. They should provide not just numbers but flags and meaningful information to be acted upon.

It makes me groan when I hear Information Systems (IS or HRIS) folks offer to spit out another report from their monstrous, data-loaded systems. Managers already have too much "information." As a society, we are trying our best to operate on the brink of information overload. One more spreadsheet filled with names and numbers isn't going to produce results. Managers still have to do something with that data; they have to interpret it to determine the message, figure out what should be done, and then take action. Usually, a report really doesn't provide a whole lot; the managers suspected they might have a problem in the first place or they wouldn't have requested the report. Providing just another spreadsheet relies too much on the abilities, alertness, time, and motivation of each individual manager for something else to happen. It assumes a manager will have the time to stop and analyze the report, and then if he has the skills to do so, know what the appropriate action to be taken is and have the motivation to take it. In my book, that's too much assuming. A breakdown in the process is almost certain to occur a good deal of the time. Remember from Chapter 3 we talked about the "messiness being in the wetwear."

On the other hand, **mission-based configuration interprets the data, identifies the action to be taken, and will go as far as management wants toward actually taking action.** In the case of overtime, for example, a basic approach is for the system to be programmed to recognize when overtime is about to happen. The system might be programmed to flag those employees who are approaching a point in the current pay cycle when overtime pay soon will be incurred. A manager may be alerted to the flag because he or she routinely monitors the system for such alerts, or he can be automatically notified electronically, thus allowing him to continue his operational tasks without the burden of having to remember to check for flags. The table in Exhibit 9.1 compares two information and decision-making solutions: Reports and Mission-Based Configuration of a WMT system. On the left-hand side the aspects of standard reports are given. The right-hand side compares that to the benefits of a WMT set up to provide information and decision support.

Let's say the workweek runs from Sunday to Saturday. The system would begin checking on Wednesday after the completion of the first shift. By that time, an employee who has already put in 30 hours, for example, is very likely to exceed 40 hours by the end of the week. The system will then check the schedule, determining how many more hours the employee is scheduled to work. Let's say it calculates that two more eight-hour shifts, which have been scheduled, will put that employee into overtime with a

EXHIBIT 9.1 The Benefits of Mission-Based Reporting

Typical Reports	Mission-Based Configuration
Paper printouts or electronic lists	On-screen filtered views of urgent data Automated notifications via e-mail, phone, text System-generated actions
Relies on the manager to: 1. Stop 2. Read the report 3. Analyze the information 4. Interpret the analysis—convert it into a decision 5. Take action	Relies on the *system* to: 1. Stop 2. Analyze incoming data 3. Convert the analysis into an action 4. Present the action for approval if required *or* 5. Take action
Requires: 1. Alertness and focus 2. Procedures 3. Ability 4. Time 5. Motivation 6. Consistency and impartiality 7. Accountability	Requires: 1. Objectives 2. Rules 3. Decision logic 4. Automated workflow
	Does not break down due to: 1. Lack of alertness or focus 2. Inability 3. Insufficient time or distraction 4. Lack of enthusiasm/engagement 5. Favoritism 6. Neglect or lack of oversight
Results: Variable	**Results: Consistent and effective**
Focus is on manual tasks, stops short of intelligent processes or action	**Focus is on manual and knowledge tasks, actions completed by system**

Mission-based configuration is a far superior answer to the need for information for analysis, decision, and action. The system doesn't suffer from the shortcomings of employees. A well-designed system delivers consistently and dependably.

total of 46 hours for the week. The system automatically generates a flag and perhaps an e-mail alert to the supervisor responsible for scheduling. The alert will draw the supervisor's attention to the probability that the employee will exceed the overtime threshold if the schedule is not changed. The schedule could also be included in the alert, and replacement candidates listed along with contact information. As my teenager would say, "How sweet is that?"

That's just one way to approach the overtime issue. Let's just say that the technology has been configured to prevent employees from being scheduled for more than a specified number of hours, because that's the way management wants it set up. In the preceding scenario, an employee may not have been scheduled for more than 40 hours but was called in to pick up an extra shift early in the week.

The mission should stay in the forefront of planning and set up for the new system. Scheduling software can be programmed to be an excellent manager of resources. With the right parameters and priorities set up, the system will select the best candidate to replace the overworked employee. It can determine who has the least amount of hours, who has the lowest hourly rate, who has the best skill set to match the position, who prefers to work that shift, and who can arrive at work the earliest. Mission-based configuration builds business logic into the processes, replacing the idiosyncrasies of each manager's scheduling style with coherent criteria for making that business decision.

There are other ways to control the amount of overtime dollars spent. Many times we find that compensation policies are loosely written and obligate an employer to overtime payments that are not required by law. As a result, either because those managing the programs don't understand the regulations or because poor control exists over the way the activity is reported to Payroll, the company is simply paying too much. When the mission is clear, exploring every option for such a control becomes a responsibility for those who are accountable for the success of the new system. Otherwise, the system is designed based on the random interests or abilities of those working on it.

Running a Test Parallel Is Essential

Having a mission usually means things will change. But some things must stay the same. Testing is vitally important to ensure that what needs to remain constant does so. This means a parallel test is in order.

What is a parallel? No, it's not a term referring to your high school geometry class, and it has nothing to do with your driver's test. (Remember parallel parking?) Parallel testing, running the old and new systems side by side, is a must when moving to any type of new system, especially when it involves employee pay. This ensures that the new system mimics the old, and that it calculates time and benefits correctly.

FULL SYSTEM PARALLEL   There are various ways to accomplish this, and I'd like to share some things we've learned in doing so. There are different degrees of parallel testing. The most extensive involves a complete end-to-end dual run of the new system and the old, whether the old system is a completely manual paper process or one that involves an older automated technology. Employees, managers, system administrators, and technical support personnel are involved.

I usually recommend selecting a small group of employees as a pilot group. Ideally, this group will represent a cross-section of employee types and lines of business in order to test as much as possible. The pilot is not expected to be a 100 percent test of the new system. Rather, it is the first phase of the complete end-to-end testing. In organizations with big employee populations or covering a large geographic area, management may chose to roll out the new system based on a phased timetable, since in complex organizations it can be difficult to orchestrate the training, support, and logistics of an all-out "flip the switch" rollout.

During the parallel period, employees record their activity in both systems, (hopefully) creating identical or nearly identical data. Supervisors review and approve both systems. Related databases interface and update background data as usual, and everyone runs through the normal paces in terms of completing the reporting and processing cycle.

Ideally, a parallel will run for two pay cycles. The first pay cycle is often practice, or a warm-up. It will generally have less than 100 percent participation, because there will be people who forget, won't comply, or have technical problems. The data employed may not be identical to that used in the current system. The second period is a truer parallel, allowing the project team to review the results, tweak the new system, and test the later results. During the second period, the new system should generate output that's closely equivalent to the old system's.

It should be noted that this type of parallel is time consuming and bothersome to personnel and not the most popular option in most field locations, unless the field is accustomed to corporate initiatives that are not well planned and prone to problems. In that case, the field may be the side rallying for a full system-proving period before a transition to a new system is made.

MOCK PARALLELS   A less extensive parallel can be undertaken by relying on a "pilot" program to prove the system before "go live" rollout begins. In this case, the company can execute a mock parallel. Mock parallels take actual-time data from the old system and input it into the new system for a pay cycle. The only difference is that the data is put into the system via a mechanized process (import) or manually by project team members instead of by employees in real time after the parallel time frame is actually complete.

Types of Parallel Testing

Full system comparison, legacy vs. new. A complete end-to-end dual run of both systems is made, comparing outputs all the way to the paycheck; employees are paid from the old system until confidence is high that the new system will pay appropriately.

Mock parallel. This uses actual data from the old system inserted into the new system to test and compare the outputs. It has no front-end employee participation and allows for a "flip the switch" turnover to the new system.

Reverse parallel. Both systems are used, but employees are paid from the new system; data from the old system is used to validate the new and ensure payments are accurate. When the new system is working well, the legacy system is retired.

The benefits of a mock parallel process are twofold. There is less disruption in the field, and there's a longer reaction time, since historical data can be input from any time period and evaluated without the stress of trying to obtain results before the next parallel period has ended. In addition, those responsible for processing the live payroll can complete that work and then focus on the new system without having to process both in relative real time. The disadvantage to this type of parallel is that it's not a true test of the input processes or the human element, which can be an important variable. Employee proficiency in using the system will not have been tested. Often, adjustments and manipulations taking place in the old system are whitewashed, eliminating the opportunity to shake out issues before going live. In addition, the mock parallel requires more involvement of the project team and may require some programming to simulate or automate the flow of data.

REVERSE PARALLEL   A reverse parallel is another model for making the transition to a new system. In this parallel testing methodology, both the old and new systems are used concurrently but there is a higher degree of readiness to go to the new system. In a reverse parallel, the old system is continued but only to produce results that will validate payments coming from the new system. The new system is the one used to send data to the payroll system for generating checks. The old system is the safeguard to ensure that everyone is paid accurately. In some situations, a reverse parallel can be used after a full parallel if there are concerns that the prior parallels did not come close enough to proving the new system. Reverse parallels also give employees more time to practice and encounter more of the special situations that may not come up every pay period. Call it a sanity check or a crutch, if you will, for management and workers to ensure that all of the kinks have been worked out.

Which method of parallel testing and proving you decide on depends on your confidence in the survey and system configuration processes, because part of what you are proving is that everything needed has been designed into the system. It also depends on how much practice you think everyone needs with the new system before you depend on it for payroll and credible data capture. This is where the human element plays a large role in parallel testing. If survey respondents did not answer honestly or completely, or if configuration analysts did not accurately understand the needs and did not translate them into appropriate system settings as a result, there will be gaps in the processes and errors in the payroll outputs.

Further, it's important to keep in mind when planning is done that the new system will be a workforce management technology tool in addition to a payroll processing system. This is something that's almost impossible to mimic without a parallel that involves users and managers in real time. Management tool elements aren't so much about data as they are about data flow, timing, access, and the parsing of data and actions in real time. The mission may be better decisions resulting in improved outcomes and only a live parallel will show these results. The tool element will be proven gradually as users gain familiarity with the system and expectations grow.

It's worth restating again: If the new system is going to do more than simply replace old processes for timekeeping and scheduling, if the new system was purchased to become a new and better decision-making tool to drive business improvements, these new improvements must also be tested. In this case, a successful parallel will demonstrate the differences. This is where having a well-defined mission for the new system and a vision of what success will look like are so critical. Mission-based configuration designs into the system the steps that must be taken to achieve success. A vision is a quantifiable picture of what will change and how much. How else can the improvements be identified and measured? This is done through parallel testing, which is a process of comparing the old processes and outcomes to the new system.

Key Idea

Parallel testing is a process of comparing the old processes and outcomes to the new system to demonstrate the differences and improvements. The goal for a parallel that is intended to make a change to a business process is not to get the same results.

Ensuring Actionable Feedback

Another important element of the parallel process is feedback. There is feedback, and then there is "feedback." Don't think that simply taking complaint calls means you are getting the feedback you need. Hoping the phone doesn't ring during the parallel and thinking that means you got good feedback isn't "feedback," either. Parallel feedback is a measurement of how things are working. Notice I said "measurement" and not "opinion." The purpose of gathering feedback isn't to placate participants who weren't happy about having to participate in a parallel or who did not feel involved in the implementation process. Feedback is a tool to ensure that the system is working effectively. Getting good information of this type requires planning.

I recall a TV show, or maybe it was a movie, in which a young lawyer was being scolded for asking the wrong question in court. The older, wiser attorney told him, "Never ask a question you don't know the answer to." For our purposes, we should modify that advice to **"Never ask a question that doesn't have a system-specific purpose."** In other words, it's important to ask questions whose answers may result in a potential change to the system or processes. If you don't intend to change a particular aspect, you don't really need to ask about it. It may be interesting to know whether users like the new system in general and whether they find it easy to use. But ask yourself, would such vague feedback prompt the implementation team to change anything?

Be specific in a way that can be measured. It may be useful to find out such things as "Were there errors in calculating hours or computing the proper net pay?" Answers to this could identify users who had to manipulate the system to make it work or who had to correct problems outside the tested system.

The answer to "Were you able to make changes to the data that you normally edit?" could alert you to problems with the user's access profile. "Were you able to toggle between modules within 30 seconds or less?" can measure the expected wait time that results from the current system infrastructure of servers, bandwidth, processing speed, and so forth.

Another might be: "Did you contact customer support for help? If so, please describe the issue, how many customer support representatives handled your call, and how long it took for customer support to resolve your issue." This question will reveal how effective training was for both users and support personnel. Common problems might prompt a revision to a section of training material. (Note: If your organization has a sophisticated problem-tracking system for customer IT support, query that database for feedback on how the system is working.)

Guidelines for Parallel Surveys

The following list will help in designing an effective survey to obtain feedback that will promote an understanding of what could be done to make the system work better. It offers some specific guidelines for creating a good parallel survey.

1. Know what you want to find out about or test.
2. Ask questions that require quantifiable answers (i.e., answers that provide measurements).
3. Ask yes-or-no questions whenever possible, but only if you plan to do something as a result of what you learn.
4. Ask open-ended questions, but be prepared to have to read all of the answers and somehow compile them.
5. Have respondents identify themselves. It's important to know the source of the feedback, even if just by title, tenure, or other important characteristics.
6. Offer an incentive to participants if possible in order to encourage feedback.
7. Publicize the results, and tell participants how the information was used to improve the system. Let them know it mattered that they spent time completing the survey and participating in the parallel.
8. Send out the survey before the parallel is performed so they will know what to expect. Prompt participants to complete the survey as soon as possible.
9. Evaluate the responses for the following:
   A. Cost implications
   B. Consistency with the overall vision and scope
   C. Problems that result from related systems or processes that are not limited to, or originating from, the current system under review
   D. Short-term versus long-term issues and goals
10. Have an escalation plan to route problems uncovered in related systems to the appropriate business owners who care and can resolve those issues.
11. Consider having participants provide feedback again after they have used the system for a longer period of time. Determine if their responses change over time and why.
12. Archive the data and review it later for "lessons learned" for future projects.

Include questions that inquire whether the decision-making tools built into the new system are having a positive impact. If overtime is to be managed better, resulting in fewer overtime hours worked, ask the survey participants if they saw that happen. Don't just use raw data—that won't give the full picture of the context of the outcome. It may be relative to the demands put on the workforce. Granted, you should also be able to account for variables in demand and partially answer that question. But you won't know fully until you ask the system users. If they are properly being held accountable for such results, they will tell you whether the system helped or hindered them in that process. Use the survey to learn from the operational experts whether the design is going to work.

This may be a good time to give a little pep talk; I often give one to customers and prospective clients.

No other system touches every employee every day. Every supervisor will be involved. The system will involve a significant investment of the company's money. If something goes wrong with the system, everyone will know it. Employees are not patient about payroll errors, and management will not be supportive if the objectives are not met or their employees are significantly inconvenienced or distracted from business activities. All this is why it's important to invest the time and the proper resources to plan effectively and manage this project carefully. It's often said and probably true that for each hour spent in the planning phase, many hours are saved in the implementation phase and in system rework.

Key Idea

A time and attendance project will likely be the most highly visible project managers will ever undertake.

Sell the Benefits of the New System

Without a doubt, the new system will bring changes that represent benefits to the company and "takeaways" to the employee. But a well-designed system will also deliver benefits to employees as well as changes that may represent costs to the company in terms of control and infrastructure. A good way to communicate the changes is to put them in terms of a balance sheet showing pros and cons to both company and employee. For example, improving the company's ability to control overtime expenses will reduce some hourly employees' earnings. On the other hand, the reduced cost due to reduced overtime will result from equalizing hours among the staff, thereby increasing the earnings of those who will now be assigned more hours. It will also increase the quality of life for those who will have to work less overtime. In addition, a reduced overtime expense may translate to more retained earnings and potentially higher base pay rates.

Another example is the elimination of pay program stacking. This control mechanism benefits the company by providing lower labor costs per hour. While it will result in a reduction in pay for those who enjoyed or engineered a lucrative alignment of their payroll stars, it also demonstrates to employees that their employer is spending its hard-earned revenue wisely and getting smart about spending. Some changes will eliminate "gaming" by a segment of the employee population. While that segment will be unhappy about the change, those who have not been manipulating things should feel positive about an increase in fairness and control. Just ask laid-off or downsized laborers whether they'd prefer less pay to no pay. This type of line item on the balance sheets assumes employees understand the value of long-term strategic financial planning. If it doesn't impress the more shortsighted wage earner, an entry opposite this on the balance sheet might be an unrelated benefit such as employee self-service or flex scheduling. Keep in mind the benefits of employee involvement and empowerment and relationships with bosses.

The point of such a balance sheet is to articulate to the workforce the impact the new system will have on them and their employer. Rest assured, nothing will go unnoticed, so it's best to get ahead of the conversation and put coming changes in the right perspective.

Maintaining Morale during the Changeover

People are naturally resistant to change, which is why obtaining buy-in from all levels of personnel will be important to the success of the new system. The new technology can result in significant changes in processes, responsibilities, and controls, and it can result in much higher visibility of individual and group performance levels and activities. The high profile of the implementation of such a system demands a good communication plan. **Putting the new system into perspective is crucial to employee acceptance.**

Key Idea

The high profile of workforce management system implementations demands a good communication plan. Putting the new system into the proper perspective is crucial to employee acceptance.

Include a clear connection to corporate goals and an indication of strong executive support for the system. The goals should be to create positive acceptance of the new system and its benefits and to clearly communicate the reasons behind its implementation along with the new policies and processes that are part of it. This is the key to obtaining a good response to the changes.

If it's true that employees will be adversely affected by the new system in any way, do not ignore or attempt to sidestep this. A reduction in net pay won't be overlooked by employees. If an individual doesn't happen to notice, coworkers will be certain to clue that person in. Plan to communicate to managers, supervisors, and employees why these changes are necessary. There is a benefit to the change; share it or at least be honest about its implications.

In today's economy, employees are aware that it's a competitive market-place. Every day brings news of layoffs and plant closings, and unions and employee groups are accepting pay cuts or reduced benefits. Unhealthy companies currently are struggling to become financially viable. If, for example, reducing overtime expenses is a financial objective to make the company more profitable, explain to employees why that's a good thing. The fact is that it's better to have a job that offers less overtime than to have no job at all. If an automated scheduling system will improve staffing and result in higher customer satisfaction, connect the dots between happier customers, more revenue, and employee job security. Don't expect front-line management to articulate these issues. This should come directly from the top and be reinforced by everyone on down the line.

If your employees don't know how competitive your industry is, what kinds of concessions others have accepted, and where the future lies if changes aren't made, it's time to educate the workforce and to put the new technology into perspective.

Using Project Champions

As touched upon previously, the implementation of a time and attendance system is a highly visible activity. Managers and employees at all levels will be talking about the changes. Those leading the project should be engaged in the conversation and working to direct sentiment in favor of the initiative and new ways of doing business. This is why the communications plan also should include a cadre of Project Champions who are fully versed in the business rationale for the changes. They need to be kept up to date at all times on the progress of system implementation and should be the first to receive communications as they are distributed throughout the organization. A clear expectation should be that these individuals will represent the project in a positive light and work to minimize negative talk or grumbling among their team members. They are also a source of feedback to the project sponsors so that concerns from the workforce can be addressed effectively.

The communications plan should be bidirectional. Politicians have perfected the use of Project Champions, whom they call "front men," and arm them with talking points to carry the torch for the issue at hand. These are hand-picked individuals, so keep in mind that titles or positions in the organizational hierarchy are not the only factors to consider. Those chosen need to be the best individuals to carry the message and must understand the importance of supporting the party line.

Key Idea

Project Champions need to be credible and enthusiastic. They must be proactive.

They should not wait to hear negative rumblings; instead, at each opportunity they should take whatever the issue might be to the staff. Project Champions state the vision of the new system in terms employees can understand by relating it to issues and concerns people have on their minds.

Obviously, Project Champions need to consider the implications of project decisions and changes and should be able to anticipate how the workforce will react. Ideal Project Champions contribute by submitting their concerns and suggestions about the system. It's a job, and a job description with clear expectations should be created for these leaders. Knowing exactly what they will be expected to do and when and how they will do it will help them perform that job well.

Gauging Success and Attitudes

Finally, some mechanism should be in place for gauging the success of these project representatives. This might be done, for example, through spot checks of how the project is perceived in the field by speaking with individuals during various phases of the project implementation who are completely uninvolved in the project. Secretaries and administrative assistants can be good barometers of employee reaction if they are in positions to hear what's going on.

A WMT system can help to boost morale and help keep employees from jumping ship, or it can cause a lot of grumbling and a negative atmosphere if it isn't sold correctly during the implementation phase. It's important to realize that both the upside and the downside are in the hands of those who design, install, and announce the system. I suggest that goals be set to use the system to improve employee retention, if that's an issue. A strategy along with specific actions also ought to be identified and implemented to keep everyone in the loop and things on a positive note while the new system goes into effect.

Key Idea

Keep in mind that change is tough for most people. What makes it more difficult is not knowing what to expect—what's on the other side.

Plan for the communication effort to evolve as the system is rolled out and to incorporate positive feedback and success stories from those operational areas that are enjoying its benefits and rewards. If certain areas had difficulty, highlight how those difficulties have been overcome and how the team is planning on avoiding those for future groups that will come on board. Praise your project team, and let the field know how hard they are working to make this a good system for the organization.

Chapter Summary

- A clearly defined mission is essential to the success of any WMT system implementation. The mission must identify specific goals and measures of success.
- To achieve that vision of success and ensure a smooth roll-out, testing and communication are essential.
- There are several types of parallel testing strategies:
  - Full system comparison
  - Mock parallel
  - Reverse parallel
- Parallel surveys are an important tool. They should be designed to capture and measure information that will be acted upon.
- A time and labor management system implementation is the most highly visible project management will ever undertake. It will affect every person, every day. It will result in how much employees are paid and how much the company spends on labor and receives in productivity.
- Project Champions have an important role to play and should provide two-way feedback about the changes impacting the organization.

PART III

From Concept to Project

CHAPTER 10

The Need for a Business Case

Up to this point we've covered the evolution of time and labor systems into an effective business tool. Companies are using them to solve a host of problems and grow revenue. The biggest challenge may not be understanding how the systems work and what others have done. It may be convincing your own organization that the time has come for it to embrace this technology. This section is designed to:

- Help anyone serious about upgrading to a state-of-the-art system develop a business case to present to top management.
- Guide you in evaluating your business relative to the unique aspects of this technology.
- Explain what it will take to ensure that the system successfully delivers improvements to the organization and supports the business mission.

Now, let's get started.

The Value of Creating a Business Case

The business case seeks to answer several questions. Does a state-of-the-art Workforce Management Technology (WMT) system make sense for your company? Will the payback be there? Will it meet the business needs and fit the culture of your company? Will it live up to the salesman's promises? After all, if you pay for a powerful system but have to implement it in a way that doesn't employ all the technology purchased or if you cannot support the system, money will have been wasted.

Today's business environment places ongoing pressure on companies to improve efficiency, timeliness, and quality and to reduce operating expenses. Simultaneously, an organization may be struggling to meet the demands of investors and customers, to abide by government regulations, and to get the job done in an ever more challenging market. Companies are expected to make money (if they are for-profit) and live within their means (especially if they are nonprofit or in the public sector). And their means of doing so must be increasingly transparent. To address the challenges, executive and middle management must maintain, improve, and grow the business using carefully crafted strategies that ensure that the organization not only survives but prospers.

Given this backdrop, new initiatives must make good business sense. At a minimum, the cost of a project and the staff time commitment required must not jeopardize productivity or the volume of output needed to maintain the status quo. Funds for special projects are limited in most organizations. Many proposed undertakings have merit, but not every one can be supported. Ideally, the investment should deliver improvements in operations and help in the effort to reduce expenses.

Key Idea

A well-written business case can make or break a project.

When the facts and pertinent information are laid out in a compelling way, a company's executives will have a relatively easy time making an appropriate decision and justifying funding. Even so, proposals often are made without much documentation or rationale to support them. This can be a huge mistake. Managers are accountable for the decisions they make, particularly when a significant investment is involved. No wonder some proposals are rejected and others simply stall and eventually die on the vine.

Laying the Groundwork

Developing a successful business case is a process that requires those charged with it to wear many hats, including those of teacher, salesman, analyst, organizer, problem solver, champion, and, with luck and hard work, hero. The best approach I've found is to tackle the job as though you were selling to another business, not to the familiar people upstairs who ride the same elevator as you every day. Most successful salespeople do a good deal of homework before they even make a call. They know how important it is to thoroughly understand an organization and to identify where and how the product they have to sell might fit. Labor management technology can answer many issues concerning costs, staffing, productivity, risk, and revenue. To maximize the likelihood of making a sale, the problems recognized as those causing the most acute pain in an organization or the challenges representing the biggest opportunities must be identified. This is step one.

Step 1: Recognize the problems causing the most pain in an organization or the challenges representing the biggest opportunities.

Next is to articulate these problems relative to workforce management technology. Why? Because you want people nodding their heads. Perhaps the most crucial factor in gaining support for your business case is an audience that recognizes the problems you believe WMT can solve. When you make your case, it shouldn't be the first time the issues come to the attention of the audience. Imagine walking into the CFO's office and saying, "Mike, I've got a business case here that will solve our attendance problems" when Mike isn't aware of any significant attendance problems. You want your business case to stand out as the savior and solution in a cacophony of communications about the issue.

If an issue isn't already front and center, you might start out by having informal conversations about it and sharing with your manager what you know, along with possible solutions. Get him or her energized about the idea that your area may be able to deliver a solution. Your job is to familiarize and educate management about what they should know about the problem. If you do not have a routine meeting with higher-ups, ask for opportunities to present introductory information up the ladder. Managers at the top must understand the problem and how not addressing it could prevent them from reaching important goals. If management does not accept that a problem exists and if they don't understand the proposed solution, your proposal may languish forever in limbo or be rejected without comment.

Step 2: Articulate the problems or challenges relative to the workforce so that management accepts that the situation exists.

Don't limit your conversations to upper management. A dialog with all those affected by the project should start at the beginning of the process. This will help build a sense of being in the loop on something important among potential supporters. Be sure to conduct these chats as two-way conversations; their perspective may give valuable information you hadn't considered. You certainly don't want to overlook anything, or to make inaccurate assumptions.

Step 3: Talk and listen to people at all levels to gain perspective and supporters.

Where does the business case fit in the project investment life cycle? (See the following.)

Project Investment Life Cycle (PILC)

- Idea management
- Project request
- Feasibility study
- Business requirements
- **Business case with ROI**
- Funding approval
- Project charter
- Activity-based work breakdown structure development

The foregoing list shows the flow of a project from the inception of an idea to the beginning of the implementation of the project. Some ideas will never evolve past the concept phase. Others will be retired when a project request is rejected. Some of the early phases may be somewhat informal and involve very few individuals until something formal is approved, such as a go-ahead to develop a business case.

You may find the complexity of this process and its formality strange. Most organizations are familiar with system development life cycle (SDLC) for systems development. New regulatory guidelines and the need for accountability have caused organizations to formalize internal processes for the selection of projects, which now more than ever before need to be based on clearly defined corporate priorities and evaluated according to their appropriateness in this regard. This new process is known as the project investment life cycle (PILC); it is a methodology for the examination of issues to ensure that decision makers make well-grounded selections.

Step 4: Recognize that you are in a competition.

You might look at preparing a business case as you would putting together a résumé for a job because, in a sense, a business case is your project's résumé. The project is a candidate, a suitor vying for a role in the organization. Your project will be competing with other candidates for acceptance. Careful consideration needs to be given to how the project stacks up against other potential initiatives that upper management may be considering. Every project that comes along cannot be funded, and it would be foolhardy to spread people who will be doing the implementation too thinly.

The business case includes several informational areas:

- Executive summary
- Purpose
- Background
- Project officers
- Business requirements
  - Strategic
  - Operational
- Justifications
- Project goals and objectives
- Scope of project

- Manpower needs
- Costs and time frame
- Business risks
- Project risks
- Alternatives
- Economic assessment
  - Costs and cash flows
  - ROI (NPV/MIRR)
  - Funding source
- Recommendation

The business case includes numerous informational areas. These areas are summarized in the preceding list. A great deal is on the list. It needs to be done correctly, with all areas covered. What's unique about WMT systems is that the current systems and processes in place may not be well understood or appreciated. Some of these subject areas may be more difficult to develop than you might expect.

Step 5: Don't underestimate how difficult it may be to develop a business case.

Developing a Feasibility Study

Once you get the nod to proceed with your suggestion, the place to start is by examining what the company is experiencing today. The first step is to conduct a feasibility survey. Such a survey consists of high-level discussion about problems, opportunities, directives, and constraints related to a system—or lack of a system—in the organization. The survey helps an organization determine whether there truly is a business need and whether it is severe enough that a resolution is required. Having the results of the survey will also provide important information to be used in system planning and for development of specifications for the purchase of software and hardware to address the needs.

Step 6: Develop a Feasibility Study to understand the need and the solution. The Feasibility Study should focus on the real problems, not the symptoms.

The important thing about a feasibility study is that it screens out issues and problems that are not the result of a system or process. It begins to focus on the real problems rather than the symptoms of problems. The feasibility study should provide the first indication that a solution truly addresses the problem from a high level.

The survey reviews issues related to performance, information management, economics, controls, efficiencies, and services to the internal and external customers of that system. The study also identifies potential solutions and suggests approaches that may address the existing issues.

Conducting a System Study

Once a feasibility survey has been completed and proves there is a rationale for finding a better solution to a problem that exists, the next step is to do a detailed system study. This analysis involves a detailed examination of the current system and processes. Conducting a system study involves reviewing all of the materials, systems, processes, and personnel involved in the current situation. Legacy systems and manual processes are identified, described, and measured. Problems and opportunities are isolated through root-cause analyses, the process of which is discussed subsequently. The key is to focus on "what is" rather than spending time and energy at this point on potential solutions. This helps assure that solutions developed later are not Band-Aids placed on symptoms.

> **Step 7: Conduct a System Study to identify, describe, and measure the current systems and processes. The Study should focus on "what is" today.**

ASK THE RIGHT QUESTIONS   Some of the questions to ask and answer in your analysis are the following:

> "What systems and processes are in place, and how do they work today?"
> "Who is involved?"
> "What are the problems and shortcomings?"
> "What is the cause?"
> "Is anything else broken?"
> "What else should it be doing?"
> "What is the impact of this problem?"
> "Where is the company headed? What are some of the larger issues at play internally?"
> "What are the possible solutions?"
> "Can the organization support the solution?"

This process is similar to what's used in Six Sigma root-cause analysis. The question "Why?" is asked at least five times until the root cause of a problem is identified. You might think of it as peeling away the layers of an onion. For example, consider a capillary tube soldered to a bellows that leaks.

Why does it leak?
> *The welding does not seal properly.*

Why doesn't it seal properly?
> *There is a deposit of a material inside the capillary tube.*

Why is a deposit on the inside the capillary tube?
> *Washing the tube did not clean it.*

Why did washing not clean it?
> *The detergent used was not working effectively.*

Why did the detergent not work effectively?
> *The detergent formula was not effective on this particular type of deposit.*

This allows a solution that will truly solve the problem to be imposed: using a detergent that will work.

Producing the Analysis, Requirements, and RFP

The deliverables produced from the system study may include a summary analysis of the current systems; a recommendation for approach, explaining how the organization should plan to acquire a solution; and possibly a survey or questionnaire based on the findings to assist in the next phase of the development of the business case. The survey's outputs focus on "what is" and are not a detailed list of new requirements. The survey's purpose is to focus on the next steps needed to find the solution to the real problems.

Step 8: Produce a Summary Analysis: What did we find out and what comes next?

Once the system study is evaluated and the approach is confirmed, next comes a requirements analysis. The purpose of this step is to document all the features and functions that will be required of the new solution. These include

- Existing functionality that must be maintained
- Features that will address the problems identified in the system study
- New capabilities that will help the organization meet its strategic goals
- Attractive features that are not required and will not justify additional expense, but if offered as part of the package offer desirable capabilities

The requirements analysis has a functional focus. It is not the same as a technical specification used to design a system, detailing specific system components. At the functional level, the company understands what is needed but is not specifying how it will be accomplished. The different vendors will provide the detail on how their product delivers the most viable solutions. The requirements analysis prioritizes the needs and assists in evaluating costs against these needs. It helps the company evaluate where they get the most bang for the buck.

Step 9: Create a Requirements Analysis: the functional perspective on what is needed and what is a priority. Where is the most bang for the buck?

The outcome of the requirements analysis is the development of the request for proposal (RFP), or request for quote (RFQ). Either one of these documents can be delivered to vendors, who in turn submit their bids for consideration. The RFP/RFQ creates a framework that each vendor must use to present products and solutions. This will result in a consistent format of responses to the same set of requirements from different vendors, making it easier to compare "apples to apples." In the same way, you will drive the focus of the presentation. It gives prospective vendors the opportunity to highlight their most relevant features, showing the customer which offers the best fit when measured against your needs. Organizations that don't control the proposal process and don't precede it with an independent evaluation of their own requirements can be easily distracted by the bells and whistles of vendor demonstrations and proposals. The result may be that the vendor proposals become the "requirements," and a customer's choice will be diverted by features that may or may not end up delivering a cost-effective solution to an organization's actual problems and needs.

Step 10: Request for proposal: invitation to vendors to submit a bid.

The final phase is the decision analysis. This effort is intended to determine the best approach (e.g., purchase a new system or fix existing processes) and assess options (e.g., evaluate vendor proposals, study new processes, etc.) to address identified problems. This is where the culmination of all of the research, internal discussions, vendor demonstrations, and customer referrals, along with the cost and return on investment analyses, takes the form of a recommendation, which is a request for approval to make a selection of a vendor and a product to move the company forward.

Step 11: Decision analysis: agreement on the approach, options, and best chance for ROI taking the form of a request for approval on the selected vendor and products.

Developing the Business Case Document

The time is near to present the recommendations to the decision makers. The next step is to develop a document to support your proposal that contains all the information that management needs to approve the project. This will contain the detailed information gathered, analyzed, and organized, showing an awareness of the benefits, impacts, risks, assumptions, and financial costs. In doing so, it will demonstrate how the solution is in sync with the organization's mission.

The purpose of this document is to define what is being proposed to support and improve the business in a way that will make a compelling argument for approval of the proposal. This document, the business case, can be considered a contract with the organization that will provide direction and parameters for implementation of the system.

Step 12: Assemble the business case document, which becomes the rationale and guide for the project.

Why This Process Makes Sense

The process just described, beginning several sections back, may be somewhat foreign to you or it may not fit the approach that is commonly taken at your organization. It may seem very formal and involved. There are a number of steps to be taken, many documents to prepare, people to involve, and a good deal of critical thinking to be done. But don't let that deter you. If this is a new concept, here are some reasons to consider introducing it to your organization:

- An approach designed around thorough discovery and analysis ensures that real problems are identified and decisions are in line with corporate objectives.
- The approach addresses concerns surrounding accountability and protects decision-makers from taking on inappropriate, risky projects.
- The detail required will cover all the bases, allowing indecision due to a lack of information or the absence of proper assessment of alternatives to be avoided.
- A document-driven approach provides a history of all the analysis, and it binds participants to the decisions, ensuring continuity and consensus.

- A professional-looking presentation will enhance credibility and show decision makers what they can expect when the project reaches execution.
- By following this approach, you may introduce a methodology that will take hold in your organization and elevate the manner in which such projects are considered.
- You are competing against other initiatives and demands for corporate resources and manpower, and you want to win. A thoughtful and thorough approach such as this has the potential to reflect well on you.

Business Case Development Is a Team Effort

A good business case is generally the result of a team effort. At the outset of a study we like to get all the stakeholders and prospective team members together in a room and introduce them to the project. This might include IT, Payroll, Accounting, and Operations. What we don't want are conflicting agendas in the various corporate fiefdoms. It's important for everyone to be on the same page and in agreement about where we are headed and where we want to arrive. We will examine the reason or reasons a hard look is being taken at this new technology and raise the question, What does each area want to get out of the effort?

This meeting is an opportunity to bring everyone into consensus in order to avoid conflicts down the road. If things go as they should, we will come out of it with everyone in agreement about the issues and their approximate order of priority. It's also important to identify who is going to lead the project and what the overriding goal is.

We try to anticipate objections some might raise about a new system and to answer as many of these as possible before they become obstacles. What we're doing falls into the area of change management and managing perceptions. After all, things will be different once the new system goes in.

Since there will always be those who are resistant to change, it doesn't hurt to do a little proactive public relations. In fact, once we are further along and have a clear picture of what the new system will entail, we will develop a full-blown communications plan and identify champions whose job it will be to communicate to others about the new system. More was said on this in Chapter 9.

For instance, people should know that the new system will bring consistency, that everyone will be treated fairly and consistently. The new system will also introduce more efficient and accurate processes. People will have more information available to them, and this will be available in real time. They won't have to wait to get answers, because they will be able to access certain data themselves. They'll be able to make better decisions and work smarter.

Team Roles and Responsibilities

The group of individuals who will work on the business case should include the project sponsor, the eventual business owner of the new system, the project manager, and the product manager. The sponsor needs to be a high-level, primary stakeholder who is most concerned with the eventual outcomes of the project and the systems to be implemented. The sponsor may be someone in a position to expect the greatest benefit from the improvements. As such, he or she should provide direction and set priorities throughout the development of the proposal and ultimately the project. The sponsor should also be expected to allocate the needed resources and ensure that the project receives ample support throughout the organization. The sponsor may be less involved on a day-to-day basis but must be available when needed to resolve conflicts and to ensure that the project succeeds.

The business owner is the individual who will lead the area that will eventually take ownership of the new system and will be responsible for its care and feeding. For a WMT system, the business owner is often the Payroll Manager or the HRIS Director. The business owner is frequently responsible for the current system and processes and is integral to understanding how the change to the new system must occur.

The project manager owns the task of leading the project from inception to completion. Once the business case has been approved, the project manager will shepherd the project from the conceptual stage through design, testing, and training to delivery. He or she will use the business case in the development of the charter, scope, and schedule of the project, and will rely on its contents to provide the vision of what is to be accomplished.

Key Idea

If the system mission is to be achieved after implementation, there cannot be a power struggle between the project sponsor and project manager. Although the project manager is accountable for the project goals (e.g., project budget, schedule, and cost) these should not take priority over the system goals (e.g., financial, strategic, and operational objectives) for which the project sponsor is accountable. A project manager with too much control will put the long-term success of the system at risk.

Finally, the product manager should play a role in the development of the business case, taking the lead in addressing issues that pertain specifically to the vendor and the system or systems to be purchased. This individual is most likely to be in tune with how the proposed solutions will fit within the existing infrastructure and will be aware of prerequisites that must be in place before change can occur.

The leaders who form this core group need to control the development of the business case and, on its approval, lead the project. They are the primary decision makers, but they do not constitute the entire task force. They represent their respective areas and serve as conduits between the business units and the other team members for the concerns and issues that may surround the proposal. Having them develop the business case and be in charge of the project will help ensure continuity, so that the original vision for the new system will be maintained. This will also involve the eventual owners, users, and caretakers of the system early in the selection and design process, thus avoiding the potential of a disconnect between those who "buy" the system and those who must "live with" the system. You might think of it as buying a house. Would it make sense to have your brother and your sister-in-law select a house for you to live in?

Casting: Involving All the Right Players

The document impacts several functional areas of an organization, some at a fairly sophisticated level. The project initiator may hail from Payroll or HR, but the gathering of information will likely involve Operations, Finance, and Information Systems (IS) among others. If those on the business case development team neither know nor have access to the information needed from their area, they must get the right people involved. This may mean bringing on an outside consultant who has the experience and technical skills to assemble the information and conduct the analysis. Mike King, who has written a book on this topic (*Project Investment Life Cycle*, Boston Publications), explains that it's a common mistake for organizations to "dumb down" the information being presented. He believes it is the responsibility of executive managers and the proposal team to educate themselves about the complexities in order to ensure the survival and prosperity of the organization.

An inclination to simplify the business case may stem from a fear that the document itself will be too overwhelming, too intimidating to complete, or too difficult to understand, or that delving deeply into the data and an analysis of it will take too much time. This may come from a concern that a great deal of detail will overcomplicate the project and makes mountains out of molehills. In some cases this may be true. What's important, however, is not to gloss over disturbing details or to brush past difficult questions. If you can't answer the tough ones now and don't invest the time to assess the impact of disturbing trends, do you really have what's needed to justify and undertake the project?

Key Idea

If you can't answer the tough questions now and don't invest the time to assess the impact of disturbing trends, do you really have what's needed to justify and undertake the project?

The purpose of the business case is to define the problem, recommend and justify a solution, and assess the potential impact of all the possible alternatives, including the option of doing nothing. The business case will answer "How much?" "Who?" "When?" and "With what result?" for each scenario. A team representing a cross-section of business areas and expertise can ensure the best answers to these questions.

Internal vs. External Subject Matter Experts

It will probably make sense to involve an expert from outside the organization. Time is one of the benefits of this. Internal resource personnel already have full-time jobs. Not only will adding the development of a business case to their plate tax them, it's likely to slow things down or prevent important tasks from getting adequate attention. Moreover, internal resources may lack expertise in important areas. Getting up to speed will take even more time and effort. Outside consultants, on the other hand, can be fully dedicated to the project. Their time will be efficiently spent because they will not be distracted by day-to-day business issues. They bring experience, knowledge, and training on the technology that can greatly accelerate the process. They will be in position to understand which issues are most critical, to quickly see potential opportunities, and to understand timetables and client expectations. They can compare what they know from prior projects to the information gathered in yours to readily spot omissions as well as gauge how reasonable the data appears. This is really important.

Key Idea

There's almost no doubt an external subject matter expert will make the process happen faster, with fewer hiccups, and the end result will likely be more thorough.

An important differentiator between internal and external subject matter experts lies in the area of expertise. An internal resource will likely be an expert when it comes to the business. He or she knows who to go to and how things work. He can maneuver effectively within the organization, garner cooperation, and encourage collaboration and openness. It is quite likely, however, he will lack technical expertise on WMT systems. After all, the technology is still new and rapidly developing. Vendors update their systems frequently, expanding capabilities and revising the underlying setup. If the company is in the investigative stage, it's likely the internal resource hasn't had his hands on it yet, unless he's a new hire from somewhere else that has a state-of-the-art system. However, by the time the new system is installed, that system may be a version or two behind.

A good external consultant can anticipate and project how business requirements can be satisfied by the technology. Based on experience, he or she should be able to uncover requirements or glitches that may create critical issues or significant obstacles. The term "best practices" is somewhat overused in today's business conversations. Nevertheless, we all know how valuable going straight to a best practice is, as opposed to stumbling through a rugged learning curve. Experienced consultants advise their partners on appropriate strategies and direct the course of the discovery process in developing the business case. Knowing the destination helps them lay out the best course to get there.

The management within some companies often assumes these projects will not require outside assistance. This may stem in part from a lack of understanding both of the technology and of the tremendous change that's about to occur. In the past, management may not have paid much attention to managing labor expenses or to what, for example, goes into getting payroll done. It just seems to happen week in and week out, fostering a misconception that a time and attendance project will fall into the same category. What it comes down to is that management doesn't know what they don't know. Not until an implementation has stalled or targets have been missed will they begin to see that the internal resources tasked with the conversion would have benefited from the experience and expertise of outside help.

Key Idea

An internal, do-it-yourself approach breeds an informal attitude that may result in a decision not to go to the trouble of developing a formal business case and request for approval.

There's something else. An internal, do-it-yourself approach breeds an informal attitude that may result in a decision not to go to the trouble of developing a formal business case and request for approval. One result of this we've seen has been that many initiators have had difficulty in getting projects off the ground. The project simply goes nowhere. The best advice is not to give in to the temptation to take the "easy way." Assemble a formal, well-represented proposal team and put forth the effort to develop a document.

Taking the Project to a Higher Level

An external consultant can provide the critical expertise and perspective necessary to build a business case that accurately connects the system to the high-level benefits executive-level decision makers care about. Such a consultant's participation can increase the credibility of assertions made in a business case, particularly when the consultant has an extensive and impressive background with the technology.

One of the current trends in the IT market is for companies to treat every IT-related project the same. More and more companies have a tendency to undertake these projects in-house. In line with this is the trend to extend "in-house" to include engaging resources only through Tier 1 or partner IT resource outfits. These organizations act as temp agencies and generally provide resources for networking, data center, specific programming needs, and off-hours (overnight and weekend) support as well as temporary technical support. Such technical resource needs are well suited to this business model, and IT sourcing firms have rosters of qualified personnel to fill these needs. But you might also say that such resources are a basic commodity. By definition an individual must have a specific skill set and be able to perform a closely defined set of tasks. Typically, such individuals are assigned to the same job over and over at different customer locations.

On the other hand, workforce management technology subject matter experts are far from "commodity" resources. No two WMT projects will ever be the same because the needs of every business, as well the strategic goals of most organizations, are certain to be different. These resources must be functional experts and have a broad range of skills and industry experience.

Key Idea

Tier I suppliers of outsourced IT resources are not the best way to find qualified WMT specialists unless they have a permanent WMT partner. While the IT headhunter model works well for "commodity" type roles such as network engineer and help desk resources, they do not supply the best WMT specialists. General IT resource suppliers are often ill-equipped to properly vet WMT experts on their own and may provide a consultant who is inexperienced and not supported.

Every day I see advertisements from IT headhunters looking for application-specific resources as though having "Product A" on one's résumé automatically qualifies an individual for a job in workforce management technology. But that is not the case. In today's business environment, where embellishment is king and former employers will provide little more than name, job title, and employment dates for fear of the legal implications of a negative referral, employers who seek resources in this manner are going to get what they pay for and probably less.

It is not uncommon to get a call from an IT resource supplier that has no idea whether the person he is talking to is qualified or not. I've literally talked to recruiters who say, "You tell *me* what skills you need to do this job" or "I have no idea if what you're telling me is correct, but I'll pass it along to the customer." Firms that engage these resource suppliers would do better to put the commission they earn into more qualified resources via a reputable WMT organization.

Another problem with assembling a WMT team via a generic IT resource supplier is that the resources are likely to be very protective of their expertise and less willing to collaborate with unfamiliar consultants who are essentially their competition. Engaging resources from a firm that specializes in WMT deployments means you get a "team within a team" and your project won't be hindered by insecurity, competition, or lack of expertise.

An important role an external consultant plays is that of translator. As with any highly specialized area, a special language is spoken that must be understood, articulated clearly, and translated for those who are not experts in the field but need to understand the ins and outs and implications. A professional consultant can help the organization learn this new language and introduce participants and decision makers to the new inventory of systems and tools. Because a successful business case will be the foundation for the next steps in the project, having such things accurately depicted ensures that there will be a match between the company's needs and the selected systems.

Key Idea

An important role an external consultant plays is that of translator.

External consultants who operate as part of a firm that specializes in workforce management systems are even better additions to the team than independent (sole operator) consultants. **Engaging resources who work with a group of WMT specialists will provide continuity to the project as it progresses.** Looking at the need for outside resources as an end-to-end solution will translate into ensuring that the project history is well understood and the objectives that are identified at inception carry through to the roll-out. Changing teams or injecting unrelated "newbies" into the project midstream means more ramp-up time, the potential for oversights, and the possible redirection of crucial system plans. Engaging a team makes the resources more vested in the project outcomes, ensures coverage during absences or vacations, and provides an added component of collaboration. Consultants who know they are there for the life of the project and understand they will be handing off specialized tasks to their team members take care to keep the project team on course and to impart project knowledge, because they are obligated to pass it along to their cohorts. Unlike what may be the case with internal project managers, they have few competing distractions and priorities. Their mission is to implement according to The Plan, and they are more mindful of issues, bottlenecks, and the customer's expectations. Given the pace of growth and change in WMT, it is virtually impossible to know it all. Therefore, a good consultant networks with other experts in the field and mentors his team. The job requires having or finding the answers and solving problems. If a good consultant doesn't know an answer, he will know someone who does. It makes sense to take advantage of this.

Key Idea

Engage resources who are WMT specialists and part of a team of WMT experts to provide continuity to the project as it progresses. No one consultant knows everything there is to know about WMT systems.

Speaking the Same Language Is Critical

I have been involved in projects for which the external consultant wasn't called in until after the vendor and product had been selected. In more than one instance, the customer and vendor had not communicated effectively on needs and functionality. Apples and oranges had been discussed, misunderstood, and misconstrued. But neither party recognized the disconnect until I started looking at the designs and the system that had been purchased.

Here's an example. One of my customers that handled the early phases of a WMT project in-house wanted labor-level validation. This means the general ledger (GL) account hierarchy needed to be enforced within the time and attendance system. In plain English that means an employee working as an RN should not be able to punch in as working in the housekeeping department. RNs are in nursing areas—always, no exceptions. This requirement, although poorly worded, was in the request for proposal (RFP).

The vendor sales team responded that their product would "validate labor levels." So, "we need labor-level validation" was responded to with "we offer labor-level validation," except this wasn't exactly true, at least not in the way the customer expected. The system would indeed "validate" the labor-level entry. If "1234—Housekeeping" wasn't a valid labor-level entry, it would be disallowed. But the system did not check to verify that a job (RN) and a department (housekeeping) were not a match. That's what the customer had meant by "validate the labor level." The result was that a product was purchased that didn't meet the business need. Ouch! What was the cost of living with that going to be? In 1607, a man named Edward Topsell referred to the reason this happened as being "penny wise and pound foolish." The company saved on consulting expenses in the early phases of the project, but those "savings" were quickly consumed.

Key Idea

Saving on consulting costs early in the process can ultimately cost much more in lost project and system savings.

When this discrepancy was identified, the relationship with this vendor was off to a shaky start. In addition, the absence of this feature may have been a valuable leverage point in negotiations with the vendor. It's what you don't know that can hurt you. Experienced consultants can ensure good communication with vendors on technical issues.

The message is, don't wait to bring in an expert consultant, and don't look for WMT experts through your partner IT outsourcing agent. They simply don't know what to look for or how to qualify candidates. Understanding the technology requires extensive training, hands-on experience, and a background in the business areas where these systems are used. If the IT outsource recruiter doesn't know the technology, how can he know what to ask or what is really required? Building a business case for a sophisticated business tool such as workforce management technology takes much more than understanding how to install a product. Leading a WMT project involves more than a technician setting up the system. Making a positive contribution to a business case and leading a complex project to deliver innovative business processes requires skills and knowledge that can come only from having previously been a key player in similar projects.

Expanding Your Vision and Finding the Right Angle

When you think of building a business case as a process, part of this is to put yourself in the position of your audience. Obviously, you get it and know why a WMT system makes sense for your organization. But your reasons for pursuing the acquisition of this technology may not be the same reasons that will sell the managers who will ultimately make the decision. Executive managers are held accountable not only for individual departments, decisions and project choices but for the overall success and profitability of the organization. They are hearing not only from you about problems, fixes, and budgets; they are also receiving competing requests for funding and resources from the entire organization. They are responsible for choosing projects that support the mission and objectives that have been laid out for the future.

Erin Govednik of Cox Communications in Atlanta participated in a panel discussion called "Workforce Management System Implementation Best Practices" in the fall of 2006. She said she'd been involved in the preparation and presentation of proposals to invest in a new WMT system for several years without success. The first unsuccessful business cases focused primarily on the need for the system from an IT, Finance, and HRIS perspective and did not cover all the potential benefits. Later, a business case was developed that explained the overall impact the system could be expected to have on the organization. This time, the proposal was accepted. Executive management bought into the wider benefits. The moral is that a business case that focuses on benefits too far down in an organization may not be able to beat out other funding requests. A winning business case will present benefits that high-level decision makers can easily understand and relate to.

What Are Executive-Level Concerns?

Nowadays, executive management is also probably worried about complying with Sarbanes-Oxley regulations and an increased level of scrutiny from corporate boards and investors. Top executives know they can be held accountable for their decisions. A business case should be designed to address these concerns and to provide detailed information.

Key Idea

A well-written case will demonstrate how the initiative will transform the organization and contribute to meeting strategic, operational, and financial objectives.

It also may help to understand that managers in the position of making decisions about strategic, company-wide initiatives make this kind of decision differently than they do those affecting operations. Operational issues are generally decided based on prior decisions, trends, and known factors having to do with maintenance, growth, and regulation. Rather than starting with a blank page, such tactical decisions often may be based primarily on a selection from a limited set of alternatives. **Conversely, a business case must compel leadership to forge into new territory.** Without a strong and thorough case having been made, the path of least resistance may be to make no decision at all, which is the same as deciding against the project.

A Good Business Case Is Both a Map and a Contract

So how is a strong case made? On any journey, it's important to know where you are before starting out. This is why a good business case will begin with an examination of where the organization is today, a place it presumably does not want to remain in. It will then provide a map to a destination that is clearly more desirable.

The map will show the way, of course, but it might also be viewed as an agreement or contract. It will outline the project and the new system for all parties and serve as a written consensus among those who support or approve the project and those who will carry it out. It can be considered a formal, auditable document focusing on ramifications of and recommending solutions to specific problems or needs.

The term "auditable" represents a new concept for many. We say it is auditable, because once it is approved the document becomes a contractual agreement that can and most likely will be reviewed and tracked to ensure that the called-for resources were made available and the corresponding results were delivered.

The business case defines scope and expectations and assures future accountability. Top managers almost always must answer to boards of directors, investors, and regulators. Such a document provides a certain amount of cover to whoever approves it, thus increasing the likelihood he or she will sign off on the request. For stakeholders it ensures continuity, because it binds current and future project leaders and participants to expectations that have been set down on paper and agreed on. In large organizations in particular, turnover is likely to happen. The approved business case prevents new team members from attempting to redirect the project in midstream.

What are some other reasons proposals fail to achieve their goal? Why are they unable to gain the support needed to move forward? It probably won't surprise anyone to read that internal politics may play a role. Players with their own personal motivations may repress or spin information and attempt to influence decisions in the direction they want things to go. Regulatory issues can also thwart an otherwise sound effort. It's important to anticipate these potential obstacles and address them early on. Often they can be mitigated during the effort made to create awareness of the "problem" the proposal is designed to solve. A good salesman knows that it makes sense to raise potential objections before someone else does and to shoot them down early.

Be Thorough—Don't Be Set Aside

A number of other factors can sidetrack a proposal. For example, if not enough information is given, decision makers may be left with unanswered questions and set the proposal aside. They may also have concerns about failed or underperforming projects in the past that were not delivered as promised. Those issues might have been overcome, but they may still need to be addressed. Indeed, as many issues as possible should be anticipated and dealt with when building a case.

Going through the process you will either demonstrate the merit of an undertaking and debunk its naysayers or demonstrate for yourself and others that, although the project may appear sound on the surface, the timing, required funding, and resources or the questioned likelihood of a desired outcome makes it inadvisable to undertake under present conditions. Although as an initiator you may feel you've failed, the process of building a business case will actually have saved the organization the time and trouble of pursuing what would likely have turned out to be an ill-timed investment.

Chapter Summary

- A business case is a tool that can help gain executive-level support and financial backing for a WMT investment.
- Developing a business case involves a number of studies and deep analysis. Some of the primary studies include a feasibility study, a system study, and a summary analysis.
- The business case is designed to address the concerns of the C-Level decision maker and put the benefits in a context about which leadership cares. The business case elevates the need for the system beyond a single department or group of employees and links it directly to the strategic, operational, and financial goals of the organization.
- The business case becomes a contract for the project team, an agreed-on agenda and mission for the new system with clearly

defined expectations and measures of success. It should provide a good road map for the project and a basis for the RFP.

- Developing a business case is a team effort. The process is involved and technical. Involving the right internal and external participants is vital.
- Tier I suppliers of outsourced IT resources are not the best way to find qualified WMT specialists unless they have a permanent WMT partner.
- Engage resources who are WMT specialists and part of a team of WMT experts to provide continuity to the project as it progresses. If you need more than one WMT expert, hire a "team within a team" rather than consultants who see each other as competitors.
- If you can answer the hard questions about the need for a new system and the challenges it is likely to face, you are ready to make your request and a good fit is ensured.

CHAPTER 11

What to Look for and Consider

Through all of the phases of getting from need awareness and concept to project, it's vitally important to spend time and energy up front thinking through the processes and systems the company now has in place. Should they be replaced, and, if so, what should replace them? In doing so, you should also consider how a new system will best be implemented. A great deal of time, energy, and money can be saved during the implementation stage and into production if a thorough job of analyzing and planning has been done.

Workforce management technology is unique. It's a conglomeration of functional and technical information and concerns. It involves old, familiar data and new possibilities for value-added data. It depends on inputs from people, external databases, and internal calculators and gauges. It is constricted by policy, contract, regulation, expectations, people, and infrastructure. It will make changes necessary in other systems, processes, and behaviors in order to deliver its powerful improvements to the operations side of the business. It is expensive, but it can deliver significant return on investment if deployed appropriately.

In this chapter we will explain where to focus your attention when planning for a new time and labor management system as well as the importance of key features. We'll also take a close look at questions to ask within the organization to fully understand the system requirements. Integration, standardization, and security will be discussed along with a brief look at portal technology. Finally we touch on hosted solutions as an alternative to outright system ownership.

Focus on Benefits and Consider the Alternatives

Envisioning what can be and communicating it effectively to decision makers is the key to obtaining approval and getting it done. The content of the business case should not be too technical in nature. It should describe technical system needs, but it is best to keep the discussion focused on what the proposal will do for the business, rather than how it will work technically. People respond positively to benefits, so focus on benefits.

For example, management will want to know how the system will allow them to implement strategies and tactics and how it will facilitate decision making. The system will do so because it will assemble and present information in a way that allows meaningful comparisons to be made that point to logical conclusions, decisions, and actions. It will solve problems that are encountered today and actually eliminate some of the decision making that resulted from those problems. It will help in other ways as well. Just how this will be accomplished is covered in the following chapter.

Executive management will expect those involved in preparing the business case to be proactive and to investigate the details. As many questions as possible should be anticipated and answered. Every reasonable viewpoint and perspective should be examined. In addition to information being well organized and logically presented, the business case should also demonstrate knowledge, capabilities, and management skills that will lessen the risk of failure and strengthen the likelihood that the project will be a success. In other words, who will do the work, and what are their qualifications?

It's also important that the case be honestly presented, regardless of whether every fact supports the author's personal objectives. Putting forth information that does not entirely support the proposal builds credibility. Most executives simply aren't going to believe a case that has no downsides. Of course, the positives must outweigh the negatives, or the project cannot be justified.

Looking at alternative directions is also important. Often, one of the biggest roadblocks to project approvals is the question, Is there something else out there that may work better? If you've identified all of the possible alternatives and show that what you are recommending is the best approach, the question will not be asked.

There is also a great deal the audience won't know and will not expect to be included, but it's your job to make certain it is included. A collaboration of internal and external subject matter experts ought to ensure this. Let's turn now to some common things to be on the lookout for in your survey and analysis.

Look Out for Hidden Practices

WMT systems are likely to impact the policies and processes now used to pay people. Workers at every level care a great deal about what they are paid. A number of factors, including the complexity, lack of standardization, and amount of individual discretion, found in many existing pay systems often aren't fully appreciated. Policies to do with payment for certain work activities may not be documented. What is down in writing may not be what's actually done in practice.

How can this be? Much of what goes on may not be visible except to a particular employee and his supervisor. It's simply buried in payroll totals. Don't be surprised to find that supervisors are putting a significant amount of creativity to work in the name of "getting the job done" when it comes to paying certain employees.

Key Idea

Hidden practices are often well entrenched, and when this is the case, they become ingrained in the psyche of managers and employees. As such, understandings are formed and held concerning what constitutes fair compensation for the jobs in question. In some cases, a practice that's been in place for a while can actually become an entitlement for employees. After a time, the company may be obligated to continue the practice in spite of its inconsistency with company policy or even union contracts. Uncovering these situations and properly handling their conversion will be an important part of the project.

The business case may not identify all of these outliers, but it should point out that a new system is not simply a "plug and play" installation or a zero-impact upgrade. If a new system cannot accommodate all of today's needs, including maintaining employee morale or getting the work done, it might not be practical to implement, given a particular business climate.

Transitioning to Electronic Approvals

Approval processes also need to be reviewed as part of the analysis. WMT systems almost always automate something that has been manual, ad hoc, or off the radar. These items didn't reach certain levels of management or the Payroll area until someone gave them the go-ahead—someone other than the employee herself. What needs to be approved, when, and by whom? Are the appropriate levels of management approving reported activity that will ultimately end up in someone's being paid? Appropriate oversight is a must.

Transitioning paper approval processes to system processes can be challenging. Paper travels a physical path and becomes inaccessible to parties once it is passed on. A stack of time sheets can be sorted, subdivided, copied, and stapled to other documents. It can contain information that is unrelated to time collection. It allows for ad hoc entries, what I call the "text messages" of yesteryear, such as workers' handwritten notes in the margins. It can be modified by the owners; columns can be used for other purposes such as adding data or information.

Key Idea

All sorts of alterations may be used in the approval process. Ways need to be provided for this when the process becomes electronic.

Streamlining Approvals

WMT can eliminate steps. A new system can make it virtually impossible for invalid data to be entered into the system, and this will eliminate the need for some forms of verification and approval. For example, when a company moves from paper time cards to data entry by telephone, automated number identification (ANI) can be used to determine the location of the telephone an employee is using. No further validation is needed that he or she was indeed onsite, because the system can be set to prevent an employee from punching in or out if he calls in from a phone other than the one designated.

The same system can also eliminate the need for an employee who moves around from one location to another to give this information when she calls in. The system will automatically know and record it, thus streamlining the process.

There are countless ways to automate the approval and qualification processes. If employee activity can be reported and it needs to be approved, that's important to know.

Where Should the Different Types of Data Reside?

The next thing to look at is the types of labor activity. In connection with this, it's important to evaluate all of an organization's pay practices. This involves poring over HR and Payroll policy manuals and documents. Sample time cards need to be studied. The general ledger account and a paycheck register should be examined to determine and understand what defines the activity that's being reported. And it doesn't stop there. All sorts of inquiries need to be made into what employees do and how it's reported.

Activities as they relate to billing and customers should be considered as well as the types of regulations and industry standards an employer is subject to. The demographics of employees and how the physical layout of the facility plays into operations should be taken into account. Who does what, where, and when and who needs to know all need to be mapped and organized into groupings, lines of business, and the hierarchal structure.

It's important to know what sort of information technology infrastructure already exists at a company, as this will determine the software options. Is it SQL, Windows-based, or on a mainframe such as an IBM?

In our discussions with clients about enhancement possibilities, we try to determine what sort of activity-based information might be helpful. For example, would the client like to track piece-rate or specific client activity? Is there value in tracking projects for work orders? What about activity tied to premium or bonus pay? Does the company care what piece of equipment the employee is using? This starts a dialog, and through these discussions we are able to communicate what the various products on the marketplace have to offer. This will often generate ideas about the possibilities, and we use the resulting feedback to determine what's important and what isn't. This is critical information to have when the time comes to make a selection between vendors. A good consultant will make sure few gaps exist between what his or her client wants and needs on the business end and what a particular vendor has to offer.

In the following chapter we will cover how a mission-based system is developed. In our discussions, we try to make it clear that such a system will deliver payroll data, but it can also focus on the activity, projects, demographics, or clients—in other words, anything that management wants to track. Once we determine what kind of data will be valuable, we assess whether it can actually be captured. The activity has to be measurable, have a defined beginning and end, and as such be consistent in how it is characterized.

- Is it a unique activity?
- Is it something that's repeated across the organization?
- Does it make sense to ask people to segment their time? Is there a specific start time and stop time for the activity? Or is the activity interspersed with others? Concurrent activities can be tracked, but not all the software available does this.
- Does someone wear several hats? Does the activity need to be charged to more than one business unit?

Data: Ask Who, What, Where, and When?

Who: Time and effort need to be spent determining where data will come from and when. **Who (or what) is reporting information into the system?** It can come from employees themselves. It can come from a separate scheduling system or another piece of technology such as work orders when entered in an ERP system. It might come from homegrown in-house systems. It could come from templates or from projected historical data.

What: If the data is to come from employees, it's important to know whether having them provide this information will impede their work. In other words, if they have to stop what they are doing and punch in every hour, the question must be raised, is that really a productive use of their time? **What does the employer need to know? Is it worth the effort?** Will what's gained be outweighed by the loss in productivity? Is there a way to soften the impact and still get the data in time?

Where: Workers can report certain types of activity when they check out at the end of a shift. This saves having to make a number of calls or trips to a data collection device during the day as they move from one activity to another. In other situations, time is more critical and employees are required to report activity throughout the day. **Where is the best place to report information?** Some customers use bar-code readers to track quantities throughout the shift from workers in production environments located right in their work area. The phone or a computer is often the easiest collection device to get to because they seem to be everywhere. Finally, there are some remote workers who cannot get to any stationary device during their workday; for these employees, remote connection devices such as PDAs, cell phones, or laptops with wireless Internet are the best solution so that data can be collected from wherever the employee is located.

When: Let's face it, we all live by the clock, at least those of us who are still working and haven't yet retired to a tropical island. We schedule our lives on the hour. Labor activity reporting can be like this, too. Everyone will be coming to work at the top or bottom of the hour. The collection of data is condensed into wedges of time, like pizza slices, near the 12 and the 6 on the clock face. **When are the peak times of activity?** Something to consider is whether stepped-up pressure will clog or bring down the system because a large number of workers will be inputting data at the same time. Let's say there are 2,500 employees in a company and they will each make four punches on average during the day. That adds up to a lot of traffic condensed into a short period of time. For a detailed discussion of the implications, see the "Scalability" section of Chapter Ten.

Those designing the infrastructure for telephony-based WMT data collection must be diligent in sizing the system to handle the call volume correctly. Erlang B calculations are used by call centers to calculate the hardware required to handle various amounts of anticipated call volume on a phone system. It's important to understand what the expected call volume will be and apply these mathematical formulas to an organization's metrics in order to design an adequate system. It's essential to consult with someone who has worked specifically with WMT technology and can share knowledge of expected call patterns and durations, hang time, busy signals, line management, and so forth.

Other data collection devices (e.g., time clocks and computers) have their own volume and location issues as well. The logistics, capacity, and speed of these systems, based on user traffic, also must be carefully evaluated when purchasing and laying out a new system. For time clocks, for example, a standard ratio in a hospital is 1:100—one clock for every 100 employees. But the ratio chosen will depend on the location of the clocks, staff scheduling, and what employees will do at the clock and when.

Caution: Labor-Level Architecture Drives More than Reports

Labor levels are loosely associated with general ledger accounts. They are used to assign labor activity and costs to cost centers—the business units that employ the labor and are responsible for the expense. In a payroll register, labor costs are charged to departments, divisions, regions, and so forth. Time and attendance systems allow the same structure to be built, but this can be broadened or broken down in different ways to capture more meaningful data. For example, management may want to assemble information that relates to a physical location that has nothing to do with the general ledger. An example might be the different wings or floors of a medical or retail complex, or a production line in an assembly plant that represents different teams or disciplines or lines of business. The different ways to break out data should be based on how employees are being expensed and managed.

Key Idea

Defining groups and locations is important, because labor levels drive such things as security and access, who will see what data, and how it will be sorted and rolled up into summaries and reports. A good labor-level design facilitates easy assignment of features within the system and exporting of information when the values accurately reflect usable groupings of employees and managers.

Organization Maps Are Powerful and Intricate

Some WMT systems have a parallel hierarchy setup commonly known as organizational mapping. These structures within the system provide the customer with two different hierarchies for two distinct purposes. The labor-level structure generally handles the expense function. The organizational map (org map) charts where people are assigned, physically. These org mappings may not line up with the general ledger. They represent how teams are structured. Org maps allow for work to be assigned in the system in the same way this occurs in the real world. Scheduling may not be built around general ledger accounts. Org maps also facilitate creating schedule templates that show job slots that need to be filled, or populated, by the assignment of a worker to a position or task.

Organizational maps are often very informal and undocumented. They can vary in structure, with one area having multiple levels and another area very few. As such, they can be disjointed and fluid, changing to accommodate business needs, and this may make them difficult to capture. The recent introduction of org maps into the technology has significantly advanced the ability to accommodate existing business practices. The ability to configure around the interplay of labor levels and org maps has allowed expense processes to "play well" with scheduling processes for the first time. This allows companies with even the most complex scheduling processes to feed the time and attendance system with the background logic needed to compare and report on worker activity, bringing dry payroll data to life and giving it value. [Bob just punched in an hour early at the wrong location, and Kathy was required to log into her secondary job when she transferred to a different department.] Schedules can now supply important real-time information. [Nobody showed up to work the front desk, and there aren't enough workers on the line to maintain production levels.] A state-of-the-art system that uses organizational maps links what managers need to know with what is being reported—now!

Defining Pay Codes

Pay codes, earnings codes, or wage types are the buckets that time goes into in order to calculate pay, report activity, or create flags. These need to be identified, standardized, and defined for the new system. This includes productive and nonproductive time, benefit time (PTO, vacation, sick, leave, jury duty, etc.) and even expenses (e.g., mileage) or units (e.g., piece rate info).

Companies can redefine pay codes to track certain types of activity. The possibilities are endless with WMT systems. Even if limits exist in related Payroll and HR systems, this doesn't keep the WMT system from parsing time into very detailed subcategories and then rolling the numbers into more generic buckets for export to outside systems. The WMT system can provide much greater detail and summary information by using more pay codes to categorize activity and time.

Key Idea

Well-defined pay codes are crucial in helping managers of an organization better understand what makes up their labor expense.

Program stacking or pyramiding is easily revealed, showing where a single shift of work activity begins to earn multiple rates of pay or pay premium. If a business operates in states or under contracts that call for multiple types of overtimes (weekly, daily, consecutive day, etc.) how can that added expense be managed if it cannot be determined when the overtime is occurring? Can it be done by better managing daily shift length or total hours per day? How about by managing weekly total hours worked? I have yet to meet a customer who broke down overtime pay by type in a manual system. This being the case, there was no obvious attempt to understand and control this cost.

WMT configuration opens up an entirely new world of labor-expense control possibilities through the use of pay codes to define discreet payments and activity. **If a manager can't see the origins of payable activity, how can he manage it?** How can anyone measure whether money is being well spent?

The System Should Be a Platform

A WMT system should be a platform for integration. Sharing information across systems and databases will reduce the duplication of effort. Instead of having the HR Department key in new hires, set up Social Security numbers and date of birth and then having department personnel do the same thing for the payroll system, it can all be done in one place and fed into the other systems. WMT systems can use the data the company already collects and maintains for employees, accounting, billing, and operations and bring it all together to provide meaning to the labor activity data.

For purposes of cost accounting and project or job management, a system can be integrated with an existing ERP system. It can also be integrated with a customer relationship management (CRM) system, so that employees might be tracked according to the customers with whom they interface. For example, suppose "issues" exist with several customers, or sales from certain customers have been trending down. It might be interesting to see if these customers are evenly divided among the sales force and customer service personnel, or if the same employees pop up frequently as being those who are interfacing with customers in decline.

What's great about integrating workforce technology into an environment that already has **ERP, CRM, and supply chain management (SCM) systems is that these existing systems may have fully matured while stopping short of intervening in the process of labor deployment.** They have great data but it has never been applied to human capital management. What WMT provides is "carrier data"—that is, collection points and processes that are easy to administer, credible, and easily dispersed. Like a carrier pigeon taking important messages from place to place, key business information is carried on the back, if you will, of WMT data to enhance decision making throughout the organization. Now the next logical step can be taken.

Key Idea

Most enterprises systems stop short of managing labor cost and deployment. WMT systems push that envelope and apply data from these matured but impotent (when it comes to labor management) systems to their labor and business needs through integration. WMT systems are a great focal point of integration, because the data is timely, accurate, and pervasive. The system touches every employee and manager every day. It works because everyone cares about the data.

All Related Systems Must Be in Sync

WMT systems draw on information in related systems such as HR, Payroll, Finance, and Operations and so must be in sync with the other repositories of business data such as employee information (e.g., name, job title, hire date, employment status, work location, supervisor, etc.). The business case should take into account these other systems in a way that dovetails with their current state. For example, if the HR system is about to be replaced, this undertaking is likely to require the time and attention of many of the same project resources. Having two systems that will closely interact in a state of redesign probably would not be smart. Granted, there is a bit of a "chicken versus egg" issue when deciding which system should be updated first. Each will depend on inputs and outputs from the other and will be required to house information so both can handle their respective processes. And each will "own" certain areas of compensation processing (i.e., calculating, assigning appropriate rates of pay, allocating, etc.), reporting, and decision making. If your organization recognizes that an upgrade to HR or Time and Attendance is imminent, my recommendation is to evaluate where these processes will reside. Which system will do the work? The risk of not understanding these needs and placing them in the wrong system can be very costly. You can lose functionality and reporting capabilities and require complex interfaces and program customization to accommodate the decisions and purchases.

Standardization Is Essential

For a system to perform up to its potential, policies and practices should be standardized across the organization. This may be difficult to accept, since many of these inconsistencies are well entrenched and have their justifications. But standardization will make administering the systems much easier, and it will make the outputs consistent and meaningful across the organization. Maintaining nonstandard systems will be much more costly both in the initial implementation phase and on an ongoing basis.

If business reasons exist that prevent complete standardization, the organization needs to assess how complex the variety of differences will be and whether the WMT system being proposed can handle the complexity.

The introduction of a global WMT system into the organization presents an opportunity to corral departments that may be fudging a bit on employee practices. When the system becomes global, the company has a strong argument for ensuring that employees are being treated equally and fairly, and this requires having standard policies and implementing them consistently in an evenhanded way. For example, what constitutes an exempt as opposed to a non-exempt employee needs to be consistent in all locations. It's also important that job titles reflect similar skill levels, training, and responsibilities. Otherwise, comparisons between areas and locations made from rolled-up reports showing jobs, departments, and divisions won't be worth as much.

Standardization can also be an issue with holidays. Many localities have their own local holidays. One way to deal with this is to go to floating holidays. Let's say a company has seven days off for holidays during the year. Are these seven holidays the same everywhere?

I had one customer who insisted during the initial discovery phase that the company had six standard holidays across what was a very large organization. This was supported in the holiday policy documentation at the corporate office, but in reality it turned out to be very different. There were more than 40 holidays observed across the organization that were based on contracts, local labor market expectations, and business practices predating the acquisition of some by the parent company. It's just fortunate that the system was able to handle them.

Some companies prefer to standardize the definition of shifts, also called zones. Others want the flexibility of having a variety. One of my customers has 150 shifts or zones, which can make things very complicated. Does the second shift start at 4 P.M. and go to midnight, or does it start at 2 P.M. and go to 10 o'clock? What if the employee clocks in a few minutes early? Is that time part of the scheduled zone or the prior zone?

Rounding is another system setting that is better when handled consistently across the organization. Should an 8:07 punch be rounded to 8:00, to 8:10, or not at all? Variation does allow the company to schedule and compensate people the way management wants, but it can make interpreting the data and passing it to other systems difficult.

As to how the day is defined (sometimes called "day divide") standardization is also important. Within the system all business units should define the day's start and stop times the same. This is often confused with shift schedules. When the third shift begins is not the same as when do hours count as Thursday hours. A day divide attributes any hours within that time frame—midnight to midnight or 7 A.M. to 7 A.M. as "Thursday hours." Day divide also defines the workweek; does it start on Saturday at midnight or Sunday at 7 A.M.? It's important because when other business data is mapped to labor, the measurement timeframe must be the same. If you start counting foot traffic into a retail store at midnight, hours worked should start counting at that point too. To compare production volumes to productive labor hours the two systems must be in sync. This was less of a factor when comparing data in large amounts of time such as a pay period. WMT systems allow the comparison to be made in smaller segments of time; thus, the variance becomes more pronounced when the counting period is off. Standardizing the day divide to align with business is also less confusing than trying to adjust for the difference.

Key Idea

Pay codes, shifts, overtimes, holidays, rounding, and day divide are but a few of the areas where standardization is important.

Standardization of components has many benefits, including ease of training, common expectations across the organization, consistent pay practices based on these standard settings, and less background maintenance being required to manage a very complex system. It also supports any centralization of the help desk, the auditing process, and prevents confusion for employees who transfer between different business units.

The Need for System Documentation

This is probably a good place to stop and mention the importance of good documentation. Preparing a written record of system setup is a best practice for any technology. On the technical side, documentation serves as a narrative that helps developer and buyer validate that requirements were communicated and configured as expected. It provides an audit trail of the history of the system as it is programmed, tweaked, upgraded, and retired.

But for WMT systems, documentation is much more. Documentation for the technicians is not enough. The system isn't touched by only a few users and administrators within the confines of one or two business processes. WMT systems touch every employee every day and end up dictating what employees are paid and how much employers spend. WMT systems are built on the translation of policies, contracts, regulations, and verbal explanations regarding how labor is to be compensated. Many people care about the accuracy, consistency, fairness, and timing of the tabulations that go on inside WMT systems. Human error and misunderstanding of these complexities happen frequently and yet the system must perform perfectly at all times, or be adjusted to reflect an accurate outcome. If the system comes up with an answer, it must be easily understood by the lowest-level user.

No matter what degree of complexity exists, a WMT system cannot be properly managed without adequate documentation. This documentation must contain not only technical specifications but the system must also be represented to its constituents (i.e., employees, managers, system administrators, and auditors) in layman's terms so that the technical becomes easily comprehensible. Naming conventions must be something that adds to the ease of maintaining and explaining the system, so they must be well thought out and adaptable to the future evolution of the system.

Done properly, documentation supports training, testing, help desk support, auditing, and change management control. Good documentation is also a source of backup for catastrophic system failure or unauthorized access.

I look at documentation as a financial tool. A properly documented WMT system will be a window into the company's compensation practices. This is where the system technicians communicate to management in a way that allows them to evaluate both the big picture and the finest detail in ways they may have never looked at in their labor spending. I've witnessed many business leaders who have experienced a revelation about their spending when WMT documentation does its job. As powerful as adding a new line item to the General Ledger to show where money is being spent, WMT documentation can have an incredible impact on people when they have a new understanding of where their dollars are going.

WMT documentation should include:

- Global Standards—system settings and rules that affect everyone in the system
- Pay Practice Statements—narrative word documents that explain in simple terms how pay programs are administered. These include aspects of eligibility, pay rates, method of reporting, and computation and exceptions. The documents should be approved and signed and updated as the pay practice policy changes. The explanation of a pay practice (such as overtime) should map directly to how the system is set up.
- Pay Matrix—a grid that shows all of the employee groups and all of the pay practices and relates them to the rules built in the system
- Change Control Log—a log sheet of changes to system setup so that changes are approved and timed appropriately, and so that any features that are impacted are also updated concurrently

Discovery and documentation are not easy tasks. The assessor must thoroughly understand the system, the policies, and the potential hidden practices. The process must be incredibly thorough and precise—leaving no gaps or ambiguity in the deliverables. As you plan for your WMT project, it is imperative to budget for enough time and the right resources to complete the documentation.

Timing Impacts Almost Everything

Dumb technology, such as paper time cards, is patient and forgiving. Paper time cards don't demand setup before they can be used. You can write all over the paper and it won't care if the "name" field hasn't been filled in. You can even wait until the very last minute of the pay period to pencil in all the data for the previous two weeks. A time card filled out at the last minute of the pay period works just as well as one that was prepared with all the right information from the very first day.

Unfortunately, computer systems are often less patient and forgiving. Mr. Nuhire won't be able to punch into the system if his information isn't in the computer yet. Much has to happen behind the scenes to get the system ready to recognize Mr. Nuhire and accept his inputs.

It's easy to dictate what the new guidelines are for submitting paperwork and inputting data into the new system in time for employees to use the system appropriately. It's not easy to ensure that it happens that way in the real world.

In the real world, employees show up for their first day of work and no one has yet told HR they have been hired. What is the employee to do that first day? Use an old paper time card? Perhaps, but then a crutch has been introduced. I've worked with some customers to set up a quick "mini hire," allowing last-minute arrivals to be set up with the bare essentials so that they can use the WMT system from the start.

Problems can occur with changes to an employee's job, too. A promotion, a wage increase, or a transfer to a new facility all have to be communicated to the WMT system, ideally before they occur.

Schedules that are imported and production data have to be timed as well. Schedules have to be in the WMT system in order to enforce punch restrictions and report exceptions. Material produced should be linked in to the WMT system to enable performance dashboards to give an accurate read of progress. How often can the two systems connect and update information without negatively impacting performance? If changes occur on one side of the connection, will the other be updated in time for the new information to pass?

What's important in the planning and design stages is to know what to ask when doing discovery. How flexible is the HR system to a "mini hire" setup? How receptive will the HR area be to such a divergence from the practice of holding Payroll hostage until all the required paperwork is received? Is someone willing to follow up, or is the system capable of making certain the mini hire converts to a full hire? How quickly can the HR system finalize inputs and export them to the WMT system? What are the options if a mini hire isn't feasible? What's the best way to accommodate these issues inside the WMT system and processes?

How often are schedules or production data entered and updated? How often do new production jobs get added? Is it possible for production information to be imported before an employee is correctly set up in the WMT system? What can be done to alleviate any time warp between WMT, HR, and other systems?

Aiming to Achieve Integration

Often, integration is accomplished through data warehousing. More and more, leaders of companies are realizing the value of the data they have in the different systems under one roof and that it makes sense for those who can put it to good use to have access to it. A data warehouse can house the information and make it available to anyone who is authorized. So instead of Payroll running a report in the time and attendance system and a budget report out of the finance system and then trying to reconcile the two, operators who use the various systems can go to the data warehouse, access and gather the information they need, combine the data, and run the report from there. This not only gives these various users access to information from throughout the company, the processing burden is taken off each individual system, thus freeing up computer power. WMT systems can be allowed to focus on managing today's operations and collecting data without being burdened with excessive reporting.

Key Idea

Migration of data and processes that drain business systems (such as WMT) of resources and performance to data warehouse systems maintains the ability of these business systems to accomplish their primary missions.

ONE VENDOR AND ITS SUITE OF SOLUTIONS VERSUS "BEST OF BREED"   A popular school of thought exists about the selection of software applications. It's not uncommon to hear people in organizations say their preference is to purchase the "best of breed" in every application. This means they want to buy the equivalent of *Consumer's Digest*'s number-one-rated application on the market. They don't want to settle for second best. I suppose the rationale is that if the product is rated highly, it must be the best solution available. Perhaps it's easier to justify large expenditures when there is a perception that "we're buying the best product out there." Is there an aura surrounding these "best in breed" products that gives a subliminal message that the organization is certain to be satisfied with and benefit from the choice? Whatever it is, I'd like to challenge the concept that "best in breed" is necessarily the best approach for every system purchase.

To support this challenge, let's examine one case where the customer decided to go with a single vendor for its workforce management systems and the pros and cons of that decision.

■ CASE STUDY: A COMMUNITY HOSPITAL IN NORTHERN OHIO   This customer began a search for a time and attendance system. A team of five key personnel representing IS, Payroll, HR, and Operations selected a leading WMT timekeeping and payroll product. Some time later, the organization decided to add access control and staff scheduling functionality to its automated solutions. Again, the organization chose the same vendor's products. In the next phase several years later the hospital wanted to upgrade its HR and Payroll systems and integrate employee cafeteria purchases into a single system. This time, the team fully committed to the existing vendor and purchased those solutions for these systems as well. Overall, they went from having more than two systems and many manual processes that were poorly integrated back in 1988 to one suite of applications from a single vendor today. What kind of advantages have they experienced? What's the down side?

Pros:

- One vendor owns any problem; there's no finger pointing.
- There's one single point of contact for system support and commonality for maintenance; the vendor has responsibility for keeping systems in sync through upgrades.
- The systems work well together; one platform supports all systems. Implementation and training effort are easier, and no translations between systems are required.
- There's no loss of functionality from any application because a related system cannot support that feature.
- Interface costs and maintenance are reduced.
- Badges work on multiple devices (time clocks, door locks, swipe for meal purchase, etc.).
- The vendor is highly vested, resulting in a stronger position for the customer in negotiations. There may also be cost efficiencies.

Cons:

- The customer is greatly impacted (multiple systems affected) if the vendor goes out of business, customer service is poor, or the relationship deteriorates. The customer must be certain the vendor is financially strong and viable for the life of the products.
- Bugs or problems with the software could be systemic and not limited to one application.
- The customer is constrained by the vendor's ability to keep pace with technology improvements.
- The customer is subject to one vendor's pricing cycle and position.
- Other vendors may offer greater functionality in one or more of the applications; the customer may miss out on desirable features by concentrating on the benefits of an application suite from a single vendor.

The hospital chose a vendor that had a full suite of solutions and the secondary purchases of additional modules (Access Control, HR/Payroll, etc.) still met their business requirements. While certain modules may not have been "best in breed" as a standalone product, the tight integration with other modules that are "best" more than compensated for the shortcomings.

The example above worked because all of the systems were within the same core business area—workforce management. The argument for relying on a single vendor for a variety of systems grows weaker as the realm of systems gets farther from a single core business area.

One example of a single-vendor model that does not always support workforce management needs is an ERP system that offers a time and attendance product. David O'Connell, Senior Analyst with Nucleus Research, cautions that buyers should be careful not to delay a WMT purchase because their ERP vendor promises that they can do it or even do it for free. Generally, companies with even a reasonable amount of pay-rule complexity need a best of breed for timekeeping. Otherwise, using a bolt-on WMT product from an ERP vendor will leave payroll errors and inflation in your systems because these "less than breeds" can't handle the pay-rule complexity. He says that waiting to make a decision or going this route can be a big deal; putting it off for even six months leaves payroll errors out there too long resulting in a huge expense. "Companies should think of best of breed WFM and ERP as complements to each other, rather than rivals to each other. If you properly deploy WFM and then wire it into your ERP system and Finance and Cost Accounting are getting information, then not only are you getting good deployment on your hands from WFM but you are extending the value of your existing investment in ERP. It's far more important to look at them as partners than as rivals."

There are advantages and disadvantages to the single-vendor suite. Risks are involved, but there also can be rewards. The point I'd like to make is simply to consider the advantages of aligning everything with a single vendor and then weigh them against the advantages of product-specific requirements. Sometimes what people in organizations think they are getting doesn't always become reality, because systems don't always integrate well, are expensive to maintain communication between, or fail to deliver the expected results because a piece of the process for delivering the desired outcome was housed in a sister application that wasn't purchased because it wasn't "best of breed."

What Does Portal Technology Have to Offer?

Time and attendance systems work well with portal technology. As mentioned previously, a number of systems may exist within an organization. Portal technology allows users to sign on in one place and maneuver between these systems. Not only are people spared the inconvenience of having to go through multiple sign-ons, the technology makes it possible to share files and data among many users. It also directs users to workspaces the company wants them to use. If managers should be monitoring the deployment of labor to ensure that it is in tune with production, they need to be in that workspace in order to get the information.

Managers and workers in the not so distant future will be using wireless technology devices to free them from the need to be at the computer. But in the meantime, periodic "attendance" in the WMT workspace can be facilitated through portal systems that make it a one-stop shop.

Another advantage of using portal technology is that everyone will have the same up-to-date version of company knowledge and decisions. This is important, because data is constantly being compiled and updated in a real-time system. Company documents and policies are routinely edited and revised. In this way, a portal system avoids the potential confusion that can come about because an individual may be working with a record or document that no longer coincides with the one someone else may be using.

Key Idea

Portal technology allows everyone to have the same, up-to-date version of company knowledge, decisions, and news inside one application login. It is efficient and secure and greatly improves communication.

A portal system can be thought of as a library that's kept constantly up to date. Cardholders are all able to check out any document, any schematic, any procedure or protocol, any report, or any legal finding they might want, and they can all do it at the same time. A portal system delivers tremendous efficiency, control, and improved communication to the organization. Some portal capabilities may already be part of the systems you already own. There is no need to buy additional software; you just need to tap into what is already there. One of our customers engaged portal technology in concert with their workforce management system training program. They learned how to use applications they already owned to deliver the program across the organization and control content from a central location. That's a space companies will enjoy operating in.

Access and Security Issues

Workers are like kids. They want to do and see what everybody else can. But employers are like parents. They know that's not always a good idea.

In the most sophisticated WMT systems, there are many available levels of security access. In one application, for example, more than 240 control points drive what a user is allowed or denied access to in its user security profile. Control points are used to enable or disable what specific users can view and what they can change. There are a few primary access categories: who, what, and, in some cases, when. One person might have access to all the employees in a department. His manager needs access to the records of employees in five departments but not his own record. Some users will be privy to hourly rates, time worked to date, PTO, and so forth. Others might need to be restricted from confidential information such as pay rates. Some will have the authority to make changes or to add comments. Others will not.

WMT systems provide different modules users need access to, such as time cards, schedules, employee records, running reports, maintaining the system settings, creating ad hoc queries, sending e-mails, and so forth. If a company has one flavor of user, then all this complexity won't be an issue. If a company has many different locations or lines of business or levels of hierarchy, the details of how access is set up can be critical. If access can't be controlled appropriately, features may have to be "turned off" for the entire company because access setup isn't robust or granular enough to accommodate the limits. Again, mission-based configuration is an approach that requires taking a careful look at the users and what they need to see and do. Controlling data and feature access is critical. Insufficient functionality will diminish the chance of reaping all the benefits from the system. Too much functionality may be risky for the organization and allow some to go beyond the boundaries of a user's true needs.

Security also comes into play beyond the application itself. Regulatory requirements and events in the news, along with the recent upsurge in the need to protect people in the workplace from terrorism and violence as well as to secure corporate secrets, are making workplace security an ever-increasing management concern. WMT companies are at the forefront of providing integrated solutions that address these issues. Paper guest books are being replaced by visitor access control systems that provide instant access to information about who is on premises, where they are, and who they visit, and so forth. Visitors can swipe a driver's license or other identification and be issued a temporary badge. The system can simultaneously send an e-mail to the person expecting the visitor letting them know their guest has arrived. Badges can even be set to expire automatically, preventing visitors from extending a stay without permission.

Sarbanes-Oxley regulations require public companies to keep records concerning who visits around the time financial reports are made public. External auditors can be given limited access to temporary offices or conference rooms, thus limiting the access they can have to sensitive areas.

Some employers use access control technology to provide a secure work environment and prevent unwanted visitors from entering large facilities. One example is a steel-processing plant with fewer than 50 employees. The firm took on the system to improve inventory control. Hiring security guards for the many exit doors simply wasn't financially viable. The vendor provided a full line of security products, including CCTVs, badge makers, and other devices that work hand-in-hand with the firm's time and attendance applications. Customers find that when they begin to manage time and labor, these processes line up naturally to provide solutions to other concerns about who goes where and when.

Software as a Service (SaaS)—Hosted Solutions Have a Lot to Offer

This list of considerations wouldn't be complete without mentioning the options for ownership of these products. It's no longer true that a majority of companies seek to purchase these products outright and administer the applications in-house. Purchasing software isn't the best option for all companies, particularly companies that are small to mid-sized in terms of the number of employees and the size of the IT and HR/Payroll areas. A growing number of providers in the market now offer time and labor management software as a hosted solution, whereby the application is configured and maintained by the vendor or a third party and accessible to employers through an Internet connection and Web browser. Some providers are very large and provide other related services, such as payroll processing and HR. Some are fairly small operations. Their customers can't afford in-house database administrators, system specialists, and product trainers. They simply don't have the budget or sophistication to take full ownership of their WMT systems.

Key Idea

SaaS providers offer a cost-efficient alternative to owning and administering time and attendance applications. Outsourcing time and attendance allows the organization to enjoy the benefits of the technology with less risk and fewer responsibilities.

If funding, resources, and expertise are lacking, it may make sense to consider a provider that will host the software. Another benefit of the hosted option is data security and access to the latest technology at no additional cost. In addition, if the organization is already outsourcing Payroll or HR services, it may make sense to have the provider host time and attendance as well.

Many companies prefer a hosted solution as a first step because it allows them to automate time and labor management processes in a phased approach. As the technology proves worthy and the capabilities are utilized by the majority of employees in the organization, the company can determine whether to stay with a hosted solution to bring the application in-house. The SaaS model may be worth considering if your company is otherwise not ready for the responsibilities of full ownership.

Chapter Summary

- Before you commit to a particular time and labor system, it's important to explore any potential benefit and every available option. Making certain the product selected is the best match is the first step in securing a positive future for the organization through the use of this technology.
- The discovery process should be undertaken methodically to uncover any hidden practices and document all findings.
- Labor-level architecture supports a number of functions within workforce management systems. It categorizes the data into the proper accounting buckets and also drives security and access, reporting, and groupings within the application. Labor levels are set in stone once they are designed; therefore, taking the long view in their setup is highly recommended.
- Organizational maps add a third dimension to organizing data and users within the system. Org maps should not be underestimated, and the long-term viability of managing them should be evaluated when selecting a system that is a good fit for your company.
- Well-defined pay codes help managers understand what is happening throughout the organization and how much they are spending on various activities and programs.
- WMT systems are a focal point of integration because the data is accurate, timely, and pervasive throughout the organization. Everyone cares about time and attendance data.
- Standardization makes life simpler and easier to manage within workforce management systems because it facilitates good communication, ease of use, and streamlined system administration.
- Industry analysts find that even a moderate amount of complexity in pay rules is enough to justify going with a best of breed product. Otherwise, the financial gains may not be fully realized.
- The single vendor solution for products within the workforce management technology area may offer benefits over best of breed within this technology realm.
- Portal technology is efficient and secure and greatly improves communication. Having the same access and versions of information keeps everyone in the organization on the same page.
- Outsourcing time and attendance systems offers a cost-effective and rapid deployment model as an alternative to in-house ownership.

CHAPTER 12

Creating a Mission-Based Workforce Management Technology System

O nce we fully understand the current system, including its strengths, weaknesses, and shortcomings, we begin to see ways new technology can be put to use. For this reason, the next stage of our work involves returning to the business case (and the vision for the system as a business tool) and creating an inventory of enhancements to be pursued that are designed to save time and money and help management run the business more effectively. The core of this used to be just time and attendance, but the scope of the possible enhancements now includes functions such as scheduling, employee self-service, absence management, automated work-flow, the budgeting process, business intelligence, and human capital management (HCM). In this chapter we focus on aligning the system's features to the organization's goals. Key elements in a well-designed system include the flow of information and creating actionable data. The chapter wraps up by going over costs, value analysis, and return on investment. What better place to end than at the bottom line?

The Business Case Defines the Mission

You might think of a business case as a story about the company and where it is today, what its problems are, what has been done to address those problems, what works, and what doesn't work. And like most stories that strike positive notes with their audiences, it's one with a happy ending. It paints a picture of the business environment both as it is today and as it is projected to be in the future, how the company will benefit, and what a better place it will be once the solution has been successfully embraced and installed.

The company may be looking for ways to control and reduce labor-related expenses and to deploy the labor force more effectively. It may recognize a need to reduce the level of effort required to manage and track labor and attendance. Or it may be looking for ways to improve its ability to attract, select, and retain the right employees in an increasingly tight labor market. Issues may also exist to do with integrating training, travel, gatekeeper controls, or even the need for billing through a centralized system. The business case will explain how a WMT system will resolve one or more of these issues. This should be done in such a way that the audience will understand how the solution will benefit the organization.

Determining System Requirements

Once the problems and issues have been determined, it's time to figure out how to deal with them. We call this a "requirements analysis." What this means is that all the functions that the new system needs to offer have to be identified. This requires isolating a solution for each problem or issue and identifying the functionality the new system needs in order to meet this and thereby move the organization forward toward accomplishing tactical and strategic goals. In addition to existing problems and issues, new requirements must be addressed. Further, those existing functions that do not need to change but have to be maintained should also be included.

Key Idea

Requirements Analysis

All of the functions that the new system needs to offer are identified. A solution for each problem or issue must be isolated via the functionality the new system must offer in order to meet this goal and move the organization forward.

This represents the first opportunity to rank the importance of the various requirements. This ranking will be instrumental in developing estimates of costs as well as time requirements for project scheduling. It will help determine what must be included versus what may only be nice to have. It will contain the deliverables to be used later in the request for proposal or request for quote. When the time comes to select a vendor, the analysis and the ranking will help the team stay focused on real needs rather than be swayed by the bells and whistles that sales people like to show off.

You may actually be surprised by the outcome of building a business case. The process can be time consuming and costly. But you have to ask, What if the wrong decision is made? What would that cost? How much difficulty could that cause?

And think about this: What if the company doesn't actually need a new system? It may be possible to fix a problem by simply tweaking what is already in place or simply taking advantage of features that were left on the shelf during the initial implementation, thereby saving a great deal of money.

WOULD YOU RELY ON A BLIND DOCTOR? Let me digress for a moment to quickly illustrate how important it is to do a little research. Imagine a doctor who is examining a child, but this doctor is blind. He places his hand on the child's forehead. It feels very warm. Is the child sick? It's easy to conclude that the child has a fever. But what if the doctor asked a few questions, did some simple tests? How did the child feel? What has he been doing? The child's hot skin could be a symptom of a sunburn as well. Is the solution a fever reducer or a sunburn remedy like aloe vera? If you don't dig into the cause, you might be trying to fix the wrong problem.

LINK PRODUCT FUNCTIONALITY TO MISSION-BASED CONFIGURATION In the requirements analysis stage, we explore the potential functionality of a new system and the scope and the vision of the project. Typically, we use a whiteboard and introduce the business pyramid hierarchy, which will be discussed shortly (refer to Exhibit 12.1), showing how driving individual decisions and tasks with specific policies and procedures can ultimately lead to the accomplishment of goals. In addition to department goals, we will explore the company's overall goals, which might include everything from cost cutting to improving productivity and sales growth or increasing employee retention, customer satisfaction, or sales. We talk about any policies and programs that are being contemplated or put in place to support these.

We may identify the specific tasks that might lead to the accomplishment of certain goals and see how these tasks might be linked to labor data. Essentially we extract from leadership a clearly defined picture of what people must do to achieve that goal at every level down to the lowest-level worker. We have to understand the tasks that are the key drivers to success. "Task" is used here broadly; I don't mean tasks such as "pick up a pencil" or "perform open heart surgery." Tasks here mean the things that should or should not be happening to achieve success. A task might be that employees should arrive to work on time or managers should schedule based on skill and cost, or total idle time should be no more than 5 percent. They might be best described as "mini goals," the things we expect people to succeed

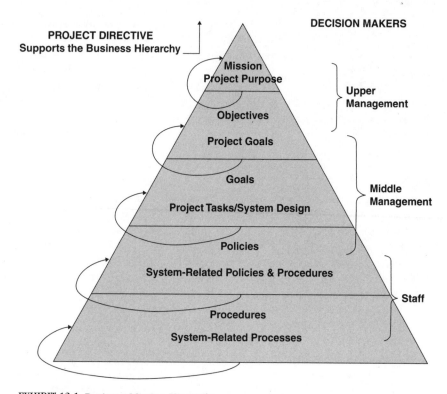

EXHIBIT 12.1 Business Mission Hierarchy

The business mission hierarchy illustrates how goals cascade down through the organization (right side) to become directives, goals, policies, and procedures. Projects mirror these relationships as system-related design and practice decisions roll up to support the mission (left side). This is how systems are aligned with the organization's mission.

at on an individual level. Mapping the goals all the way to the individual is the aim. This process avoids what happens all too often. Succeeding at those high-level goals rests too heavily on two things: a vague idea of how to succeed and the mere hope that success will happen if we make people "do their job," which are neither clearly defined nor linked to the goal.

HOW TASKS LEAD TO ACHIEVEMENT OF GOALS   Or you might say, how "mini goals" lead to achieving "big goals." Goals in an organization exist in a hierarchy that mirrors the management pyramid found in most organizations. Upper management has specific goals it wants the company to achieve. One overarching goal, for example, might be to increase profitability. This exists at the peak of a pyramid. One objective established to reach that goal might be to ensure full staffing on all shifts. This is put on the second level of the pyramid and is assigned to mid-level directors. One strategy for improved staffing coverage might be to be notified immediately of absences. This is placed at the third level and is assigned to managers. (Exhibit 12.1 illustrates the cascading of objectives down through the management pyramid.)

The directors set specific policies and targets for staffing goals. These policies are supported by procedures that relate to how managers expect to accomplish the objective. For example, a target might be a 20 percent reduction in understaffing, and the policy for reaching that goal would address absenteeism. Under the policies are the processes to support them. This forms the base of the business/system mission hierarchy. This is where front-line supervisors begin to use the system in support of the overall goal of greater profitability.

For example, to align the system with the business mission (i.e., increase profits) the system could be set up to track attendance and periodically reward employees with a financial incentive. In addition, supervisors could be immediately notified when someone fails to show up for her assigned shift. Supervisors are instructed to manage the schedule and replace the no-show with another employee with fewer hours worked. The system could be set up to automatically select and rank the best candidates for shift duty—those who meet the objectives, for example, of avoiding overtime payments, having the strongest skill match, and keeping labor expenses at a minimum. The supervisor uses the system-generated list to fix his staffing problem. Channeling the supervisor to manage his staffing inside the system keeps him thinking about the overall goal and reacting accordingly. Any supervisor who failed to take action or made a selection that was not on the list would be accountable for his divergence from the processes because his actions would be auditable in the system.

Key Idea

"Leading industry analysts estimate nearly 95 percent of workers are unaware of their company's top objectives."

Source: "3 Key Steps to Building a Pay-for-Performance Culture by Success Factors," *Workforce Management Magazine*, November, 2008

This is just one very basic example. What has been accomplished is that day-to-day activities that result in the unwanted outcomes (absences and understaffing) are channeled through a system that encourages and tracks desired behavior, alerts employees to action, guides them to the next step, analyzes the options, and provides timely solutions aligned with the overall objective.

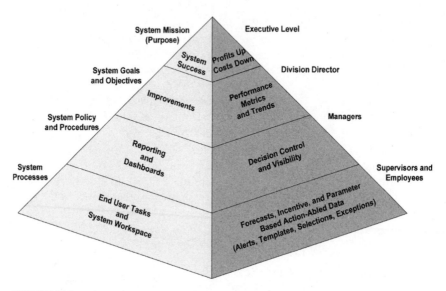

EXHIBIT 12.2 System Mission Hierarchy

On the right side of the pyramid are the company and its hierarchy of business objectives. On the left is the system. Its processes and features are paired with the business mission. From the executive level on down to supervisors and employees, and from the end-user task and system workspace on up to system success, all team members and all aspects of the system have roles to play in accomplishing the mission. Each end-user task and each instance of manager insight will now have a positive impact on the mission.

A successful system will involve every level of the hierarchy. High-level benefits are derived from actions at every level. There should be no gaps in the process of working toward the goals. The business case will illuminate this connection.

Based on this, for any new technology, the primary goal of the business case is to demonstrate how the new system will support the business and how the technology will help ensure the success of the overall corporate mission. When this is achieved, executive management will "get it," and the new WMT system will make good sense to them.

Further, these actions are entirely visible to managers, are measured against the targets, and are visible to the manager's director and to the director's boss, the CEO. The system mission hierarchy illustrates how management can link the system directly to its overall mission. If the system is designed properly, the sides of this pyramid should be in alignment. The result is that people choose and act in alignment with the big goals. (See Exhibit 12.2.)

Analyzing the Flow of Data

How are the tasks identified that support objectives and ultimately corporate goals? The first step is to clearly define the goals: Who can help reach them or keep them from being reached, the responsibilities of these individuals, and the processes they currently follow? This will allow a planner to drill down to the actions that can drive the desired results. This process will require collaboration between those who understand the business and those who can envision how the technology can become a way to help manage activities or processes. Data flow diagramming is a methodology that can map these relationships.

How should such an analysis proceed? One way is a "punch-to-paycheck analysis." This is a study, including a flowchart, of how the company collects labor data and of every step between that and the points at which the company disburses—and the employee receives—compensation. Other charts can be overlaid on this punch-to-paycheck diagram in order to integrate the management of other processes, goals, and employee activities. These charts lay out the current interplay of employees, managers, and the tools of labor activity planning and reporting. You can see that to accomplish objectives, things may need to change.

These diagrams illustrate the current flow of workers, materials, equipment, and information. They can be modified to show the change from the current condition to the recommended condition. Decomposing the charts may be required in order to show more detailed levels of complexity or ownership and personnel, which helps identify the players. These are the departments, personnel, outside vendors, and systems that are involved in the process. Decomposing also shows the bottlenecks, such as where things routinely get delayed or piled up, and the redundancies, such as where data gets collected, sorted, reviewed, or processed again and again. It identifies the gaps in communication, such as who is and who isn't in the loop. The timing is included, such as deadlines and sequencing of inputs, processes, and outputs, as are the proper audits/approvals (i.e., who is and who should be keeping tabs on various steps in the process). All the good, the bad, and the ugly aspects of labor activity and compensation are present. This analysis provides an opportunity to focus on the individual components and determine where each may be underperforming.

Another requirement is to develop specific objectives or targets for the various work areas and employee groups and for the action plans that will lead to reaching the targets. Actions, or the results of decisions made based on input provided by the new system, should be measurable. The faster such a measurement can be made, the better, because this leads to visibility.

Data flow analysis includes the goals, roles, responsibilities, and processes. Data flow diagrams include:

- Flow of workers, materials, equipment, and information
- Bottlenecks, redundancies, and gaps in communication
- Timing (deadlines, sequencing, processes, and outputs)
- Proper audits and approvals
- Specific targets
- Action plans

Such targets might be "time to complete," attendance percentages, hours worked, the amount paid out in premium pay, sales volume, production quantities, time to process (rate of work flow), throughput, quality levels, and even improved employee turnover. These tools create a blueprint for improvement, a script for managers and employees to follow. That's how tasks are identified and goals are reached. But there's more.

Making Sure the Data Is Actionable

In today's work environment, it's possible to have too much information. There can be so much it becomes impossible for any one person to digest it all, much less do anything about it. This is compounded by the fact that some managers believe the solution to every problem is to generate a report about it. That's all well and good, but the report will not be of much use if no one knows what he's supposed to do about it. That's why it's imperative to make sure whatever information the system is set up to provide is actionable. It needs to be an idiot light that says, "Hey, there's a problem here. This flag tells you there's a problem, and here's your next step."

Take, for example, the missed lunch punch we discussed earlier in this book. The supervisor needs to find out whether or not the person took lunch or worked through it. Once he does, he needs to make the necessary inputs, such as enter a comment, approval, or the facts of the missing punches into the system

The way to ensure that data is actionable is first to take a hard look at what management would like to control. Is it how much is being spent on an activity? Is it a failure to adequately schedule? Does it have to do with lost revenue or high employee turnover? Is it making sure overtime is offered to the person next in line under union contract provisions?

If, for example, the problem is too much overtime, a report about what happened last week won't do much good. What's needed is an alert that notifies managers that these people are headed into overtime unless certain interventions are taken.

Key Idea

To make data actionable determine:

1. What do you want to control?
2. Who needs to have the data? What is the person's most important job—or could someone else handle this action?
3. With the right data could the action be automated?

The next question is, Who needs to have the data? If it's department supervisors or scheduling coordinators, they need to get the alert via a mechanism they have easy access to, and they need to get it in a way that enables them to respond with the appropriate action. Sometimes this is where real changes in processes are necessary. The outputs of the technology cannot impede the recipient's primary job.

It's critical to identify the most important activity that a supervisor performs. Understanding what is required to make a good business decision when alerts are generated is also important. In a manual system, perhaps only the manager had enough information to make a judgment about the course of action. With the new technology, the information, validation, and judgment can be designed into the system, making the reaction more automatic. Maybe the best use of the manager's time is to be present on the shop floor, where he can help solve problems and open up bottlenecks. Responding to an open position on the production line is rudimentary, and the alert and action can be handled lower down the chain of command, shifting the responsibility for the process to another role and thereby freeing the manager to manage the work rather than spend his time on administrative tasks.

Finally, can an action itself be automated? Can a system be created that is intelligent enough to handle certain administrative tasks? Imagine how beneficial this would be. Not only would less time be wasted, the possibility that someone might drop the ball would be eliminated. It would mean mission accomplished 100 percent of the time.

Cost Should Be Related to Value

The cost sections of business cases and project plans are where details are perhaps most important. Cost estimates are an integral part of the contract the case represents, so you can bank on them being referred to in the future. While executive management may only review the summary, others will need the details in order to direct, structure, and drive the project. Keep in mind that no one likes surprises. And, as always with projects and contracts, "if it is not documented, it does not exist."

My husband and I have a number of friends who work for the U.S, Department of Defense. Those who have visited a lot of military bases tend to agree that the Air Force has nicer facilities than, say, the Army. The inside joke is that the Air Force builds the infrastructure first; housing and airplane hangars are erected, as are office buildings, officers' clubs, gyms, and hospitals. Then, when the money runs out, they say, "Hey, we've got to have a runway." Of course, you can hardly have an Air Force base without a runway, so more money is allocated to make the base complete. Unfortunately, most businesses don't work that way. Make sure the cost of your "runway" is included (documented).

Cost estimates should be relevant to value. There is a tendency for buyers in the market to think they know how to purchase this technology, largely on the basis of previous experience buying other systems. That could potentially be very dangerous. Treating a WMT investment as a "commodity purchase" is a pathway to disappointment. The commodity perspective assumes all products and vendors are the same except for the price. When you buy table salt, there isn't much difference between brands besides price. But WMT systems are different, and the value they bring to the customer is unique based on that customer's requirements and where the customer will realize the biggest return on its investment. A thorough business case won't simply state "we expect to spend $100,000." A properly developed proposal will link that expenditure to the expected rate of return (how much are we going to save and increase revenue and how soon?).

Considering All of the Costs

The mission of the new system has a price. Your analysis should take the costs of the new system into account. These costs can go far beyond just the software, hardware, and implementation effort. There are recurring overhead expenses related to owning any technology. With WMT systems a recurring licensing fee may be included, and it's important to consider how this cost and others will grow as the company grows.

An effective ongoing training program should be planned, for this will be needed both during the initial roll-out and over the life of the system as new users come on board. Additional personnel costs may also be involved, because it will take people to administer the system. There will be database administrators, network administrators, and system analysts who monitor the system and swing into action if the database, network, clocks, or phone lines go down. A functional expert who understands the business needs and translates them into system features will be required. This support may come from highly trained in-house personnel or from an outside consultant who partners with your company to provide ongoing system support. These experts will be able to tweak the system, administer changes, add new functions, add profiles for new business units, and so forth. The system will continually evolve just as the company does.

The budget should also include funds for attendance at user conventions and for ongoing training for personnel as new functionality is added and the product matures. Contingency plans should include reserves for handling employee turnover in highly specialized positions. A departure of key personnel may mean that temporary staff must be engaged, often consultants or vendor resources, to cover critical areas of system support. These specialized resources can be expensive and often must travel to the customer location, which can add to the cost.

It makes sense to plan as well for the possibility that existing related systems may have to be upgraded. Underlying programs and utilities may not be the latest versions or capable of handling the new software's outputs. System speed, monitor size, printers, report programs, network infrastructure, and operating systems—any one of these and more may be out of date. The cost to replace these components of the company's infrastructure may be significant. Nevertheless, with upgraded business tools the additional costs are likely to be justified. Organizations that assume new technology doesn't require additional training because the function is similar put their company at risk. When more sophisticated technology is introduced the mission changes, and without adequate training users will not be equipped to meet the challenge.

Although the number of technical sections of the business case may be limited, these areas should not be omitted even if they may be unfamiliar. It is better to educate yourself and others, if necessary, than to appear as though some ideas and concepts associated with your proposal are over your head. You must also address technical issues for the project plan. This may be an area where you will need to call in an expert, but remember, if you want others to support your initiative, the investment will be worth it. An expert should be able to tackle the technical details quickly and teach others what they know.

Don't make the mistake of simply inserting someone else's data or cost models into your proposal. I am often asked to provide a recommendation for how many people it will take to run the project or staff the department after Go Live. It's as if people expect there to be a magical number of resources for these responsibilities. Even if numbers are available from similar customers based on employee head count and industry, these numbers don't necessarily reflect what the new customer may need.

Help desk staffing, for example, will depend on the quality of the end-user training. A poorly executed training program will result in more calls to the help desk and more problems in the system. That will translate into a larger staff needed for the help desk. The timetable for the roll-out will determine how many resources are needed; you can spread out work to a smaller team if you have more time. Cost estimates must be based on the unique aspects of each project and each system.

Key Idea

Don't make the mistake of simply inserting someone else's data or cost models into your proposal.

Sometimes a project team will try to reduce the cost estimate, the time required for implementation, or the overall effort the project appears to require. Team members may argue that by keeping down the cost or by describing the time and effort as modest, winning approval is more likely. Perhaps. But unfortunately, this may mean that additional funds will be needed later, or that more time will be required and the business will be disrupted longer than expected. As a successful business executive once said, "It's a lot better to underpromise and overdeliver." The point is to err on the conservative side so that the project will be properly funded and the schedule will be workable. You will be glad of this later. After all, you can go to the well only so many times. Make certain that if you do have to go hat in hand, it won't look as though incompetence was the cause or that there was an intentional effort to mislead.

Analyzing Risk

What we've touched on are not only the known costs but the potential risks that may be involved with the new technology. There can also be unexpected expenditures or costs that are difficult to estimate accurately. Risk can also be a matter of whether the system will work well and with minimal down time. A cost estimate will be based on many assumptions. There are tools we use to identify the assumptions, the likelihood of bad things happening, and the impact on the project in terms of dollars, time, and quality. Don't ignore this. Embrace the assumptions as the foundation of your estimate, and be prepared for unexpected events to occur. It makes sense to take a conservative approach and to figure monetary contingencies into the financial picture of the business case.

Return on Investment

Our discussion isn't complete until we explore that expected return on investment. Everyone wants to know how to put this together. I wish there was one easy answer. Unfortunately, an ROI analysis is unique to each project and customer. There is no template, no simple spreadsheet, and it's not a black box of proprietary calculation tools. ROI analysis is very hands-on and specific to the needs, opportunities, and constraints of each organization.

To prepare an ROI analysis, the specific ways the WMT system will impact the organization must be understood. These can include personnel, processes, systems, and information. Each area impacted must be measured in its present condition and a value put on the present state. Then an estimate of the future condition and the rate of change, whether gradual or instantaneous, must be taken into account. Activity-based costing (ABC) is a method for obtaining this information. An industrial engineer isn't required, but an understanding of how to track activities and flow is.

The ROI analysis will require input from experts in several areas. Because it involves technology, the Information Technology (IT) department will need to assess the impact on current systems and infrastructure. The new hardware and software will have to be maintained and administered, and estimates of personnel, time and cost should be included. No doubt HR and Payroll will be impacted. Job responsibilities will shift, and personnel changes may result. Operations also needs to be included, because the system touches every person every day, and responsibilities and processes will evolve as workers engage the new technology. The impact on management at various levels should also be assessed, because of the new and improved information and the system's impact on productivity and output.

If the organization is really working strategically and aligning the system to help reach goals such as increased sales or customer satisfaction, input from Marketing and Public Relations may be required to gauge the impact.

Finally, Finance should be involved in ROI when numbers are crunched and cash flow, opportunity cost, time value of money, hurdle rates, and financing are integrated into the overall ROI analysis. Each organization has its own format and guidelines for these financial indicators, and the ROI analysis should fit these.

It's surprising to me that some companies have said they don't need an ROI analysis; they know they need the technology, and demonstrating ROI either isn't a requirement or perhaps even an expectation. Here we again encounter the pervasive idea that a WMT system is just a payroll system or just another piece of overhead, an unavoidable expense with little impact on the organization. I hope by now you will agree that a WMT system will have an impact and should produce a noticeable and perhaps significant

ROI. **The questions are really: How much and from what aspect of the implementation the return will come? How quickly will a return on investment be realized? What offers the fastest time to value?** Everyone needs to know what to expect and where to focus attention. ROI analysis figures aren't just hopeful numbers representing optimistic predictions about what the technology will deliver. They should be a target the system aims to hit and should be the ultimate definition of success.

Final Thoughts

Up to now, most workforce management technology (WMT) has taken the form of simple automation and reporting. Supplying a sufficient volume of labor and adequate payroll reporting was pretty much all that has been expected. You might say the old paradigm was concerned with how many, when, and where. The primary measurements of these processes are typically budget and trending with a few high-level relative indicators. The value of such systems is limited, however, because they are reactive rather than proactive. The lag time required to get the information all but eliminated the impact they could have on daily operations.

But WMT has developed into and can now be employed as a proactive business tool. The new WMT, what this book has been about, will allow companies to expect that organizational goals and demand (whether production, census, traffic, or any volume factor) as well as quality, employee needs, business rules, and cost will be factored into workforce decisions. There can be no doubt this will transform workforce management from part art form, part relationship-driven decision making into an applied science, infusing the business intelligence of various business systems (ERP, CRM, HR, etc.) into the process, thus pushing a business or organization to perform at peak efficiency.

This sophisticated new technology provides a forecasting tool. It can help determine what is needed, identify the best solutions, and quantify financial and operational impacts. The toolkit it provides will enable supervisors first to quantify the attributes of all available resources and the demand for them, and then to deploy and invest accordingly.

In addition, WMT enforces accountability, because decisions and performance are visible to management in real time and can be measured impartially in terms of dollars and cents. Let's face it, the big variable in workforce management is behavior. Perhaps more than anything else in recent years, managers have been searching for ways to instill and enforce accountability. WMT is the answer. More than any tool developed to date, WMT can offer the ability to influence and even to control behavior. Using it, the organization can channel management decisions and stimulate employee performance. Individuals can be made accountable for productivity, quality, and costs through a system that alerts them to operational needs, defines options, and controls actions. Companies can use this technology to plan the most productive use of capital assets, to meet customer satisfaction goals, to maximize sales, and to reduce labor costs to a minimum. And this means higher productivity and greater profits.

As our time together comes to a close, I don't think it is too much to say time and labor management systems represent the future—the future of workforce management. And after reading this book, you might say you hold the future in your hands.

A New Path for Payroll Professionals

A renaissance is underway in labor management. Leaders from varied backgrounds who possess diverse problem-solving skills and represent different market issues are coming together in this revolution, causing it to grow and flourish as the first Renaissance did 500 years ago. Then, too, people from varied backgrounds converged—artists, tradesmen, bankers, and scientists—and together brought forth a new age.

You can be a leader of this movement, participate in the discussion, and contribute to the evolution of labor time and activity management. As you've read this book, you doubtless were able to relate to many of the stories and situations that businesses find themselves in when managing staff and labor expenses. What I wanted to reveal are the problems and the opportunities that exist and to show how to get the most out of the newest technology. I also attempted to show how to ensure that the right software is selected from the many programs available and to give you the necessary questions to ask to guarantee a successful implementation. My goal was to energize you with real-world examples of companies taking labor data far beyond what's needed to calculate paychecks. And, like the Renaissance men and women of centuries ago who came together, I attempted to connect you with leaders from various fields—health care, retail, manufacturing, education—to open up new perspectives on your business and to expose you to new ideas that can help you meet goals and separate your company from the pack.

The Evolution of Payroll and HR

Let's explore the evolution of the Payroll Department. The origins of payroll and accounting, bookkeeping, and paper and coin currencies can be traced to the beginning of ancient civilizations and have evolved slowly over a long period of time. Although the practice probably dates back many thousands of years, the earliest disbursement records still intact are stone tablets dating to the Athenian state for the period 418 B.C. to 415 B.C. Of course, Rome and other empires had to pay their armies, which were scattered all over the known world. The word "salary" comes from the Latin word salarium, which literally means "salt money." Apparently it started out as money paid to Roman soldiers for their allowance of salt. According to some historians, Roman emperors had their likenesses put on coins to remind the troops who they were working for. And why not? The source of the jingle in your pocket can make a difference when the time comes to make a decision that involves a question of loyalty.

Where Is Payroll Today?

Today, the Payroll Department is much like Accounts Payable. A business activity occurs—employees work—and costs are incurred. People need to be paid, and taxes need to be disbursed. The Payroll Department is also comparable in some ways to the Human Resources area. Both departments administer employee-related services and benefit programs such as insurance and retirement programs, employment incentives, and banking services, including direct deposit and savings plans, among other things. And they manage regulatory requirements. For Payroll, this might include processing attachments such as garnishment payments and ensuring compliance with wage and hour regulations. But despite these similarities and practically an equivalent level of importance in the organization for much of the last few centuries, the two, HR and Payroll, today are positioned quite differently in most organizations.

It is not uncommon for Payroll and Accounts Payable to exist at an almost equal level in the organization, reporting up through the Finance division. Depending on the size and complexity of the organization, these departments have at least one or more layers of management between a department head and senior management. Human Resources, however, has ascended to a much higher level in many organizations.

Why Payroll and Human Resources Have Evolved so Differently

There's a logical explanation for the difference. Government and industry rules and regulations, reporting requirements, and benefit programs have exploded during the past few decades. Our political leaders and government bureaucrats at the federal, state, and local levels have been busy satisfying the demands of both their constituents and special interest groups. Businesses, institutions, nonprofits, schools, and other types of organization have become subject to regulations such as those in the Equal Employment Opportunity Commission (EEOC), the Family Medical Leave Act (FMLA), anti-discrimination and sexual harassment regulations, the Fair Labor Standards Act (FLSA), the Occupational Safety and Hazards Act (OSHA), retirement plan regulations, and on and on. Someone in each organization needed to become an expert on these rules and the demands they make on the company to keep the Feds and lawyers from the door.

Furthermore, the workforce became more highly educated and increasingly transient, and the pool of labor was no longer limited to local resources. As a result, employees demanded more competitive wages and attractive benefit packages. They could easily shop around for the best opportunity and often left unexpectedly for greener employment pastures. This resulted in a corresponding increase in the effort to manage and supply labor to the organization. All the government information and market data that was generated had to be organized and available, resulting in operational pressures that mandated the use of more technology. Regulators required reports and verification. Disgruntled employees threatened the organization with litigation and potential financial liabilities. Compliance, risk mitigation, and holding down benefit costs also became major concerns. The cost of health care, for example, has been escalating at a dizzying rate.

As the HR Department became increasingly vital and visible, its profile was raised above Payroll and Accounts Payable. Along with this, it became apparent that the director of Human Resources needed to be accessible to top management. As a result, the position was integrated with executive leadership, so much so that now the HR leader sports a C-level or VP title at many organizations.

Payroll managers, on the other hand, typically remain in relative obscurity—in the Finance Department or perhaps even reporting up through Human Resources to the HR director. The truth is, Payroll is not seen as an owner of an important part of the business and is not credited with managing much more than payroll disbursement.

In my view, this is not as it should be. Today's Payroll Department can be as vital and potentially as influential as many other areas of operations. Changing the way organizations view their Payroll Departments and the people who manage labor costs and utilization is my personal mission. I truly believe Payroll and the people who manage labor costs and utilization will become important in almost every organization in surprising ways as the future unfolds.

I'd like to see the Payroll Manager's job elevated in terms of respect. That has been one intent of this book: **to provide evidence that Payroll is the owner and conduit of valuable labor management data and can become empowered by using the latest technology to bring significant**

benefits to the organization. I haven't just written about payroll theory, nor have I speculated about what might happen. Rather, I have related case studies that come from real companies and explained the successes they have achieved so that you would be able to see how the technology can be applied to your situation.

Payroll Should Be Positioned as a Strategic Player

Payroll Departments handle huge sums of money. In many organizations, labor costs are the single largest expense. Despite the complexities, frequent changes, and tight deadlines that Payroll Departments operate under, the work they do is highly accurate and timely. At the same time, Payroll may be the least "managed" cost. It is treated more like a fixed cost and a flat biweekly obligation than a controllable disbursement of the company's valuable funds.

How often will an employee overlook an error on his paycheck? Never, unless the error is in his or her favor. Think about it. The IRS doesn't accept estimates, inaccurate wage calculations, or late deposits of tax withholding. Everyone who depends on the Payroll Department expects perfection. This puts on the pressure, but the good news is that this perception can be a big plus. When it comes to numbers, Payroll has credibility out of the gate. Payroll is assumed to be staffed with administrators who are sticklers for precision and timeliness. Who, then, would be better to put in charge of labor data technology?

The right processes, controls, and procedures can make a big difference to a company's bottom line. In addition, the value of the data that Payroll can provide is tremendous, because the efficiencies and cost savings can be enormous if the data is used correctly.

As previously mentioned, Payroll tends to be viewed currently the way Accounts Payable is viewed. Accounts Payable doesn't drive sales. It doesn't increase revenues or make the business end of the organization operate any better. Accounts Payable pays vendors. Payroll pays employees. But this perception is about to change. I'm not an expert on Accounts Payable, and there are certainly professionals in this area who perform important functions. But assuming they are not actively involved in front-end procurement—the buying decisions, contract negotiations with vendors, and supply chain management—their job is to expedite the processing of payable invoices. Accounts Payable may have influence over the terms of payment. The people in Accounts Payable may determine the legitimacy of charges and the allocation of expenses to the general ledger. There may be value to improving the data collection process for this area as well, but that's for another book. The big difference between Payroll and Accounts Payable is that AP has little opportunity to proactively impact the costs incurred by the organization, given that traditional AP departments are the central and final repository of costs incurred by other areas. The regulatory requirements and competitive demands driving these purchases are already being managed by the areas incurring the costs. Industry is already aware of lean manufacturing, just-in-time (JIT) supply chain management, competitive material bidding, and so forth.

Payroll, on the other hand, is in charge of what has been up until now an unmanaged expense (annual budgets don't count as an equivalent to real-time lean initiatives). But the opportunity exists to change this, for Payroll to actually provide the tool to manage this expense.

The all too common and pervasive attitude toward wages has been that they represent a fixed expense relative to the number or type of employees. An employee is hired at a fixed rate, either an annual salary amount or an hourly amount. The hourly employee may be eligible for some additional wages via overtime, shift premiums, and an occasional bonus, but these are also seen as static and are usually "budgeted" with an expectation of only small variations from the prior year or some high-level trends. In addition, the payroll expense is a continuing obligation eliminated only in extreme situations. Wouldn't vendors love to be assured their services would be needed 40 hours a week indefinitely?

Payroll has remained unmanaged from within the organization, perhaps because outside entities took the first steps to dictate how labor expenses would be paid. States and localities have imposed numerous industry standards and practices on employers. The resulting rules and responsibilities for compliance on the organization and the Payroll Department have been substantial. Each state has a unique set of guidelines dictating the terms of employment and governing such things as rest breaks, overtime, minimum wage, how minors are treated, the types of activity different classifications of employees can perform, total hours, and so forth. Add to this the complexities of union contracts which must be applied to the payment, scheduling, and treatment of employees. No wonder we have been lulled into thinking someone is managing labor costs. By way of proxy, Payroll has thus become the administrator for these outside management guidelines.

Key Idea

Government regulations, bargaining agreements, and industry standards that dictate how employers must pay their workforce were never written to support the profitability or success of the employer.

When regulators imposed rules on labor practices and payments, they did so from the perspective of the worker, the state, and the public. Few, if any, of the wage and hour guidelines or union contract mandates were designed to use labor resources more efficiently or to improve operations. **Certainly, no one outside the organization can be credited with collecting any data, designing compensation programs, or constructing work scenarios that are intended to make the company more profitable.** Allowing the process of administering third-party regulations, which Payroll does quite nicely, to substitute for conscious management of labor expenses and utilization by the company seems absolutely absurd to me. So why have we been allowing it to be this way for so long?

Key Idea

Payroll processing and administration of government, policy, and industry rules is not a substitute for conscious management of labor spending and utilization.

Payroll data is the natural convergence of labor cost and business activity. It's where the mechanism for getting an organization's product to the market (i.e., employee performance) meets the cost of that undertaking in the form of production labor costs. When rules were imposed from the outside, payroll administration was logically identified as the most efficient place to monitor and administer them. To comply with these controls, which are more accurately described as constraints and penalties, takes time and effort. They are written in the way the laws that tell us the penalty that will occur if we exceed the speed limit are written. The result is that emphasis is typically placed on making sure whatever is triggered by exceeding a limit is complied with, rather than putting mechanisms in place to be sure the limits are not exceeded in the first place. This is a lot like driving a car with the attitude "I'll slow down when I get a speeding ticket." At this point, it's too late. A penalty has been incurred, and points have been posted on that person's driving record. That's why most of us don't go much over the speed limit. It's safer, it's more fuel efficient, and we will avoid the extra cost of the speeding ticket or, better yet, a costly or deadly accident. It doesn't make sense to slow down only if and when we get pulled over by the man in blue.

Wouldn't it likewise be better if we operated our businesses the way we drive our cars? But we keep paying the proverbial "ticket" every pay period, over and over again. As though our business only operates at one speed—reckless!

WMT Professionals Should Participate in Managing Labor Costs

Let's step back and consider why Payroll is the best place to begin to manage these constraints. Let's face it, employee activity determines everything. Machines don't run on their own. Customers don't buy a product with robots standing by. Patients don't get well just by lying in a hospital bed. Widgets don't travel to stores on their own two legs. The point is, your organization uses people to make it happen, and it costs money every time they show up at work. Every strategic initiative the organization undertakes requires employees to get it done. Because Payroll is the point where activity and costs merge, it's the right place for integrating all the information and decisions related to labor activity and expense. The truth is it has held this position for a very long time, but without the ability to take advantage of it until now. Recent developments in workforce management technology now make it feasible. This is why the time has come to reevaluate the payroll function and workforce management. I'll say it again. During the past five years, developments in technology have transformed labor data into a valuable tool for controlling a major expense while at the same time influencing performance in a positive way.

The time has come to stop managing labor using shorthand, manual typewriters, and adding machines with a crank. It's time to collect and analyze labor data and then wisely put it to use. It might even be time for payroll managers to become a little more assertive regarding their role in the organization, and for C-level executives to reassess how they can—no, how they should—leverage this knowledge to their companies' advantage.

The Future of WMT Professionals within the Organization—The WMT Office

I'd like to be so bold as to predict that we will see the creation of a new business unit morphing out of the payroll department as a result of the emerging importance of workforce management technology. Twenty-some years ago, project managers began a grass-roots effort to have their area of expertise recognized as a specialty. This effort resulted in the creation of the Project Management Office (PMO) within many organizations. A body of knowledge and standard practices was adopted throughout the industry, and companies recognized that projects needed to be managed by professionals. These professionals applied a unique set of skills, technologies, and business acumen.

Professionals who deploy and administer workforce managements systems will evolve much the same way. Workforce management technology requires specific technical and fundamental skills and knowledge. This expertise overlaps many business areas: Payroll, Human Resources, Finance, IT, and Operations. It is unique by industry but shares much common ground as well. What we will see is the creation of workforce management technology offices, perhaps by some other name, chartered with the responsibility to deploy and manage WMT systems in alignment with organizational goals and constraints. Professionals in the Payroll area today are well positioned to be a big part of this evolution, because their domain knowledge is key to the success of this business unit.

Especially for Owners and C-Level Executives

Having good labor cost and productivity data can be valuable in positioning a company for sale. How so?

A lot of time and effort is spent tending to the assets of the company, but what about tending to the company as an asset? Business leaders, including those in small, privately owned companies, not to mention corporate executives of large, publicly held institutions, benefit when they look at their companies as they would a commodity on the market for sale. These "owners" are responsible for the health and appearance of the company. When a company is available for purchase, outsiders will examine it closely from an operational and financial perspective.

Within smaller, privately held companies, owners are eventually going to be concerned with succession planning or with positioning their company for sale at retirement. **Why should workforce management technology be part of the business brokerage process?**

You've heard it said, no doubt, that the three most important things to consider when buying a house are location, location, location. When buying a business, it's not so simple. Prospective buyers of a business will look at profitability and cash flow. As has been said, the only way to obtain a return is through profitable operations, and the only way to pay bills is through positive cash flow.

WMT can provide data that will help a prospective purchaser understand the business and what its true costs are, as well as its sources of profitability and true profit potential. The numbers can be scrutinized from every angle. They can be reviewed by business line, profit center, individual product, or whatever the case may be, which should give a prospective purchaser a high degree of comfort about what he will actually be getting. If the buyer has a question, such as how much is spent to staff this or that unit or what is the cost of maintenance or rework, it should be relatively easy to answer.

Another concern from a buyer's perspective has to do with the distinctive competencies of the company's management. **Labor data merged with business data can draw the connection between managers and profit centers and reveal the productivity of groups and individuals.** This can give prospective buyers an opportunity to identify key personnel as well as workers who may be more expendable. This will help buyers understand who is essential **in maintaining continuity** following the acquisition or merger. Buyers have a common set of concerns when looking at a company for sale; these include continuity of management, cash flow, and the ability to ensure future revenue opportunities.

The Buyer's Primary Concerns

1. **Management.** Management's ability is usually the key asset sought after in an acquisition.
2. **Cash flow.** Cash flow or potential cash flow of the acquired assets is critical. Profitable operations are essential to obtain a return, and positive cash flow is the only way bills get paid. The time period for positive cash flow is unique to the acquirer.
3. **Opportunity/Strategy/Capital.** Is there a meaningful opportunity, and are there effective strategies and appropriate capital assets to reach desired objectives? Key aspects of a strategy might include customers, products, services, footprint, competition, business model, and so forth.

WMT answers the call within each of these buyer concerns. A time and labor system will **make the transition to a new owner go more smoothly since a methodology for controlling labor deployment and labor costs will be in place.** New management will not have to learn through trial and error while getting up to speed. The sophisticated WMT system can automatically schedule people, enforce policies and union rules, and manage such things as projects and billable activity. WMT technology can also act as an effective change agent for companies that must administer major transitions when merging two companies together. Managing labor deployment, activity, and costs within these systems gives leadership the ability to direct those efforts across the organization consistently and continually without physically micromanaging every supervisor and worker on the shop floor. If the parent organization has a better way of doing business, those guidelines can be set up within the system and applied to every manager's workspace. Their actions will be automatically aligned with the new order of business and instantly observable.

Employee-centric business tools combine data and decisions in the hands of the drivers of change in the organization. Production or Operations, HR, and financial system initiatives alone are not enough to maintain the economic viability of many organizations. Because the time to value is short, the savings from WMT systems are immediate, and funds become available for other transformations. Cash flow is more likely to be positive. **Using the technology to save time and money frees up company resources for other projects.**

A good realtor tells his client to pay attention to curb appeal. A good business broker should consider how WMT dresses up a business and gives potential buyers a positive picture of the "property."

About the Author

L isa Disselkamp is President of Athena Enterprises, LLC, a consulting firm specializing in time and labor management technology implementations. She is a nationally recognized subject matter expert on workforce management business practices and a visionary in the industry. Throughout her career she has taken time and labor systems beyond the typical boundaries of automation and helped companies strengthen their bottom line through the strategic use of the technology.

She is the author of *Working the Clock*, the first book focusing solely on workforce management technology.

Disselkamp is a charter Advisory Board Member of the Workforce Productivity Technology Council and a member of the APA's Emerging Technology Subcommittee. She is also on the Advisory Board of the Payroll Manager's Report and IOMA's HR/Payroll forum. She is a member of VISTA—Society of Industry Leaders, where she serves as a consultant to industry analysts.

In 2005, Disselkamp was invited by Newt Gingrich to make a presentation to the Center for Health Transformation in Washington, D.C., on workforce management technology. She has also been an invited speaker and webinar presenter for the Human Capital Institute, HR.com, the Institute of Management & Administration, The Service Corp. of Retired Executives, the American Payroll Association, State Society for Human Resource Management conferences, vendor conventions, the Institute of Management Accountants, and the Society of CPAs.

Disselkamp graduated with honors from Earlham College with a degree in Japanese and International Management and was a National American Business Women's Scholar. In 2008, she was recognized as the "Woman of the Year—Technology Star."

Index